Agricultural Exports, Farm Income,
and the Eisenhower Administration

Agricultural Exports, Farm Income, and the Eisenhower Administration

Trudy Huskamp Peterson

UNIVERSITY OF NEBRASKA PRESS
Lincoln and London

Library of Congress Cataloging in Publication Data

Peterson, Trudy Huskamp, 1945–
  Agricultural exports, farm income, and the Eisenhower administration.

  Bibliography: p. 197
  Includes index.
  1. Agriculture—Economic aspects—United States—History. 2. Agriculture and state—United States—History. 3. Farm income—United States—History. 4. United States—Economic policy—1945–1960. I. Title.
HD1761.P42   338.1'873   79–15825
ISBN 0–8032–3659–X

To my parents

Contents

Contents

Preface

ONE OF THE CHARACTERISTICS of American agriculture is its reliance on markets abroad. The colonial sotweed factor exported his tobacco, and antebellum cotton farmers depended heavily on English cotton spinners for their income. In the 1890s nearly a third of the wheat and more than half the cotton grown in the United States went abroad; by the middle of the twentieth century more than a third of America's wheat and cotton and more than a fourth of its tobacco and soybeans found foreign buyers. And by the late 1970s, two-thirds of the wheat, a third of the corn, and two-fifths of the soybeans grown in the United States were exported. These markets were and are vital to the stability of American agriculture, and the continuing quest for outlets abroad has absorbed farmers and their allies for decades.

This work examines the Eisenhower administration's attempt to maintain agricultural income at home by expanding foreign markets. This course had several features that recommended it to the Republican officials. First, it seemed to provide an alternative to statist controls over agricultural production without obstructing the modernizing process, with its commitment to greater efficiency and hence greater production. If markets could be captured or developed abroad, the reasoning ran, excess domestic production could be utilized, production and marketing controls could be reduced and then eliminated, and, as the foreign

markets grew, the increasing surplus resulting from technological advances would be absorbed. In addition, the Eisenhower officials believed that expanded export marketing
could strengthen the private export trade, and encouraging
private enterprise was one of the administration's goals.
Finally, the Republicans thought that by increasing agricultural exports they could ensure the support of rural groups,
agribusiness, and free traders—the groups that formed the
political power base of the administration. Naturally not
everyone agreed that trade expansion was the way to a
healthy rural economy, and conflicts both within and without the administration plagued the Republican planners.
And, in the end, gaps persisted between the goals and the
programs that were adopted.

Historians have written little about the Eisenhower years
and still less about the agricultural policy of the era. Yet
several features of the Eisenhower period make it a useful
one through which to study the workings of agricultural export policy. For one thing, it was the first Republican administration in twenty years, and its officials were anxious
to put a new Republican stamp on government programs.
This meant they were careful to distinguish their programs
and ideals from those of their predecessors, and in the process they clarified their underlying assumptions about the
agricultural economy. In the second place, the staff of the
administration had remarkable longevity. Ezra Taft Benson
was secretary of agriculture for the entire eight years; John
Foster Dulles was secretary of state for more than seven;
such major advisors as Clarence Francis, Clarence Randall,
and Don Paarlberg were in the administration for all or
most of Eisenhower's two terms. This meant that the administration had time to develop and enunciate a clear policy
and to make adjustments as time passed. This also means
that one factor often cited as a reason for changes in
policy—the change of the person or persons at the top—can
be eliminated, and other factors influencing policy can thus
be seen more clearly. In particular, one can observe the
structure of decision-making and the institutional influence
of bureaucracy on policy. Third, the Eisenhower administra-

tion was coterminous with some of the coldest years of the cold war. Agricultural exports were affected by that foreign policy climate; so, too, new export programs such as Public Law 480, usually known as Food for Peace, reflected the prevailing anticommunist chill. Here one can examine the relationships between foreign and domestic policy and the complex set of influences that work both on and between the two. And here also one can consider the emerging revisionism about the Eisenhower presidency that insists that, far from being a "do-nothing" president, Eisenhower was a skillful conciliator at home and a clear-minded internalist who maneuvered to prevent a retreat into isolationism and yet to avoid the hazards of military commitment abroad.

Any study of export policy must deal with the clamorous New Left or neo-Beardian interpretations of recent American history. In simple terms, the neo-Beardians allege that United States foreign policy responds directly to domestic influences, primarily to a felt need for foreign markets. With increasing United States productivity, they argue, both agrarians and industrialists believed that the only way to prevent recurring depressions was to expand markets abroad under the protection of the United States government. The government responded to these domestic pressure groups by attempting to enforce an Open Door policy abroad, which led to an informal American empire of trade and investment. This marketplace mentality, the neo-Beardians contend, is a unifying theme in modern American history, linking Cleveland to McKinley, Wilson to Harding, Hoover to Truman. The differences between these administrations, they conclude, were over the way to achieve an Open Door world, not over the end itself.

Agricultural trade presents perhaps the strongest argument for the Open Door thesis because of its easily demonstrated dependence on foreign markets throughout the nation's history. Yet too great a reliance on the economic motivation for United States trade policy tends to force events into an unnecessarily narrow mold. In the 1950s, for example, important ideological influences retarded market expansion, especially in communist areas; here political considerations played a major role in determining policy. Then, too, neither the government nor the agriculturalists were as logical and controlled as a purely economic motivation suggests; indeed, decision-making on agricultural trade policy was characterized by conflict and by inconsistent, sequential problem-solving rather than by a clear determination of economic need.

This study focuses on the officials of the Eisenhower administration as they seek markets abroad. The first chapter introduces the policymakers of the administration, their attitudes toward agriculture, their ideas about trade policy, and the constraints within which they operated. The second and third chapters examine the tools and levers the officials inherited, their early and frustrating attempts to use them, and the legislation that resulted. The fourth and fifth chapters focus on export efforts through government programs, principally PL 480. The sixth and seventh chapters examine efforts to expand commercial trade, including trade with nations of the communist bloc, the internal debates that resulted, and the developments in domestic politics and international relations that influenced the course. Finally, the conclusion enumerates the major characteristics of the Eisenhower trade program, explains why the system developed as it did, and outlines other options that might have been taken.

The agricultural trade program of the Eisenhower administration was beset by problems. Some were resolved, but others remained to plague the Kennedy administration. The Eisenhower men left Washington in frustration, and Don Paarlberg spoke for them all when he summed up the export program in this way:

We sold what we could for cash. What we couldn't sell for cash we sold for credit. What we couldn't sell for dollars we sold for foreign currency. What we couldn't get money for we bartered. What we couldn't get anything for we gave away. What we couldn't export by any means we stored. And still the stocks increased.[1]

Agricultural Exports, Farm Income, and the Eisenhower Administration

Introduction
Searching for Stability

VOLATILE PRICES, volatile incomes: this is a chronic problem
of commercial agriculture. As the farm economy moves from
peak to trough and back to peak again, individual farmers
find themselves rocked by market forces beyond their control. Farmers and their allies have long sought a way to
stabilize the market, to smooth out the extremes of the
economic cycles. In their search for a balance wheel, they
have been most concerned with cushioning the bottom of the
cycle, thereby maintaining a minimum return on production. Inevitably they have turned to institutional remedies;
yet at the same time they have hoped to protect the independence of the individual farmer within the marketing
structure. Their goal has been regulation without domina-
tion, stability without autocracy.

The search for stability has taken many forms. In the
nineteenth century, futures markets developed to guarantee
year-long supplies to agricultural processors and to allow
farmers to market commodities when prices seemed most
advantageous. The futures market enabled farmers to distribute their incomes throughout the year (provided they
had a way to store their crops), but it did not stabilize the
level of farm income.

During the first years of the twentieth century, maintaining a minimum level of farm income was not a problem in
the United States. In fact, the relationship between the
price of farm commodities and the price of industrial goods

1

was so favorable to farmers that parity was subsequently figured on the 1909–14 price ratio. World War I changed that comfortable situation, for wartime demands led to an improved technology that enabled farmers to produce more than the postwar market could absorb. In the 1920s tractors, combines, insecticides, and scientifically bred plants and animals joined to drive production and productivity upward, and—unhappily for farm prices—while production expanded demand contracted. European agriculture revived and European producers successfully lobbied their governments to erect tariff walls. Competition increased from producers in Canada, Australia, and Latin America; high United States tariffs prevented foreign nations from earning the dollars to buy corn and wheat. And, to make matters worse, domestic demands were shifting, as gas-eating tractors replaced grain-eating horses and an increasingly urban nation lost its country appetite. Farm income fell; the prewar hopes for a stable, prosperous agriculture faded.

Now maintaining a minimum level of farm income became critical. Discussion of the problem, however, was usually couched in terms of curbing production or maintaining commodity prices rather than maintaining income. Indeed, most farmers did not want to protect farm income if it meant underwriting the inefficient producer. They preferred the concept of parity return for production, which was income support one step removed. Consequently, solutions were based on manipulating production and marketing, principally restraining production, restraining competition, or expanding markets.

Before the 1920s, farmers had tried to stabilize farm income by organizing private institutions such as cooperatives and commodity exchanges. But the magnitude of the agricultural distress in the 1920s made most agrarians turn to the federal government for relief. Three schemes, each requiring government intervention, found wide support: domestic price supports, protective tariffs, and export subsidies. Many plans featuring one or more of these devices were proposed, such as the McNary-Haugen program, the export debenture plan, and the domestic allotment program, and they were to be debated almost continuously for the next half century.

The New Deal gave proponents of governmental activism the power to test some of the agricultural schemes of the 1920s. The first Agricultural Adjustment Act (AAA) established parity as the goal of the farm program; it authorized a domestic allotment plan whereby farmers were assigned acreage or production allotments and (under subsequent amendments) marketing quotas. The government also provided storage loans on agricultural products via the Commodity Credit Corporation (CCC), enabling a farmer to get an immediate loan with the option to sell to the government at a set price if the market fell or to redeem the loan and sell to a private dealer if the market rose. The AAA authorized the use of export subsidies where possible, and through a Federal Surplus Relief Corporation the government could buy surplus commodities and divert them into relief activities.

Although much of this initial legislation was held to be unconstitutional, the second AAA in 1938 adopted many of the same features, including support loans, acreage allotments, and marketing quotas. To dispose of surpluses already accumulated, it authorized a school lunch plan, some relief distribution, an experimental food stamp program, research projects, and export subsidies. It also authorized the president to impose import quotas whenever domestic price support operations were threatened by an influx of foreign products.

Just as American agriculture was settling down to find out how these government controls would work over an extended period, the Second World War arrived. Controls were hastily removed and production incentives substituted, and farm prosperity rose to the highest level since the end of the First World War. As the war drew to a close, administration officials discussed reducing incentives, but because they thought the postwar world would need more food they decided to continue stimulating agricultural output.

After the war, shiploads of agricultural commodities

were delivered to Europe and Asia, empty bellies were filled with American food, and at home farm prices remained high. But once more the bubble burst. Surpluses again started accumulating in government bins, and farm income declined by nearly a third between 1947 and 1950. The volume of agricultural exports fell rapidly in 1951 and 1952, and their dollar value plummeted nearly 30 percent. The decline was due in part to the reduction of American economic aid to Western Europe; in part, too, exports contracted because agricultural production and protectionism recovered in Western Europe; the dollar was scarce in importing countries; domestic price supports set American commodities above world prices; and American export controls limited trade with the Soviet Union and her allies.[1]

For certain crops and areas, of course, the effect of this decline in exports was much greater than for others. Meat and poultry producers, for example, were not heavily dependent on foreign markets. But when wheat and flour exports dropped from 475 million bushels in 1951–52 to 325 million bushels in 1952–53 and when cotton exports declined from 5.5 million bales to 3.5 million bales over the same period, these were staggering blows for the economies of the agricultural South, Great Plains, and Pacific Northwest.[2]

Wartime demands—this time in Korea—had buffered some of the decline in prices, but the prospect of peace in 1953 seemed to presage agricultural depression. Except in periods of conflict, agriculture had been depressed for more than thirty years, and many people assumed that the government must somehow intervene to keep agriculture solvent.

One thing the government could do to stop the downward slide of prices was to purchase commodities through the Commodity Credit Corporation. Acting under the authority of the Stabilization Act of 1942, the CCC began acquiring large holdings of wheat, cotton, tobacco, corn, vegetable oils, and dairy products. By the end of 1952 the CCC had a crop year carryover of 5.6 million bales of cotton and 605.5 million bushels of wheat—in both cases, an amount double that of the previous season. Although legislation authorized acreage controls and marketing quotas to relieve such pressures, loopholes in these laws allowed production to continue unchecked.[3]

Technology, it seemed, joined with politics to make the problem worse. By 1953 a chemical revolution had produced effective ways to control weeds, plant diseases, insects, and parasites; new developments in genetics further improved livestock and plant stock; Southern agriculture was transformed by the adoption of effective mechanical cotton pickers. Crop production per acre was 110 percent of that in 1950, while output per hour was up fully 25 percent. These changes further increased the amount of capital necessary to farm profitably, and farm concentration proceeded.[4]

As the repercussions of the decline in exports and the growth of surplus stocks rolled across the entire farm economy, farm spokesmen began demanding that the government act to stabilize farm income. Once again the remedies of the 1920s were trotted out: production controls, marketing quotas, import controls, export market expansion. Some observers began to wonder whether midcentury American agriculture could prosper only in times of war. Others wondered whether agriculture's slide into depression would pull the entire economy along with it. All assumed that the government would take steps to maintain farm income. The new Eisenhower administration had to find a way to meet that expectation.

Chapter 1

The Influences

City people and foreign people need to see that some form of price stability is necessary for world economic stability.
—*John H. Davis, Assistant Secretary of Agriculture, 1953*

FOREIGN ECONOMIC POLICY is a compromise of compromises. It spans domestic and foreign policy issues, troubles private citizens and public servants, agitates foreign governments and domestic pressure groups, engages Congress and international organizations. It is a constantly changing balance of ideology and expediency reflecting the shifting influence of institutions and individuals.

Agricultural trade policy illustrates the point exactly. Of primary interest to the Department of Agriculture, its congressional allies, various farm and food interest groups, and consumers, it is also important to the departments of State, Commerce, and Treasury, to the economic aid agencies, and to foreign governments and international bodies. And just as these entities affect the course of agricultural trade policy, so the policy forces adjustments in their goals and methods.

No administration can have a single, coherent agricultural trade policy. What passes for policy at any one time is the result of personal philosophies, interagency logrolling, standard operating procedures, sequential problem-solving involving no specific consideration of long-range objectives.

6

and bureaucratic indecision. During the Eisenhower administration, however, there was a remarkably high and consistent level of policy discussion, reflecting the Eisenhower officials' desire to resolve these conflicting pressures without relinquishing their ideals or diminishing the power and prestige of the administration.

Eisenhower himself was not deeply interested in agricultural problems. True, he made the requisite speeches and congressional statements, but he had little more than a cursory knowledge of agricultural issues.[1] Consequently, on matters of farm policy Eisenhower's most important decision was his choice of the secretary of agriculture. Eisenhower believed in selecting associates who were sympathetic to his brand of Republicanism, giving them administrative freedom, and defending them against their critics until further defense was clearly untenable. Cabinet members were not to bring departmental business to him, and after initial rebuffs they did not. He believed differences should be resolved as far down the hierarchy as possible; it was only when issues could not be handled at lower levels that White House staff or the president were to be involved.[2]

Eisenhower chose Ezra Taft Benson as his secretary of agriculture. Benson was above all else a Mormon clergyman, but in his secular life he was a dedicated agriculturalist. He grew up on a farm, took an M.S. in agricultural economics at Iowa State College, operated a farm, worked for the Idaho extension service, and served as the executive secretary of the National Council of Farmer Cooperatives. Although not a politician, he was slightly involved in Republican political activities, participating in the Thomas Dewey campaign in 1948 and supporting Taft in 1952. He was a friend of Eisenhower's brother Milton, and it was probably this connection that led to his selection as secretary.

In personal philosophy, Benson stood close to Herbert Hoover. Like the former president, he was deeply committed to a cooperative capitalism in which the federal government merely lent aid to private enterprise. The public and private sectors, he believed, must work together to export agricul-

tural products, the government opening doors and helping
to build future markets, the trade competing fairly with
quality products. Food and fiber, he thought, should move
through "free competitive markets, not government warehouses," and, like Hoover, he had a deep belief in the efficacy of "old-fashioned American salesmanship," provided
it could retain its Yankee aggressiveness. Both men had an
abiding faith in the power of information and education to
raise production, expand markets, and strengthen the nation's economic mechanisms. There was a religious fervor in
Benson's belief that the "farmer's best hope of getting his
fair share of the national income is through efficient production—balanced production—and better marketing—made
possible through research, education, cooperation and free
initiative."[3] Essentially this was an agricultural restate-
ment of Hoover's philosophy of "voluntaryism," with its
emphasis on production efficiency, private initiative, industry cooperation, and federal leadership as elements of industrial self-regulation for the national good.

Also like Hoover, Benson favored study commissions and
advisory panels of private citizens as a means of injecting
new ideas into government, and these committees and commissions became usual features of Benson's department.
But Benson's appointees tended to have views much like his
own and so were hardly a source of new ideas. The committees and commissions were primarily a rubber stamp for departmental policies, a public relations ploy to create a false
sense of public participation, and possibly a psychological
placebo whereby department officials could believe they had
consulted "the people."

Finally, both Benson and Hoover were accused of being
more responsive to suffering overseas than to suffering at
home. Just as Hoover had been involved in relief during and
after the First World War, Benson had worked in relief programs following the Second. Both had a deep sympathy for
those who suffered from hunger. But both also believed that
hunger would ultimately be eliminated by private initiative, with the national government intervening only to aid
private efforts.[4]

In short, Ezra Taft Benson—religious leader, agricultural cooperative official, farm economist—held conflicting ideals of individualistic competition, cooperation, and humanitarianism. His belief in the yeoman farmer struggled with his promotion of aggressive agribusiness practices. The desire to assist the farmer tempered the belief that the government must leave him the "freedom to farm." The humanitarian impulse to share America's agricultural technology with other nations contradicted the fear that increasing foreign production would decrease American exports. The conviction that the hungry must be fed confounded the conviction that it was morally preferable to sell rather than to donate. Within himself, Benson debated most of the issues that marked the public controversy over agricultural policy.

Benson was far from the only strong-minded member of the Eisenhower cabinet. Like him, Secretary of State John Foster Dulles, Secretary of Commerce Sinclair Weeks, and Secretary of the Treasury George Humphrey firmly believed in capitalist trade, the immorality of the Soviet Union, the obligation of the United States to lead the "free world," and the necessity for an expanded trade between free world allies. A balance of exports over imports, such men held, was desirable, but the disparity could not be so large that trade partners found it difficult to earn American dollars. Nor could the United States revert to its earlier economic nationalism. Indeed, by ignoring the isolationist wing of the Republican party they legitimized the internationalism of the postwar period in a manner no Democratic administration could have achieved.

Yet there were substantial differences in the positions of these cabinet members. Weeks, for example, was not willing to trade with the Soviet bloc, a possibility Benson was willing to explore. Humphrey opposed foreign economic assistance, to the dismay of Dulles. And howls of anguish could be heard from nearly all cabinet members when Humphrey demanded that the federal budget be cut substantially.[5] The cabinet also divided on the issue of agricultural exports. Benson made increasing exports one of his major goals. But Humphrey stubbornly opposed using Treasury funds to sub-

sidize shipments; Secretary of Defense Charles Wilson
viewed overseas sales chiefly as a means of providing
revenue to pay military bills in foreign countries; and
Dulles saw them as a foreign policy weapon, albeit one
whose use was fraught with headaches (Sherman Adams reports that whenever the subject came up "Dulles had a nervous tremor"[6]). Benson and Dulles both believed it sinful to
destroy food in a world where people were hungry, though
they preferred that surpluses be sold rather than donated.
Yet they differed on the means to increase sales, Benson
pressing to lower foreign trade barriers (which he believed
unduly restrictive), and Dulles stalling because he feared
foreign retaliation to an abruptly expanded export program.
These were self-assured, obstinate men, convinced of the
"rightness" of their ideas; the road to a common administration position on agricultural exports could not be smooth.

In addition to the ideological influence of these cabinet
members, three men just outside the cabinet circle also
brought their personal philosophies to bear on the development of the administration's export policy. They were Don
Paarlberg, an economic adviser to Benson who became an
assistant secretary of agriculture, a White House staff member, and finally the first director of Food for Peace; Clarence
Francis, special adviser to Eisenhower on agricultural surplus disposal; and Clarence Randall, special assistant to Eisenhower for foreign economic policy.

An agricultural economist from Purdue, Paarlberg was
invited to serve as Benson's economic adviser on the
strength of a paper on the International Wheat Agreement
that he wrote with Earl Butz and J. W. Hicks. In it the
economists recommended that the agreement be emasculated but the facade preserved so that the United States
would not be criticized for refusing to renew the agreement
in any form, a pragmatic approach that appealed to Benson.[7]
Moreover, Paarlberg's general economic views were similar
to the secretary's. "Every bushel we export, even at zero return," he declared, "is a net gain, better than costly and end-
less storage." And while he did not think exports were a
complete solution to the twin problems of farm surpluses

and low farm income (that would come only when price support levels could be reduced and supply and demand allowed to find a free market balance), he believed they were a vital transition measure. Later Paarlberg became increasingly enthusiastic about the international political advantage of export transactions. Since "agriculture represents our greatest absolute and relative advantage over the Communist world," he argued, it should be used to advance foreign economic policy, either by supplying farm products at concessional prices or by outright donation to allies and noncommunist developing nations.[8]

Clarence Francis, the second of the influential figures outside the cabinet, was brought into the administration in 1954 from the chairmanship of General Foods to coordinate surplus disposal efforts. With his background in business and sales, he was convinced that modern management techniques could quickly eliminate the surplus. Asked by the White House to estimate the time needed to reduce burdensome stocks, he blithely suggested ninety days. He was ready to "get rid of surpluses" in any way he could, and while making a nod toward respecting the traditional markets of other nations, he was soon stretching the definition of "traditional" American markets as far as possible. Francis also argued that agricultural surpluses should be sold to the Soviet bloc (after all, he said, it was a market).[9]

The third influential figure was Clarence Randall, a former head of Inland Steel. Early in the administration, Eisenhower established a commission to study foreign economic policy and named Randall its chairman, in part because in his book *A Creed for Free Enterprise,* Randall had written that American aid to Europe was "justified for no other purpose than to advance American security." Although Randall saw the Soviet bloc as the "enemy," he did suggest that trade with the bloc was not unthinkable.[10]

Two years later, in his 1954 Walgreen lectures at the University of Chicago, Randall reemphasized his commitment to the private sector. The nation's goals, he insisted, were security and a steadily rising standard of living, goals that could be achieved only by "the maximum possible reliance upon private initiative, vigorous competition, and the free market." Hence the foreign economic policy of the United States should strive to expand trade reciprocity so that other nations might earn dollars, to dismantle the price supports and marketing controls whose maintenance was "too un-American to contemplate," and to reintegrate American agriculture into the world trading community. While moving in this direction, the United States should avoid both state trading ("lest such a pattern of conduct, adopted as a temporary expedient, become a permanent part of our government structure") and the "mad processes of export subsidies, import quotas, manipulations, and regulations."[11]

While Benson and Dulles, Humphrey and Weeks, Paarlberg, Francis, and Randall all operated within a similar philosophic framework, their emphases were different. It was inevitable that the goals of national security, fiscal conservatism, domestic farm relief, aid to suffering humanity, and overall trade expansion would create tension and conflict within the administration.

But more than just individual ideals and ideologies shaped foreign economic policy during the fifties. Each of the departments and agencies of government that had an interest in foreign trade also exerted an institutional influence, and each of these bodies had a penumbra of congressional committees, client organizations, extranational counterparts, and private citizens that lived in a symbiotic relationship with the institution and helped influence its policy position.

Of the departments involved in the formulation of agricultural export policy, the two most influential were State and Agriculture, and the upper hand tended to belong to the stronger. At the beginning of the administration, the power was flowing toward Agriculture, in large measure because it had strong congressional support. It consistently received appropriations that exceeded the previous year's budget and occasionally even exceeded the department's requests. The State Department, on the other hand, suffered from more enemies than friends (at least on the House floor), and throughout the period it had great difficulty in obtaining money from Congress.[12] Congressional support also significantly expanded the Department of Agriculture's bureaucratic territory during 1953–54. In two major actions, Congress awarded the department the oversight of agricultural attachés, which were transferred to it from the Department of State, and the supervision of overseas disposal of farm surpluses through PL 480. At the same time, the House Agriculture Committee acquired jurisdiction over legislation on overseas disposal of agricultural products; consequently, Agriculture would formulate the policy on surplus disposal and report to its own oversight committee rather than watch State formulate policy under the guidance of its committee. In interagency warfare, the ability to formulate policy could be crucial.

Another factor contributing to the strength of the Department of Agriculture was its ability to rely on a forceful external constituency that helped to mold agricultural policy and shared in its implementation.[13] The general farm organizations, commodity groups, and representatives of agribusiness often served as advisory, lobbyist, and regulatory arms of the departmental structure. And, given the practice of drawing upon their members to fill department positions, the frequency of consultation, and the interlocking network of friendships, goals, and informal contacts, it was sometimes difficult to discern the line between public and private organizations. Yet, much as the department drew strength from their support, it also found itself in many respects their prisoner, heeding their wishes and pleading their cases in order to insure their support.

Of these private adjuncts and pressure groups, the American Farm Bureau Federation (AFBF) was clearly the most important during the Eisenhower years. For one thing, the bureau and its friends dominated Benson's appointments. Not only was a former AFBF vice-president now an assistant secretary, but two other assistant secretaries had been state Farm Bureau directors, one head of the Foreign Agricultural Service had been employed by the national office, and the advisory committees of the department were heavily staffed with persons who had either state or national bureau connections. In addition, since the county-level bureaus have historically been allied with the county extension agents, who were tied to the agricultural colleges, Farm Bureau policies were often backed by representatives of these institutions. And though advice was solicited from other farm organizations, the department usually ended up adopting the bureau's position and at times directly incorporated bureau language into departmental issuances. As one USDA official admitted, "We try to start out with our programs being independent of all the farm pressure groups, but we usually end up buying just about what the Farm Bureau advocates."[14] The bureau, in short, exhibited all the characteristics of an effective lobbyist. Its leaders knew "the optimum stage of the decision for delivery of their message"; knew "the officials or their advisers who [were] involved in the decision and who [were] most likely to be receptive to the messages"; had a "clear and open channel" of communication; attracted attention; composed messages that were "credible and legitimate"; and supplemented official messages by grass-roots communications and messages from like-minded elites.[15] And on agricultural export policy the bureau's message was clear: sell through the private trade.

As much as the Farm Bureau was in, the National Farmers Union (NFU) was out. Appointments of its members to departmental positions were few, and at least one may have been calculated to irritate the national leadership.[16] Its lack of influence was partly because of its Democratic ties, partly because former Secretary of Agriculture Brannan was now NFU counsel and other Brannan staffers held NFU policy posts, and partly because the general NFU ideology was anathema to Benson and his staff.[17]

Somewhere between these two in influence stood the National Grange and the central organization of agricultural cooperatives. The Grange had some representatives appointed to committees and commissions, but its philosophy was not as close to Benson's as was the Farm Bureau's, and it did not attain the bureau's strikingly close relationship with the department.[18] The most prominent representative of national farm cooperative organizations in the Department of Agriculture was Benson himself, but there were also a number of other men from cooperatives in the top echelons. Since cooperatives tend to specialize by commodity, they mainly attempted to influence the department on specific commodity issues and through the various commodity committees rather than to advise on overall policy as the Farm Bureau did. When the National Council of Farmer Cooperatives did express an opinion on agricultural export policy, however, it supported private investment and private foreign sales promotion "in a favorable climate created by the Departments of Agriculture, Commerce, and State," a position identical to Benson's own.[19]

In addition to the cooperatives, other commodity-based organizations attempted to influence department policy-making, their homogeneous memberships giving their demands a more specific focus than those of the general farm groups and their geographic concentration giving them particularly good ties with members of Congress. Groups representing stockmen, wheat and cotton growers, dairymen, and orchardmen—all of whom produced commodities that were in surplus during the fifties—were particularly strident in their demands, and the department usually heard them out.

The growing power of agribusiness in the farm economy was reflected in its rapidly rising influence on the Department of Agriculture. Agribusiness lobbyists included the traditional agricultural processors, the transportation industries, warehousing and port facilities (the increase in surplus holdings in leased warehouses created a powerful lobby as the industry grew to depend on these revenues), exporter organizations (especially those for cotton), and a number of banks. Agribusinessmen were named to prominent positions in the department and on its committees, and at the close of the administration many USDA officials found places for themselves in the agribusiness community. Labor groups, on the other hand, rarely lobbied on agricultural export issues, and the department was not notably responsive to their entreaties.[20] Nor were consumers particularly vocal.

Good lobbyists, of course, spread their activities throughout the government. General farm organizations, commodity groups, and agribusiness representatives lobbied the

White House and the departments of State and Commerce on export issues, but their main locus of activity was the Department of Agriculture. Likewise, several lobbyists whose primary target was the State Department lobbied the Department of Agriculture on agricultural export policy. The most prominent of the latter were the private relief agencies, both secular and religious, foreign governments, and international organizations with associated general agricultural and commodity groups.

The voluntary relief agencies depended upon the availability of cheap commodities to supply their overseas programs. They lobbied individually (the most persistent of the group was CARE) and through the American Council of Voluntary Agencies. Some donations were made directly to them by the Department of Agriculture under the provisions of the Agricultural Act of 1949, but the agencies purchased the remainder, principally wheat, rice, and dried milk.

Foreign governments also attempted to influence export policy. State and Agriculture both dealt directly with foreign emissaries, and although both exporters of competitive products and potential importers made representations, the former were the principal lobbyists.[21] Sometimes the approach would be made by the embassy in Washington, sometimes by a counterpart organization within the foreign government (the Canadian Wheat Board contacting the USDA's Grain Division, for example), sometimes—although less frequently—by the foreign government to the American embassy in its capital, sometimes through the medium of an international organization. Private interests within foreign countries also attempted to influence policy. Among the most active of these were the cotton exchanges in Liverpool and Le Havre, the textile and soybean processors in Japan, and various national dairy groups.

An astonishing array of international agricultural organizations ineffectually attempted to shape United States agricultural policy in the 1950s. Generally these bodies were subdivisions of an international organization of which the United States was a member. The United States participated reluctantly in these agricultural adjuncts, usually choosing to support those in which there was some hope of American control. The policy positions they took often offended the American planners, for among their statements during the decade were ones condemning dumping, supporting international trade regulation, and advocating world food reserves.

In addition, there were various international commodity organizations that, like the great international agricultural groups, represented at least theoretical influences on American export policy. During the interwar period attempts had been made to establish international trade agreements on sugar, wheat, and cotton, but only a wheat agreement was in effect when the Eisenhower administration took office, and that was about to expire. Negotiations were under way on its extension, however, and the administration would have to take a position on United States participation in it.

The responsibility for formulating and executing agricultural trade policy lay with Ezra Taft Benson and the Department of Agriculture. Closer in spirit to the New Deal's reciprocal trade philosophy than to its economic nationalism, Benson sought to move gradually from the inherited New Deal regulation of agriculture to an economy in which farmers would have, in his favorite phrase, "freedom to farm." Others in the administration hoped to modify his policies in certain not altogether harmonious ways, while members of Congress, agricultural organizations and commodity groups, humanitarian organizations, foreign nations and producer groups, and a variety of international organizations attempted to influence the administration's policy for their own ends.

Through conflict and compromise, choices would be made: difficult, fundamental choices about the role of government in the nation's agricultural economy. And in the process of making these choices, the administration would thoroughly debate the ideological and economic influences on America's export policy.

Chapter 2

The Inheritance

Read the headlines during the Coolidge and Hoover Administrations and see how similar they are to today's. Washington thinking even in Agriculture is that as long as industry is booming agriculture will be OK. That didn't happen in the '20's and will not happen now either.
　　　　　　—*William G. Lodwick, Department of Agriculture, 1953*

THE MODERNIZING PROCESS in agriculture tends to increase the production and productivity of the farmer, increase the capital concentration in agriculture, and squeeze the marginal farmer out of the system. But the peculiar position of agriculture within the American political economy creates strong resistance to this evolution. In part the resistance is the result of nostalgia for an earlier, rural America, where agriculture was not just another industry but a way of life shared by most citizens; in part, too, it reflects the theory of agricultural fundamentalism that argues that traditional agriculture is the foundation of national prosperity upon which all other industries depend; and, probably, in part it reveals a fear that the increased consolidation of agriculture will bring the end of the family farm, replacing it with a faceless, unknown corporate unit that will then dominate America's supply of food and fiber to the detriment of the consumer. The political effect of these beliefs is consider-

18

able, and officials of the Eisenhower administration knew this. As they saw it, their job was to ensure the freedom to farm, and with it the freedom to modernize, within the context of the traditional rural social structure.

One way to resist the consolidation process without sacrificing the commitment to modernization is to ensure markets for all agricultural production. If surpluses build up, the argument goes, prices fall, creating pressures throughout agriculture but making the position of the small farmer especially untenable. If, however, all products find a market, the productive small farmer will receive his fair share of return for production and so can continue to operate and to modernize on a small scale. Guaranteed markets, in other words, tend to compensate for economies of scale.

If this theory of guaranteed markets is adopted, market strategy becomes central to policy-making. One method to ensure markets is to limit production to an amount that current outlets can absorb; an alternative is to develop additional markets and new products to utilize all that farmers can produce. Although during the 1920s and 1930s a number of schemes to limit production were promoted, traditionally Americans have chosen to seek supplementary markets, mostly abroad.

Ezra Taft Benson firmly believed that the greatest assistance the government could give to agriculture would be to free production and marketing from government controls. It was only through the free market, he thought, that commercial marketing could be expanded, farm income enhanced, and government costs reduced. He had an early opportunity to move in this direction when the International Wheat Agreement (IWA) came up for renewal in January 1953.

Although agricultural leaders held widely divergent views of the efficacy of the agreement, Benson decided to support its renewal if it was revised to allow prices to fluctuate with the world market. In this way, he believed, most of the constraints would be eliminated but a facade of international cooperation would be maintained.[1] Formal meetings on renewal began on January 30, 1953. Ultimately the United Kingdom refused to accept the negotiated price range and withdrew, leaving the agreement without the adherence of the world's major wheat importer. A provision for yearly price adjustments was included in the final agreement at United States insistence, and the United States ratified it in July. Late in the year, as market-breaking surpluses accumulated, the United States announced that it would sell government-owned wheat at the agreement subsidy level to nations not signatories of the agreement (e.g., the United Kingdom). At the same time, Canada and the United States established a Joint United States–Canada Committee on Trade and Economic Affairs, pledging to consult with each other on the disposal of surpluses and to refrain from interfering with "normal commercial marketings" in attempts to move surplus stocks.[2] This meant that international wheat prices were actually those established by the Canadian price-maintenance policy, the United States sales policy toward nonagreement nations, and United States–Canadian cooperation. Wheat moved under the IWA now dropped to half the quantity of previous years. The USDA had managed to nod to international cooperation by signing the agreement and yet to retain real pricing power in a tight exporter cabal. True to Don Paarlberg's suggestion, the agreement was emasculated.[3]

With the IWA negotiations well under way, Benson and his aides began to examine the export levers they had inherited. They were optimistic. Not fully perceiving the lethal combination of exploding agricultural technology, reviving agricultural production and protectionism abroad, and conflicting commitments of the parties involved, they believed that the surplus was a temporary phenomenon, a "hump on the curve," as Assistant Secretary of Agriculture John H. Davis put it.[4] They felt that it was possible to refine the use of the tools available to them and to adopt new ones selectively, and that these would take care of the short-range glut. Thereafter, as the State Department sanguinely observed, they assumed that Benson would "be successful in devising a domestic program that will not continue to build up surpluses."[5] Four possible trade stimulants seemed especially useful to the Eisenhower officials: Export-Import loans, barter arrangements, export subsidies, and relief donations. These, they hoped, would allow the administration to support and supplement commercial marketing activity but not to supplant it.

The first of these export levers was the export-import loan program of the Export-Import Bank, an institution established in 1934 specifically to promote American exports by providing loans to foreign governments and businesses for purchases in the United States. In making loan decisions, the bank took into account depression in a domestic industry, and during the preceding two decades several loans had been made to assist cotton exports. Now, in March 1953, Benson urged Secretary of the Treasury Humphrey to speed consideration of new Export-Import Bank cotton loans by the National Advisory Council on International Monetary and Financial Problems (NAC). Favorable NAC action, Benson argued, would "reduce the need for less desirable and more costly methods of export promotion," and in May the council authorized a $12 million cotton loan to Spain and a $40 million loan to Japan. In fact, between August 1953 and July 1954, Japan purchased nearly a quarter of all American cotton exported, largely through Ex-Im loans, and, as Assistant Secretary of Agriculture John H. Davis told the bank's director, these loans "enabled American cotton to compete with cotton of other growths." "The savings in financing, provided by the Export-Import Bank credit, more than offset the lower price of the non–United States cotton," he declared.[6]

A second inherited export stimulant was the 1949 amendment to the Commodity Credit Corporation charter that authorized the CCC to barter agricultural products for "strategic and critical materials" for the national stockpile.[7] This had not been extensively used before 1953; clear procedural guidelines had never been established; and each barter proposal had to be handled de novo. Two efforts were made to barter surplus commodities in 1953, one to pay a portion of the construction cost for United States air bases in Spain in commodities, the other to exchange wheat for Brazilian rare

earths or industrial diamonds for the defense stockpile. Both
were fraught with complications, and only a small Brazilian
barter was later completed.[8]

A third export weapon was section 32 of the Agricultural
Adjustment Act of 1935, which appropriated 30 percent of
yearly customs revenue for use by the secretary of agriculture.[9] In the 1930s these funds had been used twice for
export subsidies—once for cotton and once for wheat. And
following a 1949 amendment directing that they be used
principally for perishable nonbasics (i.e., commodities other
than wheat, cotton, corn, tobacco, rice, and peanuts), the
funds provided subsidies for fruits, nuts, and honey. Since
none of the CCC-stockpiled commodites was involved, the
program depended on the commercial exporter's ability to
obtain supplies, make contacts in USDA-approved importing countries, and carry the financial burden until reimbursed by the government. Given these restrictions, only
about $25 million per year was actually spent in subsidy
payments in the immediate postwar period.[10]

The new Republican administration considered supporting wheat and cotton exports through section 32 subsidies,
but they did not immediately adopt the idea.[11] Export subsidies establish a two-price system, and the State Department
feared that such measures would incur criticism from the
United States' partners in the General Agreement on Tariffs and Trade (GATT) at the GATT meeting scheduled for
late September 1953. In a letter to Benson (with a copy to
the White House), Secretary of State John Foster Dulles
warned that export subsidies could have "serious effects on
our international relations" and "might result in action inconsistent with a principle of the General Agreement on
Tariffs and Trade and the objectives it seeks to promote."[12]
For the time being new export subsidy plans were shelved,
and at the GATT session the United States escaped with
some criticisms of United States trade practices and a formal resolution asking for American "regard" of GATT policies and requesting consultation and a progress report at the
next session.[13]

With the GATT safely over, the Department of Agriculture quickly returned to its subsidy plans. The USDA began selling butter at world market prices in the spring of 1954 despite protests from Denmark and New Zealand; Canada quickly began offering its own butter on the same basis; and France prepared to follow suit.[14] A trade war seemed to be in the offing, and the threat of GATT censure was not a serious deterrent.

The final export lever, relief sales and donations, developed from the provision of the Surplus Property Act of 1944 and the Agricultural Act of 1949 that authorized the CCC to sell stockpiled surplus commodites for export below the domestic market price. Under this provision the CCC periodically announced quantities and prices of stocks offered for sale to private traders for export; thereafter it was the responsibility of the trader to export the stocks acquired. The CCC could also make sales directly to foreign governments and to international organizations for relief work and could donate commodites to voluntary agencies for the same purpose. Although this was potentially a powerful weapon, it had not been widely used before 1953.[15]

Because the fourth lever was limited to sales or to donation through a voluntary agency, it was not an effective way to provide commodities to poor countries for disaster relief. Consequently, when Pakistan suffered a serious drought in the spring of 1953 and its government requested a million tons of United States wheat for relief feeding, Eisenhower appealed to Congress for a special Pakistan relief bill. Dulles urged its passage because of Pakistan's "strategic location," declaring that the Pakistanis would "resist the menace of communism as their strength permits."[16] The legislation passed, but its implementation was delayed while Agriculture and the Foreign Operations Administration (FOA) squabbled over whether hard or soft wheat would be shipped, FOA favoring the former and Agriculture the latter because it "was causing a real storage problem." Long interagency negotiations followed, and finally the administration compromised and shipped both kinds.[17] Argentina complained that the donation ruined a possible Argentine-Pakistan barter arrangement,[18] and although the protest had no effect it foreshadowed aid-trade conflicts to come.

Shortly after the Pakistan measure was signed, the president requested general legislation authorizing him to use agricultural commodities for emergency relief. This encountered stiff opposition from "streams of ambassadors" expressing fear that the bill would be used as a dumping device and from organizations such as the National Grain Trade Council and the Farm Bureau. The latter, in particular, argued that "foreign countries would magnify their needs in an effort to qualify for U.S. gratuity," dollar markets would be impaired, and any future legislation designed to sell surplus agricultural stocks and expand trade would be jeopardized. Such opposition, however, failed to outweigh the support of State, Agriculture, the Foreign Operations Administration, and such lobbyists as CARE, the National Milk Producers' Federation, the Millers' National Federation and the NFU,[19] and the Famine Emergency Relief Act passed easily. Under it Eisenhower soon made commodities available to Jordan, Libya, and Bolivia.[20]

Another special relief program evolved during the June 1953 uprisings in East Germany. West German Chancellor Konrad Adenauer requested food shipments for the East Germans, and in what was surely a most unusual use of the authority granted under section 513(b) of the Mutual Security Act, Eisenhower decided that the allocation of up to $15 million for East German food relief was "important to the security of the United States." The administration first offered to provide the food through the auspices of the Soviet government, but this was rejected by the Soviets. The United States then cooperated with West German and West Berlin authorities to make food packages available to any East German who would cross into West Berlin to collect them. Nearly six million packages were distributed in this remarkable humanitarian-propaganda effort, one that had nothing to do with immediate United States security and everything to do with a long-term effort to entice East Germany into the Western orbit by persuasion or revolution.[21]

Another possible outlet for surplus agricultural commodities suggested by the relief operations was the American military establishment, which could use food for sale, donation, or barter both to meet the needs of American and allied armies and to feed occupied populations and help cover the costs of military procurement abroad. In the spring of 1953, the administration decided to seek legislation authorizing such disposals, but it could not decide whether to seek a separate bill or an amendment to the pending Mutual Security Act. Benson, who had already begun urging the Defense Department to tie its purchases of foreign military materials to reciprocal purchases of surplus American foodstuffs, supported a surplus disposal amendment to the Mutual Security bill. However, the Bureau of the Budget warned that such amendments would seriously weaken the Mutual Security program by making it "appear to be little more than a surplus dumping operation."

Don Paarlberg, too, was wary. He doubted that large quantities of commodities could be introduced into the world market without disturbing commercial marketing to some degree, and he worried that an amendment would pressure the Mutual Security Administration into making "deals" at the expense of "our regular commercial exports," especially if Agriculture was not given the authority to rule on and limit the operations. He questioned the idea that the proposed sales for local currencies would mean a net increase in consumption, except perhaps to the extent that it would allow artificial restrictions to be lifted. And regular American exporters, he warned, would suffer because of falling local prices owing to greater supply.[22]

Agreeing with Paarlberg's reservations, the White House now would have preferred to leave an agricultural surplus provision out of the Mutual Security bill altogether. Congress, however, had now seized on the surplus-disposal-cum-relief idea, and the administration decided that it could "live with it."[23] Consequently, the new Mutual Security Act (MSA) contained section 550, which authorized the sale for local currencies of between $100 million and $250 million worth of surplus agricultural commodites, provided these

went to friendly countries and did not interfere unduly with
the normal marketings of the United States and its friends.
Where possible, private trade channels were to be used, new
market areas were to be cultivated, and transshipment
guarantees were to be sought. Proceeds could be used to
finance overseas military purchases, provide foreign military assistance, purchase material for the United States
stockpile, provide production loans or grants-in-aid for
friendly countries, or develop markets "on a mutually bene-
ficial basis."[24]

The farm organizations had backed the section 550 legislation and were eager to see the new provision utilized.[25]
They were to be disappointed. By January 1, 1954, only programs for West Germany and the United Kingdom had been
approved, and just two purchase authorizations (both for the
United Kingdom) had been issued, one for $20 million worth
of tobacco and the other for $5 million worth of prunes.[26] Un-
derstandably, the USDA's Foreign Agricultural Service
(FAS) and the farm organizations were unhappy that the
program was not moving more rapidly and was not moving
items in the greatest surplus. While acknowledging Assistant Secretary of Agriculture John Davis's explanation that
the program had to take into consideration "foreign policy
and military objectives . . . as well as the matter of farm surpluses," the service urged numerous changes. In particular,
it believed that the State Department and the Foreign
Operations Administration (which was responsible for the
program) were paying too much heed to diplomatic niceties
and far too little to the surplus disposal the legislation demanded.[27]

The FAS criticisms, however, were unduly harsh. Actually the whole process of handling an application took only
about a month, which seemed interminable to those sitting
on a melting pile of butter but seemed rapid to the slow-
paced diplomatic machinery. Contrary to Agriculture's belief, moreover, the State Department did at times overrule
protests from competitor nations about pending sales. It approved an Italian cotton sale over Pakistani protests and a
United Kingdom beef sale in spite of Australian objections.

And at times it did bypass consultation with other suppliers in favor of rapid transactions. It did not consult with Australia, for example, on a Japanese wheat sale, and the Australians were indignant.[28]
During the first months of 1954 the program moved a bit more rapidly. Procurement authorizations were issued for more than $40 million in commodities, including beef to the United Kingdom, cotton to West Germany and Italy, tobacco and cotton for Finland, and wheat for Japan and Afghanistan. Still, the pace was slow, and Agriculture received complaints from the grain trade and from agricultural attachés abroad that the Section 550 program was shrouded in confusion and delay. Furthermore, some governments were hesitant about participating because under the program surplus agricultural commodities could be substituted for appropriated funds that might otherwise be available as military or economic aid. It already seemed clear that this limited program could not provide the answer to the surplus disposal problem.[29]

The four major export levers—Ex-Im loans, barter, export subsidies, and relief donations—had now been tried and found unequal to the task of maintaining farm income. The administration did not have to rely solely on export stimulants, however. The Eisenhower officials had also inherited a number of import controls designed to protect domestic agriculture from influxes of foreign commodities, and experiments were going on in these areas, too. Three import control laws were especially important. First, section 22 of the Agricultural Adjustment Act gave the president the authority to establish import fees or impose import quotas if the Tariff Commission found that imports of a commodity would be in such volume as to "render ineffective, tend to render ineffective, or materially interfere with" domestic price support programs. Second, escape clauses and peril-point procedures of the Trade Agreements Act, which were written into all trade agreements completed by the United States after 1945, allowed domestic industries to request that the government modify or withdraw a trade agreement concession in order to remedy serious injury to a domestic

industry. Third, section 104 of the Defense Production Act of
1950 extended wartime import embargoes on peanuts, butter, flaxseed, and rice; established a new one on nonfat dry
milk solids; and authorized country-by-country import quotas for cheese.[30]

As surplus commodites continued to flow into USDA
hands in the fall of 1953, Benson recommended that section
22 import controls be invoked on oats, rye, and long-staple
cotton. The State Department vigorously opposed a cotton
quota. Peru and Egypt depended heavily on cotton for foreign exchange earnings, it said, and Peru "has given the
United States strong political support in Latin American affairs," "follows a policy of ensuring a very favorable climate
for U.S. private investment," and would "justifiably" look
upon the quota as an impairment of a GATT concession.
Even more serious, the State Department said, limiting the
importation of Egyptian cotton might impair the ability of
the United States to influence a settlement between Egypt
and the United Kingdom over the Suez Canal. With White
House mediation, a compromise was finally reached
whereby Agriculture would request a Tariff Commission investigation, Eisenhower would request further information,
and a decision would be postponed until "summer or fall."[31]

Evasive action was also taken on the oat problem. The
Tariff Commission agreed with Benson that oat imports
were adversely affecting the domestic price support program; so to forestall any difficulties with Canada that a
quota might cause, the United States managed to work out a
gentlemen's agreement whereby Canada would voluntarily
limit oat exports to the United States for ten months and the
new United States import quota of 2.5 million bushels would
apply only to non-Canadian oats. This, however, brought
immediate protests from the importers of Argentine oats,
prompting the Foreign Agricultural Service to expound
upon the difficulties of gentlemen's agreements and the pre-
ferability of "restrictive actions applied equally to all importing and exporting interests concerned."[32] FAS had a
point: at the least, such an agreement violated the GATT
philosophy of nondiscrimination and open covenants.

A United States rye quota would also affect Canada. But, having discussed this at the time of the oat quota negoatiations, the administration concluded that the Canadians would not object, bowed to pressure from Congress and producers, and ordered a Tariff Commission investigation. To its surprise, Canada *did* object. At the mid-March 1954 meeting of the United States–Canada Joint Economic Committee, the Canadians filed a stinging protest. Eisenhower, however, approved the rye quota and merely sent a conciliatory letter to the Canadian prime minister explaining his action.[33]

By late spring of 1954, with surplus problems worsening, relations between Agriculture and State were extremely tense. The *Farm Journal* called for the State Department to stop hindering farmers, and congressmen and agricultural groups raised questions over slow-moving sales.[34] Benson told Dulles he was "firmly convinced" of the necessity to impose section 22 controls "from time to time over the next few years." If this conflicted with United States GATT commitments, he declared, "these should be amended in order that this Government may be consistent in its international agreements."[35] And at the April 1 meeting of the National Security Council, when Clarence Francis declared that the State Department was either completely stopping or unduly delaying almost every sale, Dulles "came to the edge of his chair."[36]

One result of the April 1 discussion was an interagency agreement that sales were to be consummated "provided no *material* injury" to a friendly power resulted. But this scarcely improved relations. On April 19 Dulles told Benson that USDA charges of State Department obstructionism could "affect most adversely" the work of State. In reply, Benson warned that relegating American farmers "to the role of residual suppliers" was "unthinkable."[37]

The commodity reports for that spring showed that the sources of the friction were not likely to go away. The cotton carryover was approximately 9.6 million bales, about three times more than necessary under a normal supply and demand situation. Surpluses of wheat, fats and oils, tobacco, and some of the minor crops loomed almost as large. And daily carrying charges, so the CCC estimated, would rise by half during fiscal year 1955, from a 1954 average of $852,000 to an amazing $1,207,000.[38]

As foreign observers pointed out, moreover, American policy-makers were not disposed to seek solutions through expanding the domestic market, an approach that in theory might have removed the source of the foreign policy conflicts. In the case of the two most important commodity problems, wheat and cotton, the Department of Agriculture believed that domestic consumption was relatively inelastic. And while campaigns had been launched to increase domestic consumption of dairy and livestock products (which would indirectly stimulate consumption of feed grains and, to a lesser degree, wheat), the only serious proposals for domestic surplus distribution came from members of Congress, but their bills slid into legislative purgatory.

Proposed solutions continued to run in terms of overseas disposal. Yet except for the Ex-Im loans on cotton, all the levers available for this seemed to call into play countervailing forces that rendered them largely ineffective. Attempted actions using section 32 funds as export subsidies, for example, brought vigorous protests from competitor nations and from the State Department as being contary to American obligations under GATT. Sales for local currency, which had been authorized by the cabinet in February 1954, faced the same opposition.[39] Barter efforts were stalled in interagency discussions, and disaster relief efforts were sporadic. The most promising new export weapon was section 550 of the Mutual Security Act, but it too was hampered by friction between the departments.[40]

Similarly, efforts to dislodge foreign restrictions on imports clashed with foreign efforts to maintain stable currencies, thereby encountering stiff opposition from nations struggling to overcome dollar shortages and from officials concerned with international financial health. During 1953, to be sure, some gains were made. The United Kingdom, for example, did allow dollars to be used to purchase feed grains, some fats and oils, and a few fruit items, and the

Netherlands did the same for tobacco, cotton, and corn. Yet numerous controls of this sort remained, specially in West Germany and France. And though a May 1954 meeting of the Organization for European Economic Cooperation (OEEC) council of ministers did recommend that member countries should relax the existing quantitative restrictions on imports from the dollar area, this was only a recommendation.[41]

Even in the underdeveloped world, there seemed to be a growing disposition to indulge in gentle international blackmail, requesting irrigation projects or industrial development loans before agreeing to accept the agricultural products the United States so desperately wished to deliver. Colombia, for example, asked for a large-scale assistance program, including irrigation and drainage construction, agricultural machinery and fertilizer, in return for importing United States food products. Egypt informed a USDA trade mission that unless it could purchase wheat and flour at competitive prices for local currency, it would not buy at all, adding that "Russia stands ready to offer wheat for sale to Egypt."[42] And some Third World countries interested in one commodity hoped to block disposal of another: Pakistan and Egypt, for example, might gain cheap wheat but lose their cotton outlets.

The international realm also held some promising signs for the Department of Agriculture. For one, the International Wheat Agreement had been successfully emasculated through the unwitting cooperation of the British and the witting cooperation of the Canadians. For another, the GATT negotiations had produced no more than the expected rebuke. International commodity agreements and international organizations, which had received strong Democratic support during the postwar years, would apparently not be an impediment to Benson's plan for free trade.

The Eisenhower officials were learning to feel their way through the bureaucratic undergrowth. They had tried the current agricultural export levers and had found them wanting. The new Mutual Security legislation was too limited in scope to do the massive short-term export job they envisioned. It was time, they decided, to try to steer some major surplus disposal legislation through the policy process.

Chapter 3

The Legislation

Surplus agricultural commodities are the next most important national problem to that of balancing the budget.
—*Samuel Waugh, Assistant Secretary of State, 1953*

WITH A REPUBLICAN CONGRESS on the Hill and with high interest in the problem of surplus disposal, the officials of the Eisenhower administration reasoned that new export legislation would not be hard to secure. They still believed the surplus difficulties could be solved by "a one shotter," and they set out to devise a program that would provide the final answer. They argued strenuously to insure that their personal philosophies and the positions of their agencies and clienteles would be reflected in the proposed legislation. As policy was reviewed and as a proposal took shape, was introduced, and became law, they engaged in the first serious, structured discussions of the surplus question, and in the process options were clarified and underlying assumptions brought to light.

This leisurely review was made possible by previous Eisenhower commitments to maintain temporarily the current farm program. During the 1952 presidential campaign and again in the first State of the Union message, Eisenhower had declared that price supports on farm commodities would continue until 1954. The goal thereafter, he had indicated, was full parity for the farmer, a goal that listeners

variously interpreted as 100 percent parity price supports or
as a full income parity with industrial workers. In any
event, the administration had a grace period in which to
study the problems and recommend new directions.[1]

Accordingly, in the summer and fall of 1953 the USDA,
the Commission on Foreign Economic Policy, and an interdepartmental committee on the surplus all wrestled with
program proposals for agriculture and with two underlying
questions that had to be answered. One was the old problem
of farm income: Should the federal government support
farm income, and if so, how? The second concerned the extent
to which consumption could be expanded at home and
abroad, given the fact of surplus production. Inevitably the
answers would be primarily political and moral, and only
secondarily economic.

The results, as finally announced in the president's message on agriculture in January 1954, derived from an extremely wide survey of agricultural alternatives. In June
1953 Benson asked the Farm Bureau, the Grange, and the
NFU to hold local discussions on five areas of farm policy—farm income stability and improvements, production
and marketing adjustments, conservation and improvement
of farm resources, capital needs of agriculture, and trade or
aid—and to report the results of this nationwide, grass-
roots survey to him. The departmental commodity advisory
committees and the National Agricultural Advisory Commission also made recommendations, and mail flooded into
the department as every self-styled agricultural economist
gave the USDA the true, simple, and complete solution to
the farm problem.[2]

The range of positions on these questions was very broad.
On the one hand, the Farm Bureau leadership and businessmen like Clarence Randall came very close to saying no, the
federal government should not support farm income, the
only federal involvement should be to remove barriers to
free market operations within which the fittest would sur-
vive. Benson leaned in this direction. On the opposite extreme were the Brannan Plan advocates, who believed that
the need for government support for agricultural income

was inescapable and that the cheapest way to provide this was by direct payments to farmers to maintain their income at an acceptable level. Neil Jacoby of the Council of Economic Advisors supported this, a rather lonely position in Republican ranks.[3]

Between these two extremes lay a wide range of positions whose common denominator was a commodity base for farm income support. Persons taking these positions thought federal support for farm income was necessary but argued both that it was morally preferable to pay the farmer for what he produced rather than to give him a direct income guarantee and also that such supports could be used to help correct the surplus problem. Supports could take the form either of direct payments to farmers (advocated by the Department of Commerce as cheapest in the long run) or of indirect payments under a price support program. In either case their manipulation could stimulate production in certain crops and discourage it in those already in oversupply, something that could not be done if payments were geared to income rather than commodities.

Critics pointed out several weaknesses in such programs. In the first place, they noted, nearly all commodities were in surplus. Hence no genuinely profitable crop substitution was possible, and if payments were to be tied to production and marketing quotas, this would mean paying farmers *not* to produce, a position Republicans found difficult to support, especially since it seemed to smack of Henry A. Wallace and the AAA. In the second place, as the State Department incessantly reiterated, any mechanism that guaranteed a domestic price tended to peg that price above world levels, thus inviting a wave of foreign imports unless import controls were invoked, which in turn tended to provoke foreign retaliation. Furthermore, it meant that American products could compete on the world market only with the aid of export subsidies, a costly program that provoked foreign charges of dumping. Third, critics said, the benefits from commodity price supports went primarily to the large commercial farmer. Such programs left the rural poor almost untouched and were therefore a highly inequitable means of supporting farm income. And, finally, they argued, the rise in domestic retail prices caused by commodity support programs hurt the American consumer, both urban and rural.[4]

Despite such weaknesses, however, commodity programs were amazingly popular. Enjoying particularly wide support, for example, was the Grange's export subsidy plan, which proposed that domestic prices be supported at predetermined levels, that exporters sell at world market prices, and that subsidies make up the difference. Similar, too, were a variety of two-price plans, schemes that would support a domestic (and higher) price for the percentage of a commodity normally marketed in the United States and allow the remainder (ostensibly exported) to be sold at the world price. In addition there was the NFU proposal for negotiating international marketing agreements, based on the International Wheat Agreement format and designed to stabilize the world price for each commodity and create international purchasing guarantees. And still others advocated tinkering with the price support mechanisms already in operation, inserting sliding instead of rigid support scales or basing parity ratios on more recent years ("modernized parity").[5]

By mid-fall the USDA's survey showed that the two-price plan, with concomitant production quotas and price supports, was the favorite of farmers throughout the country. In an August referendum, 87.2 percent of the wheat growers supported production quotas and price supports at 90 percent of parity. Later in the year, cotton growers did likewise by an amazing 93.2 percent, and from the department's advisory groups came a steady stream of recommendations for two-price systems. The wheat advisory committee, for example, advocated supporting the domestically consumed portion of wheat production at 100 percent of parity; the rice, cotton, and peanuts committees would support domestic marketings at 90 percent; and the corn committee recommended flexible supports with a range of 75–100 percent. The National Agricultural Advisory Commission also seriously considered a two-price plan for cotton and wheat.

In the face of these national agricultural attitudes, the policies ultimately recommended in the president's agricultural message differed from current programs only in degree, recommending flexible price supports, limitations on use of acreage allotments, and the modernized parity formula. No one in the administration was completely satisfied with the program, but those involved bowed to the political realities. The most significant new proposal was a "set aside" of $2.5 billion in Commodity Credit Corporation stocks, to be "insulated" from commercial markets and used for disaster relief, foreign aid, domestic school lunch programs, and stockpile reserves. This was not to figure in price support calculations and would therefore give a surreptitious boost to the price support level.[6]

Meanwhile, as the results of the USDA study found their way into the president's January message, the work of the second major group considering agricultural policy was nearing completion. This was the Commission on Foreign Economic Policy, generally known as the Randall Commission in deference to its strong-minded chairman, Clarence Randall.

The commission's structure insured that agricultural interests would be given weighty consideration. Although Randall himself was not an agricultural specialist, the vice-chairman, Lamar Fleming, was a well-known cotton merchant; the staff included such prominent agricultural economists as Ernest T. Baughman, Oscar B. Jesness, and Joseph C. Davis; four of the five senators on the commission were from states with an important agricultural sector; and at least two of the five representatives had rural constituencies.[7]

Hearings were held,[8] the staff prepared working papers, and the public members wrote report sections and submitted them for discussion by the entire membership. Issued on January 23, 1954, the commission's report included a five-page section on agricultural policy that, though brief, elicited written dissents from eight members of the seventeen-man commission. The report argued that "a dynamic foreign economic policy as it relates to agriculture cannot be built out of a maze of restrictive devices such as inflexible price-support programs which result in fixed prices, open or concealed export subsidies, import quotas at home and abroad, excessive use of tariffs here and abroad, exchange restrictions, and state trading." It recommended the complete "elimination of such devices as a part of, or supplement to, our own agricultural policy" and suggested that the International Wheat Agreement "be kept under critical review," with "consideration" of termination in 1956. In the written dissents, Senator Bourke B. Hickenlooper and Representative Jere Cooper objected to the implied elimination of price supports; Senators Walter F. George and Laurie C. Battle scolded the commission for failing to "point the way in the direction of a constructive solution of our farm program"; Senator Eugene D. Millikin and Representatives Daniel A. Reed and Richard M. Simpson withheld support from the entire report; and public member David McDonald of the Steelworkers called the proposal to abandon price supports and international commodity agreements "disastrous," not only for domestic food supplies but also for "America's leading role in supplying foodstuffs . . . throughout the world."[9]

With a mixed reaction from the participants, domestic newspapers gave the commission mixed reviews, congressional reaction was "predominantly hostile," and the Soviet press chuckled over European discomfiture with the report's tone.[10] In the end, the Department of Agriculture effectively nullified the report's agricultural recommendations by insisting that any inconsistencies between the report and the president's January 11 agricultural message be resolved in favor of the latter. When Randall agreed to this at a cabinet meeting on February 26, the agricultural section of the report was dead.[11]

In the meantime, the third group studying agricultural policy, the interdepartmental committee on the surplus, had been working on legislation. The study group was Benson's idea, and he had persuaded Eisenhower to establish it at the subcabinet level under the chairmanship of Under Secretary of Agriculture True D. Morse.[12] The situation facing the committee was this: in the spring of 1953, as a result of Farm Bureau lobbying, the spring Senate hearings on foreign trade in agricultural products, and the interest of individual senators, a Senate bill had been drafted that authorized the export and sale for foreign currency of $500 million worth of CCC and privately held surplus commodities. Benson had tried to block its introduction, arguing that section 550 of the Mutual Security Act should be given a trial before further legislation was enacted, but he had failed. Introduced on July 24 and discussed briefly on July 28 (one senator mildly complained, "I had never heard about this bill until today"), it had passed on a voice vote. However, Congress adjourned before the House had time to act on it. This Hill recess gave the administration the opportunity to seize the initiative and control the content of any surplus disposal legislation, and it was up to Morse's committee to develop a suitable legislative vehicle.[13]

Realizing that the House Agriculture Committee would take up the Senate bill as soon as Congress came back in January, Morse quickly called the first meeting of the committee on November 30, 1953, just two days after it had been established. The problem, committee members agreed, was to "dispose of this surplus without affecting normal operations or marketing." Although they frankly leaned in the direction of "exporting our problems," the committee asked the Department of Agriculture to study increased domestic disposal, the Office of Defense Mobilization (ODM) to look into stockpiling, especially in Europe, and the Commerce Department to examine the possibilities of barter. A second meeting soon followed, and by the third meeting on December 14 the committee had in hand the first draft of an administration surplus disposal bill.

After several more drafts, the committee agreed in detail on the $2.5 billion set-aside that was incorporated in the president's agricultural message and agreed in principle on a three-year program for disposing of $1 billion worth of surplus commodities, a program that was outlined in the president's 1954 budget message.[14] But despite Eisenhower's call for "fast action," the committee could not agree on a final draft bill. What commodities would be included? Who would have the administrative authority? Should the United States take title to the local currencies? How would they be managed? What kind of marketing safeguards would be acceptable? To what extent should the private sector be involved? Should famine relief authority be included? On all these questions, meetings were held and position papers exchanged, but little progress was made in resolving the "substantial differences" between Agriculture, State, Treasury, the Foreign Operations Administration, and the Office of Defense Mobilization.

Fundamentally, the issue was one of bureaucratic authority. Agriculture and FOA each believed it was the correct agency to administer the program (Agriculture because it held the commodities; FOA because of its MSA experience); State wanted to retain its authority over foreign policy and to be in a position to safeguard normal marketings; Treasury hoped to ensure that at least part of the funds derived from sales were earmarked for the account of the United States; and the Office of Defense Mobilization was interested in using the commodities in its defense stockpile barter program. In addition, there were disputes over how the program would be defined and who would define it. Agriculture, in particular, wanted to ensure that the disposal funds would be in *addition* to the $2.5 billion set aside, that the secretary alone would determine what was in surplus and thus was eligible for programming, and that privately held stocks and private traders would be included in the distribution operation.[15]

Finally, Joseph Dodge of the Bureau of the Budget appealed to Sherman Adams to have the differences "resolved at the White House level." Adams agreed that the situation was out of hand, and he asked Clarence Francis to come to Washington to serve as the White House surplus disposal coordinator.[16]

While the administration squabbled, the House began considering various surplus disposal bills. Representative William Harrison introduced a bill developed by the American Farm Bureau Federation that would increase total

surplus sales to $1.5 billion over a three-year period, and in
support the bureau mobilized its local organizations in a
mass mail campaign. The Department of Agriculture, dis-
satisfied with the drafts coming out of the interdepartmental committee, also urged the administration to support
the Harrison bill; this, the department argued, would "tie in
with the strength" of the Farm Bureau effort and would test
"whether the opportunities of sale for foreign currencies do
exist." The State and FOA bills, it thought, reflected those
agencies' belief that "sales for foreign currencies cannot be
made in substantial volume without interfering either with
United States export trade or that of friendly foreign countries." Francis, hoping to expedite matters, explored the possibility of using the Farm Bureau bill as a basis for reconciling the opposing views of the agencies, but the effort
failed.[17]

As spring wore on, some sixty bills on surplus disposal
were introduced in the House of Representatives. None of
these had been endorsed by the interminably wrangling administration by the time hearings began during the last
week of April. Given such a vacuum, the House Agriculture
Committee set out to draft its own omnibus farm bill, one
that would include domestic programs, surplus disposal,
foreign trade—everything. The administration, it seemed,
was about to lose all control, and this finally spurred the
interdepartmental group to compromise. In mid-May an administration draft was presented to various interested congressmen for discussion. This was followed by a redraft, a
compromise version that tried to steer through the muddy
waters between the Farm Bureau bill and the desires of
various agencies. And once this was worked out, it moved
through the legislative mills fairly quickly. Introduced by
Representative William Hill, it was discussed by the House
Agriculture Committee on June 3, reported out, debated for
two days by the House as a Committee of the Whole, and
passed on June 16. Following rapid Senate action, the conference committee then made some further adjustments, the
bill was agreed to by both houses, and the president approved it on July 10.[18]

As passed, the Agricultural Trade Development and Assistance Act of 1954 (PL 480) had three titles. The first authorized sales of surplus agricultural commodities for foreign currency to "friendly" nations (i.e., any country other than the USSR or one "dominated or controlled by the foreign government or foreign organization controlling the world Communist movement"). The president was to negotiate the sales agreements, taking "reasonable precautions" to "safeguard usual marketings of the United States" and not to "unduly disturb world prices"; CCC stocks were to move through private channels, "to the maximum extent practicable"; new market areas were to receive "appropriate emphasis," and transshipment guarantees were to be secured; CCC reimbursement for the three-year period was to be limited to $700,000,000; and the foreign currencies acquired were to be used for market development, stockpile purchases, military procurement, debt payments, educational exchanges, new loans, and aid to friendly third countries.

In its second title, the act renewed the famine and other "urgent" relief programs for "friendly" nations and for "friendly but needy populations without regard to the friendliness of their government." The amount that could be spent here was limited to $300,000,000, and intergovernmental and voluntary relief organizations were to be used "to the extent practicable."

Title III was a catchall. It authorized the CCC to donate commodities to the Bureau of Indian Affairs, to areas declared by the president to be disaster or "acute distress" areas, and to various federal, state, and private agencies for school lunch programs and assistance for the needy, either at home or abroad. In the latter case, however, the secretary of agriculture was to "obtain such assurance as he deems necessary that the recipients thereof will not diminish their normal expenditures for food by reason of such donation," and the processing and transportation cost would be paid only to the point of export, not to the destination, as the voluntary agencies had urged. Title III also gave the secretary of agriculture discretion to engage in barter transactions "for strategic or other materials" and to make commodities available to any other federal agency "for use in making payment for commodities not produced in the United States" when he deemed such actions "in the public interest" or useful "to protect the funds and assets" of the CCC. Finally, the secretary was ordered to assist farm cooperatives in completing barter transactions, and the president was required to "assist friendly nations to be independent of trade" with nonfriendly nations and "to assure that agricultural commodities sold or transferred hereunder do not result in increased availability of those or like commodities to unfriendly nations."[19]

As written, the bill represented the best in legislative logrolling and buck-passing. The President still had to decide which agency would administer the various titles, and debates over bureaucratic jurisdiction now reappeared as the administration sought to work out an executive order setting up the necessary administrative machinery. State wanted assurance that it would be responsible for the international negotiations, would determine overseas famine and relief requirements ("the international relations aspects of such determinations are of overriding importance"), would be consulted on the determination of eligible countries and the use of foreign currency proceeds, and would be allowed to consult with countries potentially affected by PL 480 transactions. Commerce, which had been squeezed out of the barter section of the law, wanted a "clear statement" of barter responsibilities. FOA wanted to administer the title II famine relief program, something that State and Agriculture opposed. And no one was sure how to coordinate the MSA 550 sales with those to be made under the new law. Harold Stassen, who was FOA director, accurately observed that "in the final analysis" any "successful administration" would depend upon "good will and friendly cooperation by departments within the Executive Branch," but this did not stop him from insisting on as much FOA control as he could get.[20]

The discussions of the executive order, which had begun in late June, dragged on through August. The USDA and the FOA were particularly at odds, and an impatient Earl

Butz finally dropped "diplomatic niceties" and confronted
the FOA directly. This led the Bureau of the Budget to
intervene, and they persuaded Benson and Stassen to meet
and exchange letters of understanding. The letters specified that Agriculture would have "the prime authority and
responsibility" over title I and FOA would advise and
consult. For "certain key free countries" FOA would prepare comprehensive programs, but Agriculture would retain veto power. In developing programs for all other countries, Agriculture would keep FOA informed. FOA would
administer title II. Such an arrangement was probably un-
workable, but it did serve as agreement enough for the
White House to release an executive order.[21]

Issued September 9, 1954, executive order 10560 gave
Agriculture title I authority; FOA, title II; State, "the
functions of negotiating and entering into agreements";
Budget, the agency-use allocation of foreign currencies;
Treasury, the regulation of "purchase, custody, deposit,
transfer, and sale" of the currencies; the Office of Defense
Mobilization, stockpile purchase authority; Defense, the
military procurement authority; and various agencies authority for other foreign currency uses. In an accompanying
letter, the president elaborated on how the agencies might
cooperate. Under State Department leadership, he "assumed" the "other agencies directly concerned with the
substance of the negotiation" would conduct the day-to-day
discussions. In addition, the secretary of agriculture was
"to utilize to the maximum extent practicable the facilities,
services and experience of the Foreign Operations Administration." ODM was to use the "facilities and services" of
the General Services Administration, and, in what appears
to be considered disregard of Congress's instruction to the
USDA, the president called upon the secretary of commerce
to serve as the "focal point" for "assisting private enterprise with respect to barter transactions referred to in the
act."[22] The latter reflected Clarence Francis's thinking, but
it was almost certain to lead to trouble. Commerce had
warned Francis that the CCC was not sold on the idea, and
that unless the conflict could be resolved "so as to permit us

to function without distressing shackles, we would prefer to be excused." And, sure enough, less than a month after the order was released, Commerce wrote Francis that "the Department of Agriculture and the CCC really do not believe that the Commerce Department ought to be in the picture at all" and that Commerce would withdraw and merely "provide such specialized knowledge of non-agricultural commodities which may be requested by the CCC."[23]

The executive order and accompanying documents also formalized the position of the interdepartmental committee that had been working for nearly a year. Known now as the Interagency Committee on Agricultural Surplus Disposal (ICASD), it was to continue to formulate policy in the field under the chairmanship of Clarence Francis. Actual direction of the surplus disposal operation, however, would be handled by an Interagency Staff Committee on Agricultural Surplus Disposal (ISC), composed of one representative from each agency in the ICASD and chaired by a representative of the Department of Agriculture. Any operating question that the ISC could not resolve, and all matters of policy, would be referred to the ICASD. Any agency could appeal the decisions of either group, and the appeal would go either to the cabinet or to the president. William Lodwick, a Foreign Agricultural Service official, was appointed both administrator of the service and chairman of the ISC.[24]

One other thorny problem was also finessed in the documents accompanying the executive order: a "well defined policy as guidance for the disposal of agricultural surpluses abroad." Throughout the summer a committee chaired by Assistant Secretary of Agriculture John H. Davis had struggled with the problem, seeking some way through "the undergrowth of interagency differences."[25] The basic issue was consumption. Not always well-defined, the question of the elasticity of commodity consumption had run through all the discussions of agricultural policy, whether in the USDA survey, the Randall Commission, or the interdepartmental committees on surplus disposal. Could consumption be expanded domestically? In other industrial nations? In underdeveloped nations? To what extent? For all commodities? For certain commodities? Greatly? Narrowly? What would be the effect?

Advisors with backgrounds in marketing, like Francis and Randall, tended toward a view that consumption was infinitely expandable if trade barriers were removed, the price was right, and good sales techniques were used. Benson leaned this way too, as did ISC Chairman Lodwick, but Benson pulled back where the domestic market was concerned. Sell abroad, yes, and use Francis's planned advertising campaign to sell more dairy products at home; but domestic consumption, he thought, was not elastic enough to permit unrestricted imports, either of the same products (e.g., oats) or of similar products (e.g., Italian cheeses). Most congressmen agreed with Benson.

Others were not so sure. John H. Davis thought that worldwide consumption could probably be greatly expanded if commodities were sold "at a greatly reduced price," but he felt that for economic, political, and security reasons international prices should be maintained "near present levels." At home, he believed, consumption could be expanded little except for dairy and specialty products. Don Paarlberg, like many agricultural economists, was persuaded that demand for agricultural products was basically inelastic, which made him fear that surplus disposal operations would eat into commercial exports, whether the disposal was by sale, barter, or grant. Dennis FitzGerald of FOA, another agricultural economist, also thought that consumption increases were sharply limited both at home and abroad. The State Department, too, agreed with the theory of a basic inelasticity in consumption. There might be an expansion in consumption abroad at a lower price, State agreed with Davis, but that lower price could not be tolerated, and allowance had to be made for the fact that supplier nations like Australia assumed narrow limits for short-term consumption expansion and therefore viewed every PL 480 bushel as a threat to their normal markets. On the other hand, the State Department believed the domestic market to be more flexible than did almost anyone in Agriculture. It argued, for example, that increased importation of Italian cheese would result in additional overall purchases rather than a substitution of the foreign product for the domestic one.[26]

Now the operative principle in PL 480 legislation was that of additionality—the notion, in other words, that the surplus commodities distributed would be an addition to those amounts the recipient nations would normally purchase. This was a principle of increased consumption, designed to protect the normal commercial marketings of the United States and other supplier nations. Furthermore, through additionality the United States hoped to prevent a disastrous break in world market prices. The administration wanted both price maintenance and expanded sales; yet, if the economists and the State Department were right, any expansion of sales without "greatly reduced prices" would be very small and, to prevent international discord, would have to be meted out among the suppliers.

On August 17 a general policy statement was agreed upon by the interdepartmental committee. It commended "orderly and gradual" surplus disposal with "the full knowledge of friendly nations"; it announced that the United States would sell at competitive prices but would not disrupt world prices; it urged international cooperation with friendly countries to increase consumption "in those areas where there is demonstrable under-consumption and where practical opportunities for increased consumption exist or can be developed in a constructive manner"; it recognized the role of private enterprise in foreign trade and said the United States government would "seek to assure conditions of commerce permitting the private trader to function effectively." It satisfied everyone—and no one. William Lodwick of Agriculture complained that "the matter of consumption is something that the purchasing country may worry about. Our interest is sales." He refused to accept the State Department's definition of a "traditional market," charging that "at one time many of those markets were ours" and that the State Department had unfairly chosen to start "their 'tradition' " at "a more recent date." State, for its part, wrote another memo on the "problems which we may expect to encounter in the operation of PL 480." Nothing had actually been settled.[27]

In the meantime, on August 28, the president signed the Agricultural Act of 1954, a measure that included the $2.5 billion CCC "set aside" that the president had recommended in his agricultural message in January.[28] With that, PL 480, and the renewal of MSA's section 550, surplus disposal legislation was finally in place. It was now clear government policy to "export the surplus." The private trade was officially recognized as the preferred export vehicle, and the foreign currencies received were to promote market development abroad. Relief programs were authorized, and voluntary agencies were to be used when "practicable."

But beneath this commercial and humanitarian veneer, other strains were apparent. The government's broad authority to negotiate title I sales agreements brought the clear possibility that sales would be below cost and determined by noncommercial (disposal) rather than commercial (demand) factors. With this large role for the administration, it seemed reasonable to conclude that PL 480, title I, was a euphemism for dumping and state trading. Then, too, the caveats in title I and title II about sales and donations only to "friendly" nations and peoples reflected the possibility that both commercial and humanitarian aims would be bent to accommodate the foreign policy ends of this cold war administration.

Finally, most of the underlying questions about consumption, the role of the various government agencies and the private relief groups, the importance of barter, and the conflicting aims of disposal and foreign policy were left unsettled. Only a fragile mechanism, the Interagency Committee on Agricultural Surplus Disposal, was left to monitor these divergent commitments. Interagency friction was far from over.

Chapter 4

The Implementation

You can say one thing: trade is the greatest weapon in the hands of the diplomat.
  —Dwight Eisenhower, President of the United States, 1955

PERHAPS THE HARDEST LESSON a bureaucrat must learn is that the freedom to make policy is very limited. The men who entered the USDA with Ezra Taft Benson were primarily academics, farm organization men, and agribusiness leaders used to a great deal of flexibility in decision-making and a good deal of freedom to consider and adopt wide-ranging policy positions. Suddenly they were forced to administer programs they found offensive, such as production and marketing controls, and to adopt policy positions only after long rounds of discussion and compromise within the administration. But what they began to discover and what they would fully realize in carrying out PL 480 was that their real control over policy came in the way they chose to administer legislated programs and in the policy positions they would put forward for executive branch consideration. It was a circumscribed freedom, based on timing and legislative lacunae, but it was real and powerful.

In the fall of 1954 the administration turned to the task of implementing PL 480. Interagency issues were far from resolved, with serious disagreements brewing between the

trade expanders, the fiscal conservatives, and the foreign
policy advocates. But it was here, in implementing the
legislated program, that the administration's real policy
freedom lay. The programming priorities, the allocation of
resources, the selection of tools, all were left to the discretion of the Republican administrators. Four key questions
had to be resolved: what commodities would be programmed; what title would be used for which program;
what nations would be benefited; and how the accumulated
foreign currencies would be used. The criteria that gov-
erned the answers to these questions varied by agency, by
time, and by philosophy.

The controversy over which commodites would be eligible for programming began as soon as the legislation was
signed. In the earlier MSA disposals a conflict had arisen
between those who hoped to limit disposal to "hard core"
surplus disposal problems and those who hoped to use disposal to better agriculture's general economic position.
Now this disagreement shifted to the PL 480 disposals under title I.

State, Treasury, and Budget all favored limiting the
range of commodities eligible for financing to those already
in the CCC inventory, those under loan, or those that,
without title I disposal, would be placed under loan. This,
they argued, was in line with the program's primary aim,
that of moving surpluses already in the hands of the government. Agriculture, on the other hand, was anxious to
expand agricultural trade and to prevent further accumulations in government warehouses; so it wanted the title I
and MSA programs to include all commodities that might
in fact be in surplus supply, whether or not there was a
government investment. FOA, considering the consumption requirements in recipient countries, also urged an expanded list. And as word leaked out that an eligibility list
was under consideration, a variety of commodity groups
brought "tremendous pressure" to bear as they urged that
their needs not be forgotten.

In the face of such conflicts, the interagency committee
decided to publish no list at all. Instead, it concluded that

any government could propose a title I program for any commodity, at which time the Interagency Staff Committee would determine whether that commodity was eligible for programming. In effect, the decision forced foreign governments into a game of blindman's buff, but it did preserve flexibility, and, since most programs originated in Washington, it was probably not detrimental.[1]

The eligibility question was by no means totally resolved, however. After PL 480 had been in full operation for about a year, during which time Commerce and its clientele continued to pressure the USDA to limit programming to those commodities owned by or under loan to the CCC, the Bureau of the Budget brought the issue up again. It reported that 35 percent of PL 480 programming was in commodities other than those in "hard core" surplus difficulties, which Budget thought was objectionable "in view of our budgetary objectives and the current budget situation." A round of interagency discussions followed, leading to an agreement that any non–CCC-owned items included in title I had to be specifically approved for that purpose by the secretary of agriculture. Inside the USDA, Assistant Secretary Earl Butz warned the Foreign Agricultural Service to "be careful not to abuse" the programming of non-CCC commodities but to utilize it fully when the USDA could "get a public relations plus out of such inclusion."[2]

A year later the question surfaced again. This time the Council on Foreign Economic Policy took up a proposal to limit title I programming to CCC-owned or CCC-committed commodities, and State urged its adoption, once again arguing that including non-CCC commodities was expensive, inflated price supports by increasing exports (one factor in support price calculation), and circumvented the "normal procedures for initiating a price support program by, in effect, supporting the prices of additional commodities." Agriculture and its White House ally, staff member Jack Z. Anderson, saw State's latest challenge as a move to eliminate fruit from PL 480 programs—something, they insisted, that would be contrary to congressional intent. They also claimed that moving commodities directly from private stocks saved the money that would be spent to move them into and then out of government warehouses; that the sales of commodities not covered by price supports were a very small part of total title I sales; that agreements were easier to conclude if non-CCC commodities were used to "sweeten" the deal; and that market development occurred as these products were introduced into new markets. Clarence Francis sided with Agriculture, and the council followed suit. This time the question stayed buried. While State's analysis may have been economically correct, it ignored the political reality that programming non-CCC commodities strengthened support for the program both at home and abroad, and that point was decisive.[3] Economics was no match for politics.

The second major administrative issue in the application of PL 480 legislation was what criteria distinguished a title I program from a title II or title III program. On the surface, this looked easy. Title I was to be used for sales, title II for direct donations, government-to-government, and title III for donations abroad through nonprofit voluntary agencies (among others). In practice, however, the distinctions blurred.

During the hearings on PL 480, Congress had made clear its preference for sales under title I, and FOA had promised that title II would be used only when the recipients did not have enough local currency to cover the transactions. On this basis the ICASD early determined that "as a policy" programs under title I would not allow waiver of payments (such a waiver would have made the "sale" a grant) and that, under title II, commodites would be available as grants only for emergencies and for school lunch programs. Soon, however, the ICASD realized that grants could be a useful foreign policy weapon, certainly more potent than sales, but that many countries where grants might be made for political reasons did not qualify under either the emergency or the school lunch criteria. Consequently, the committee revised its title II guidelines to include grants serving the "political or security" interests of the United

States as certified by the State Department or other foreign affairs authority.[4]

Title II thus formed an escape clause from the sales requirements of title I. It could be used to reward friends and woo the wayward. Surprisingly, the title II programs rarely caused criticism, even when the donated food and fiber were used more as aid substitutes than as emergency relief. Its government-to-government conveyance was clearly state trading and certainly evaded the posture of support for the private trade that the administration tried to maintain. But its countervailing virtues were that it was quiet, quick, and clothed in humanitarian rhetoric. Although potentially a point of collision between the conflicting demands of surplus disposal, international relations, and humanitarianism, its low public visibility kept the disagreements to a minimum. Useful in one way or another to most of the interested agencies, in favor with Congress and the public on humanitarian grounds, it was the most easily administered title of PL 480.

The criteria for the people-to-people donation programs of title III derived from similar programs established under the Agricultural Act of 1949 that were absorbed into PL 480. Charitable groups seeking to obtain commodities registered with the Advisory Committee on Voluntary Foreign Aid, and the Committee certified the eligibility of these groups to the joint administrators of the program, the Department of Agriculture and the Foreign Operations Administration or, later, the FOA's successor, the International Cooperation Administration (ICA).[5] Before a donation was made, the prospective distributor was required to submit a plan describing the basis of recipient eligibility, the duration of the feeding, and other particulars. A contract was then signed with the USDA, in which the distributor promised not to "sell, exchange, or dispose" of the commodities except by noncommercial distribution free of cost to needy people and certified that such donations would not reduce the "normal expenditures for food" of either the relief agency or the recipients. Here, as elsewhere, the concept of additionality was firmly entrenched.[6]

During the first two years of operation, the program was broadened to include feed grains[7] and to authorize the use of federal funds to pay the costs of ocean transportation and consumer packaging. As a result, distribution through voluntary agencies nearly quadrupled, and soon the small supervisory staffs in the ICA and the USDA were pressed to cope with more applications, more commodities, and more program reviews than they could handle. As supervision broke down, the voluntary groups sometimes violated the guidelines, most often by selling the donated commodities to foreign consumers for a pittance.[8] And as the voluntary agencies came to depend heavily upon this source of supply, they protested when declining stocks or disposition through other channels led to suspensions of expected donations and left them short of particular commodities.[9]

By spring 1958 the situation was dangerously out of hand.[10] The ICASD met with representatives of the voluntary agencies to discuss future operations, and at the meeting ICA proposed that both the child-feeding and the large-scale foreign government relief programs (for which the voluntary agencies sometimes acted as brokers) be transferred to title II, where the United States government had direct control. In the remaining title III programs, the ICA suggested, the voluntary agencies should be required to enter into written agreements with foreign governments that would be "subject to review and approval by the U.S. Government prior to final negotiations." Shocked, the representatives of the voluntary groups argued forcefully that such changes were neither desirable nor practicable.[11] In June 1958 the ICASD approved ICA's proposal to shift many of the programs to title II, but before this could be implemented the ICA changed its mind. Now ICA offered to transfer all responsibility for title III programs to Agriculture, rather than to transfer them to title II. On August 11, 1958, the ICA director, J. H. Smith, Jr., formally requested Benson to relieve ICA of title III "to ease the burden of our overworked staff and improve the Agency's efficiency by discontinuing or transferring to agencies with more direct responsibility those activities which are peripheral to this Agency's central task of operating programs of technical and economic (developmental) assistance."

The problem was that Agriculture did not want the program either. As the Agricultural Marketing Service's administrator accurately observed, the trouble with title III was that it had not become a "major program of any agency or group except in effect the voluntary agencies themselves."[12] The USDA stalled, and early in 1959 ICA agreed to continue to administer the program if USDA would pay the administrative costs.[13] Agriculture, however, could not transfer the funds without congressional authorization, and this the administration was unable to obtain. So, for the short run, Budget allowed MSA program funds to be used by ICA to cover title III programs, there was no further talk of moving them to title II, and there the matter rested.[14]

The third major administrative issue in implementing PL 480 was what nations would be benefited, or, in simpler terms, who would get how much. The initial PL 480 appropriation was $700 million for title I and $300 million for title II, each amount to be spent over a three-year period. But how much was to be programmed each year was not specified, nor was it clear whether the ceilings applied to total transactions or to allowable CCC losses. Asked its opinion, the Justice Department ruled that the sums applied to CCC losses; so the ISC, anticipating a 10 percent return, projected $770 million as the title I limit.[15]

By October 12, 1954, the Staff Committee had proposed seven major programs at a total cost of $589 million, of which $78 million was anticipated to be reimbursed. The State Department was horrified by the proposal. If implemented, they charged, it would be merely a dumping operation that would create chaos in world markets. It was a "completely unjustifiable total sum, an economic foreign policy torpedo," that (in the words of Assistant Secretary of State Thorsten Kalijarvi) amounted to "total irresponsibility." Treasury complained that the proposal made the program a "give-away" at the expense of the American taxpayer, and Clarence Francis worried aloud that normal sales would fall off "when people know you are a Santa Claus." In defense of the proposal, FOA argued that the $589 million represented projections, not negotiated amounts, and it thought that actual negotiations would probably substantially reduce the total. Agriculture's William Lodwick also defended the proposal, insisting that the three-year period was permissive, not mandatory, and that there was no reason not to program the entire amount in one year if it could be done.

After two weeks of wrangling, the ICASD decided that title I programming for the first year would be $400 million and that the primary emphasis would be on increasing exports of wheat, cotton, and dairy products. State, Agriculture, and the FOA were asked to submit lists of country programs for the current fiscal year to the ICASD, recommending dollar amounts and the title under which they would be programmed.[16]

By this time a Japanese delegation seeking a PL 480 agreement was already in Washington, but the State Department refused to negotiate until it had had time to complete a global review under the $400 million ceiling. ISC Chairman Lodwick, furious, told the State Department what he "thought of the Russian practice of 'abstaining' and put [the State] Department in the same class." "We in Agriculture," he complained to Clarence Francis, "are wondering who is selling—State or us. Who determines what markets and what commodities and in what amounts—State or us." "State," he continued, "has successfully hamstrung the Staff Committee except in cases they want like Jugoslavia and Pakistan," and "some of us are ready to refuse to participate in some of these deals—and State has some more—until there is a change." Agricultural purchasing worldwide was affected, he charged, and if this continued, it would be necessary to "go around" the obstructionists. "Defense, FOA, and ourselves [sic] can make monkeys out of State if we so desire," he threatened, and there would be no more "going along" unless there was a "change."[17]

After several weeks of fruitless interagency negotiations, during which Dulles had to be talked out of bringing the whole matter to the cabinet,[18] the ICASD met on December 7 and agreed on an initial distribution of funds. This was a costly agreement, however, because it was achieved only by raising the title I ceiling for the year to $453 million. Commerce strongly objected to this compromise, arguing that dollar sales were "already being affected" as countries held off on purchases "to see what they can get under 480," and Treasury was even more opposed. "The economics of P.L. 480," the Treasury Department argued, were "self-contradictory."[19] But once ICASD had agreed, the cabinet added its approval on December 17 and the program was underway.[20]

These initial decisions heavily favored Europe and the NATO partners. European programs totaled $235.8 million, 52 percent of title I allocations, and the only non-bloc countries without projected title I sales were Sweden, Switzerland, Greece, Belgium, the Netherlands, Portugal, and West Germany.[21] One Francis Committee member admitted he could not "quite see where the UK figures in the program," but the large European commitment probably reflected both the belief that food was an effective instrument of mutual security assistance and the related notion that permanent commercial market expansion would be most successful in relatively affluent societies.

Asia had the largest single program—Japan's $100 million—but received only 38 percent of title I funds. All the ICASD agencies agreed that the United States had "to give Japan financial support whether we like it or not," and Pakistan, like Yugoslavia and Spain, already had longstanding United States commitments.[22] The Indian and Thai programs were based on economic development criteria and reflected generalized "foreign policy" considerations.[23]

Three Latin American countries—Chile, Peru, and Brazil—rounded out the title I list with 10 percent of the funds. The Chilean and Brazilian programs resulted from negotiations at the meeting of ministers of finance and economy in Rio de Janeiro in late November 1954. There George Humphrey and Under Secretary of State Herbert Hoover, Jr., promised to supply commodities to Chile because she was running out of wheat and to Brazil because of her financial "emergency." These commitments also reflected United States hopes of moving from a residual to a main supplier of agricultural products to Brazil, a position that would damage Argentine marketings, in clear violation of the stated aims of PL 480.[24] As a whole, the projected title I programs were an uneasy compromise between the belief that the way to a man's heart is through his stomach, and the belief that a real Yankee trader could sell pigskin to a hog. The compromise was not destined to become easier over the years.

As the PL 480 country negotiations progressed, they followed the pattern established by the FOA in its administration of the Mutual Security Act. Under this procedure, program proposals were first shaped by the interagency committee and proposed to the potential recipients. Agreements would then be negotiated covering commodities and quantities, currency uses, exchange rates and currency guarantees, and any other stipulations considered essential by either side. Applications by the foreign government to the administrator of the Foreign Agricultural Service for purchase authorizations would follow, with the FAS making public the specific terms and conditions. And once applications were approved, the purchasing agents would negotiate contracts with American exporters, who were required in turn to purchase CCC commodities of the same quality and quantity as those exported. In effect, the CCC also acted as the financing agent for the transactions. It issued letters of commitment to American banks on behalf of the banks of foreign nations. Exporters obtained from the American banks letters of credit, which, after shipment, could be converted into American dollars. The American banks were then reimbursed by the CCC, and it in turn received payment for the goods and for service fees in foreign currencies, which were deposited in special American accounts in foreign banks.[25]

The general procedure was relatively clear, but by January 10, 1955, when the president's first semiannual report on PL 480 was released, title I agreements had been signed only with Japan, Turkey, Pakistan, and Yugoslavia, and no deliveries had yet been made.[26] With other nations, agreements were stalled for an incredible variety of reasons. Some countries rejected the American commodity proposals. India, for example, did not want tobacco, while Britain rejected wheat and dried beans. Others, such as Spain and Brazil, objected to exchange rates and currency value guarantees. And still others were irritated by the requirement that 50 percent of the commodites be shipped in American bottoms. Britain balked over this provision but finally gave in, but Denmark refused to participate in title I so long as the requirement was in effect. In addition, some programs were held up pending Mutual Security allocations. Others, which were to include exchanges of commodities for strategic materials, were delayed while the Office of Defense Mobilization checked prices and stockpile supplies. And in nearly every negotiation, quarrels developed over the proposed uses of the soft currency received. What percentage would go for United States uses? How much would go to the foreign government as grants and how much as loans? What kind of control would the United States exert over the uses of the lent and granted currency?[27]

To add further to these formidable difficulties, neither State nor Agriculture was willing to consider the cabinet-approved program absolutely binding. When, for example, FOA presented the program proposal for India, State suggested that it be developed for calendar (not fiscal) year 1955 because the "political and economic importance of India to both the Soviet bloc and the free nations of the world" made a longer-term commitment desirable. United States Ambassador to Italy Clare Boothe Luce also appeared before the staff committee to plead for an additional

$10 million for Italy, with the proceeds to go for a developmental loan that "would be of considerable help in the fight against Communism." The committee, impressed, agreed to the Italian increase, thus breaking the ceiling. It had lasted just over a month.[28]

By this time, too, countries not included in the original cabinet-approved list were requesting title I programs. Some, like Israel and the Philippines, appealed to their ties with the United States; others, like Colombia, appealed to the administration's cold warriors by reminding them that "the International position of Colombia is and has been so fundamentally anticommunist and so essentially inspired in the highest purpose of continental solidarity that Colombian soldiers and sailors have been fighting in Korea side by side with the United States soldiers and sailors to repel the communist aggression." Having held out as long as possible, Francis decided in mid-February that the ceiling was "largely obsolete" and authorized the staff committee to consider whatever proposals it chose. Agreements with Colombia, Israel, the Philippines, Ecuador, Korea, and Indonesia were immediately proposed.[29]

Once the gates were open, however, the old arguments about disrupting the trade of other nations quickly surfaced again. State called a proposal for shipping 200,000 bales of cotton to Italy "the most blatant case of displacing sales of other countries" yet and forced the addition of a negotiating clause to guarantee that Italy would continue to purchase 350,000 bales from third countries. State and Commerce objected to a similar proposal for Israel that would (they believed) displace Turkish cotton sales, and Commerce also suggested that a $3.4 million sale of wheat to Israel would displace Canadian sales. In addition, the inclusion of tobacco in the title I program for Greece brought complaints from State and FOA that it would compete with Greece's domestic tobacco, which was "produced in an area in which the Communists are most aggressive and the shipment of any tobacco from the U.S. to Greece would be used as Communist propaganda against the U.S."[30]

A few instances of international arm-twisting were also involved in title I delays. An Ecuadorian negotiation was postponed "pending completion of discussions between the Department of State and Ecuador concerning a recent fishing vessel incident," and a Colombian agreement was delayed when there was "apparent abrogation of existing cottonseed oil flakes contracts with a U.S. firm."[31]

As in most human endeavors, moreover, personal conflicts entered into the programming. In mid-January 1955, Senator James Eastland criticized the State Department for slowing down surplus disposal. He demanded that representatives of the department call on him at his office to answer questions on their PL 480 activities and attitudes, and when they arrived he told them frankly that he had been receiving reports from the Department of Agriculture on the supposedly confidential discussions in the ICASD and the ISC. At the next meeting of the ICASD, the State Department representative raised the question of leaks, only to receive another call from Eastland saying that he knew leaks had been discussed and suggesting that "a Cabinet Member, unnamed, might be subject to attack on the floor of the Senate." The Farm Bureau's executive committee also indicated that it had knowledge of confidential committee discussions. When Francis expressed "deep concern" about the problem at the February 8 meeting of the ICASD, State reported that a Senate committee had been set up to investigate charges of State Department obstructionism. Suspicion about the origin of the leaks focused on Lodwick, who had so outspokenly opposed State at almost every turn.[32]

Throughout the spring the situation continued to deteriorate, and as interagency trust waned programming slowed even further. On April 5 the ICASD discussed rice subsidies, and one day later Congressman E. C. Gathings sent a blistering letter to Dulles, charging that by delaying PL 480 programming the State Department was refusing "to honor a law of the Nation by Administrative action." Senators Eastland and Ellender also protested the rice proposal, indicating knowledge of the discussion. Pressure for Lodwick's ouster mounted, and on April 15 he was transferred to the post of United States agricultural attaché to Mexico. Gwynn Garnett from the American Farm Bureau Federation took over as FAS chief. And though the interagency disputes never fully subsided, the bitterest period of interagency recrimination was now over.[33]

The program, however, was still not moving well. By mid-May 1955, title I agreements had been signed with only ten countries, for commodities with an export market value of $176 million. To complicate matters even further, the new Democratic Congress now increased title I funding from $700 to $1,500 million and stipulated that this was not to be "apportioned by year" but was "an objective as well as a limitation, to be reached as rapidly as possible." Congress also gave the secretary of agriculture specific final authority "to determine the nations with whom agreements shall be negotiated, and to determine the commodities and quantities thereof" after consultation with other interested agencies. This was clearly an indication of congressional desires to speed disposal and strengthen Agriculture's hand, perhaps a sign that some of Lodwick's leaks (if they were indeed his) were persuasive.[34] Subsequently, the CCC proposed to commit wheat, rice, and cotton to three-year programs on the condition that all obligation to deliver would lapse in the case of an "international conflict." The ISC agreed, overriding State's counterproposal for two-year planning, and on the basis of the CCC proposal long-term programming was begun.[35]

The programming reflected an ever-shifting compromise between the desires of the trade expansionists and the concern for international political influence. An especially important element in the latter was the United States perception of the relationship of a particular nation to the Soviet Union, and this became an even more critical consideration in 1956.

Concern among American policy-makers over a rapidly developing Soviet trade offensive had been growing throughout 1955, as Near Eastern and South Asian trade appeared to shift toward the communist bloc. The importance attached to this apparent redirection is revealed in the formal letter the American delegation to the United Nations sent to Dulles in December 1955, warning him of a "shift in the Cold War, in which economic and social problems have moved to the forefront." The Russians, they reported, had been strengthening their relationships with India, Egypt, and Burma, and they were challenging the United States in a "bitterly competitive" contest over "economic development of underdeveloped countries." "Defeat in this contest," they warned, "could be as disastrous as defeat in an armaments race." Dulles agreed with this analysis. To Dulles and to Chairman Joseph Dodge of the Council on Foreign Economic Policy, the new Soviet aid program was intended "to subvert and communize the nations that are its targets." Pressure now grew to counter it by using MSA and PL 480 disposals as levers for strengthening alliances and military defenses in the underdeveloped world.[36]

Responding to this pressure, MSA programs in the Far East increased 150 percent in value during fiscal 1956, surpassing European MSA programs for the first time; programming for the Middle East–Africa–India–Pakistan area also increased by one and a half times. Furthermore, PL 480 commodities and currencies were adapted to provide defense support. For example, Congress's rejection of a Defense Department request for a new defense appropriation for Iran was followed by a title I program designed to supplement the Iranian army's defense rations and provide soft-currency loans that would enable the Iranian government to meet the military budget and payroll. In Greece a similar program was developed "on the basis of the requirements of a total aid program to Greece and justification for the maintenance of the Greek Military Forces at their present level." In Formosa and Korea, grants of PL 480 funds were made for the "common defense."[37] And by the summer of 1956 Burma, India and Egypt (the nations with whom the American United Nations delegation had been most concerned) were all involved in projected schemes that would tie surplus disposal to defense objectives.

As negotiated, the Indian program was to deliver $360 million worth of commodites over a three-year period, including 500,000 bales of cotton (which India did not want, but upon which the United States insisted), 3.5 million tons of wheat, and 200,000 tons of rice. In operation, it seemed likely to have adverse effects on Egyptian cotton sales, Burmese and Thai rice markets, and the Australian wheat market in India; and for this reason the State Department had urged India to guarantee that normal imports would be maintained. The Indians, however, had refused to do so and had broken down American resistance by indicating that they might "acquire their agricultural needs from Communist China." When it was learned that the Indian minister of agriculture was actually in Peking awaiting word on the PL 480 negotiations, the program was quickly settled. Competitor nations would have to fend for themselves.[38]

Such cold war considerations were also of major importance in the programming for Egypt. During the 1956 hearings on the Mutual Security legislation, the administration argued that the "concerted Soviet efforts to penetrate the Middle East economically and politically" made it "more important than ever" that the United States extend aid to Egypt. Events like the Soviet bloc arms deal or Egypt's recognition of Communist China must not outweigh these larger considerations, it declared. And while Agriculture was unhappy about American funding of an Aswan Dam that would mean more competition from Egyptian cotton, it too went along with the administration's position.[39]

However, if aid could be used to win friends, it could also be used to pressure nations that had become dependent on it. In July 1956 Dulles withdrew American backing for the Aswan loan, and after Egyptian seizure of the Suez Canal on July 26 the United States immediately blocked dollar balances held by Egypt and suspended both PL 480 and MSA programs. This, so Dulles said, was not economic warfare. But limiting wheat purchases to those that could be made with dollars acquired since July 31, 1956, was a distinctly unfriendly position, involving no subsidies or currency breaks at all and placing Egypt in the same category as the Soviet bloc countries. The United States, to be sure, did not use its cotton surplus to break the Egyptian cotton market, but this was hardly necessary, since cotton prices were already excruciatingly low and still dropping. Furthermore, United States cotton did benefit from the Suez crisis. Britain cut off Egyptian imports, and British cotton spinners turned to United States growths as replacements.[40]

The fourth major administrative problem confronting those who sought to manage PL 480 was the use of foreign currencies obtained as payment for title I sales. Early in 1956 the Commodity Credit Corporation, in an effort to increase the amount of shipping available, supported a scheme whereby the soft currencies resulting from sales of commodities to Japan and Italy would be used to finance a ten-year, $150 million loan to American shipping firms, who would use it to purchase cargo ships or tankers built in those countries. In April the proposal came before the ISC, supported by the Bank of America and the Bankers Trust Company but opposed by the Commerce Department as involving a serious possibility of dollar sale replacement. The ISC forwarded the plan to the ICASD, which in turn sent it to the National Advisory Council on International Monetary and Financial Problems. There, on July 9, 1956, a decision was reached that some portion of the local currency proceeds of PL 480 sales should be made available for loans to private enterprise, both domestic and foreign, in "friendly" countries. The loans would be provided through lending institutions in the foreign country, including branches of United States banks, with terms based on the money market in the country.[41]

Over the next year, about $200 million, or 10 percent of the foreign currencies derived from PL 480 sales in sixteen countries, was earmarked for private lending. Only $23 million, however, was actually lent, and none of this went to United States companies, despite their great interest in obtaining part of the funds. Local pressures, it seems, made it "difficult" to lend to anyone other than nationals of the countries concerned. But the resultant complaints from United States firms became a demand for legislative action.[42]

Consequently, in the extension of PL 480 in the Agricultural Trade Development and Assistance Act of 1957, these loans were institutionalized. Known as "Cooley loans," in honor of House Agriculture Committee Chairman Harold Cooley, they were to be financed from a reserved 25 percent of title I foreign currency receipts and were to go to private firms, either foreign or United States, for the purpose of establishing foreign facilities that would aid "in the utilization, distribution, or otherwise increasing the consumption of, and markets, for, United States agricultural products." Repayment could be made in foreign currency, but no loans were to be extended for "the manufacture of any products to be exported to the United States in competition with products produced in the United States or for the manufacture or production of any commodity to be marketed in competition with United States agricultural commodities or products thereof." If scrupulously administered, this would seem to rule out loans for agricultural development of any temperate-zone crop, even if such development would help fill a normal food or fiber deficit. ICA heartily disliked the Cooley program, predicting that it would "further complicate the already difficult administration of PL 480."[43]

Called upon to implement the new provision, the ISC decided that the loans would extend for three years and that the host country would have sixty days to react to loans proposed by the Export-Import Bank. The chief item of debate, which arose in conjunction with a proposed United Kingdom fruit agreement, concerned the obligation to reserve a full 25 percent of currency receipts for such loans. As State saw it, the projected sterling proceeds could be "better" used to pay for United States military housing, to retire United States obligations, and to purchase British goods for export to aid recipients than as Cooley loans.

Eventually the ICASD agreed, ruling that variations from the general 25 percent reservation could be made "in exceptional cases" for "compelling reasons" relating to surplus disposal, foreign policy, or alternative uses of sales proceeds. The first priority for title I currencies would be United States uses, ISC said, second would be Cooley loans, and third would be loans to foreign governments.[44]

Abroad, however, the United States encountered strong opposition to Cooley loans. Spain saw "U.S. colonialism" in them and insisted that the money be used to retire United States obligations in Spain rather than being lent to private businesses. France and Italy, although "strongly opposed," finally acquiesced in order to get agreements at all. And other nations put up varying degrees of resistance. After one year of experience with the Cooley amendment, twelve countries had agreed to the 25 percent reserve, Turkey and Greece had agreed to 15 percent, and Korea, where State and Defense felt that uses for "common defense" should have priority, had only a 4 percent reserve. Finland had accepted a 25 percent reserve but was holding the funds in escrow until the United States resolved "Battle Act problems." And, like Spain, four other countries (Britain, Burma, Poland, and Yugoslavia) had negotiated agreements containing no Cooley provisions at all.[45]

By the end of fiscal 1958, 159 applications had been received for loans in eleven countries (72 for Israel alone; 43 for Mexico). These came initially to the Export-Import Bank, which then sent resumes to the Department of Agriculture for determination of the degree of competition present. In the department, opinions were solicited from the appropriate regional, commodity, and technical divisions, and a recommendation was then prepared by the Foreign Agricultural Service.[46]

In practice, as in theory, each case was judged individually, with protecting United States agricultural interests the primary concern. An Israeli corporation that wanted to double its Haifa silo found no opposition, nor did a proposal to establish an Israeli cigar factory that could expand U.S. markets. But an American tobacco firm's proposal to build two warehouses in Greece was rejected, Agriculture finding in this case that ample facilities already existed and that Greek tobacco products competed with American products. On this matter, moreover, Agriculture was unyielding. It stuck to its position despite pleas from the Greek ambassador, the State Department, and the Export-Import Bank, all of whom suggested that the loan "would have a salutary effect in this critical area where the Communists are making a strong effort to win the support of the tobacco growers." In Mexico, on the other hand, initial rejection of a Cooley loan to Mexican affiliates of Ralston-Purina and the Archer-Daniels-Midland Company gave way to approval after an appeal from the United States Embassy. In this case, the USDA decided that the possible competition would be "minimized by permitting the expansion of feed mixing facilities in Mexico to remain in the hands of firms affiliated with the parent firm in the U.S." Whatever the decision, the whole process took time, and it was not until June 19, 1958, nearly a year after passage of the amendment, that Ex-Im authorized the first Cooley loans, eleven separate grants of Mexican pesos totaling $3.3 million.[47]

These, then, were the four major administrative problems with PL 480. In each case, the Eisenhower administration found virtually complete freedom from congressional pressures in adopting and executing policy within the legislative mandate. The choice of commodities, the use of the titles, the sensitive distribution politics, and the disposition of accumulated currencies were all internal matters for the executive branch to handle, with Congress exercising oversight and, in the case of the Cooley loans, essentially confirming and emphasizing an executive branch policy. Congress became directly involved only when it believed that the administration was ignoring or evading legislative intent, such as during the early programming debates. Pressures from commodity groups and agribusiness were felt, but they were neither as important nor as concerted as the pressures the same groups brought to bear on commercial questions. Humanitarian groups were vocal but only marginally influential.

In administering PL 480, the administration continuously balanced conflicting objectives. The legislation was all things to all people: surplus disposal, humanitarian relief, cold war weapon, domestic farm income stabilizer. The interagency debates reflected this mix of aims, and policy swayed and veered as first one and then another group gained temporary advantage. The administration was keenly aware of these serious underlying disagreements, and early and repeatedly it engaged in program review and analysis. Perhaps not since the days of the WPA had there been such a consistent devotion to self-scrutiny and momentary catharsis. And as early as 1955, not even a year after the legislation was passed, the self-examination began.

Chapter 5

Reassessment and Retrenchment

I think it likely the animus for talking about Food For Peace is largely, if not wholly, domestically political: a high falutin term designed primarily to cover the attempt or the promise to dispose of more surpluses.
—Clarence Francis, Chairman, Interagency Committee on Agricultural Surplus Disposal, 1960

MAJOR PROGRAM REVIEWS are unpleasant to conduct and unpleasant to endure. The surplus disposal and food aid program, with its inherent conflicts and high political visibility, endured more reviews than anyone anticipated at the outset. It survived these reassessments with its policies more or less intact, and in the end the reviews accomplished very little. Still, the process of review was executive branch "earnest money," showing a skeptical Congress that the administration was expediting surplus disposal, and the continuous reviews clarified and momentarily resolved the serious interagency conflicts over the means and goals of the program.

The first major program review came less than a year after PL 480 was passed. In the spring of 1955, the Council on Foreign Economic Policy (CFEP), concerned that the various surplus-disposal programs were not moving well, formally requested a report from the ICASD on "the extent to which it is practicable and desirable to depend upon for-

70

eign disposal to meet the domestic agricultural surplus problem and the most appropriate and effective means of accomplishing such disposal." In turn, Clarence Francis asked each interested agency to submit to him a statement on disposal efforts, and he persuaded Ernest Baughman, a former Randall Commission economist now with the Federal Reserve Bank in Chicago, to write the report.[1]

Baughman spent the summer studying the agency responses, and on October 31, 1955, Francis forwarded the completed report to the CFEP. Pessimistic in tone, it reported that CCC loans and inventories had increased by $6 billion in the three years ending June 30, 1955, and that further increases were probable. Surplus commodity stocks above domestic need were now so great that, exporting at 150 percent of the 1954–55 volume, it would require "five years or more" to liquidate the stocks of wheat, cotton, and feed grains and about four years to liquidate the rice and tobacco. Nor did it seem that expansion of this sort could be achieved. Of the $3,143 million in agricultural goods exported during 1954–55, more than 40 percent ($1,343 million) had been exported under a government subsidy or program. And, though the export total was up $207 million from the previous year, exports under "special" export programs (not including those of section 32 or other subsidies) had increased $275 million, reflecting lower dollar earnings for commercial exports.[2] "Some" agricultural expansion was possible, Baughman concluded, but the increased volume would not be enough "to provide substantial relief to the problem of agricultural surpluses in the United States." The best possibility for increasing exports, he believed, lay in "low-volume, low-consumption areas . . . if appropriate programs to increase demand are developed." Along this line he recommended that noncommercial exports of surplus commodities be committed to three-to-five-year programs of economic development, that export subsidies be used sparingly, that barter be used only when "consistent with United States foreign economic policy and with the maintenance of dollar sales," that legislation be enacted to make Soviet bloc trade discretionary with the president, and that the fifty-fifty shipping requirement for PL 480 and the Mutual Security Act be repealed.[3]

The Baughman recommendations raised a question that the administration had been discussing for some time—the extent to which the United States was willing to make long-term commitments to accelerate economic development. In the fall of 1954, Joseph Dodge and Nelson Rockefeller had undertaken a special study of executive branch organization and coordination in the development of foreign economic policy, and in the course of that review the Defense Department had pointed out the "mutuality" of military and economic aid in order to "attract allies and bind them to the United States." At about the same time, Secretary of State Dulles had also publicly emphasized the need to use American capital in development abroad. And, since then, the cabinet had approved a paper by Clarence Randall calling for incentives to encourage private investment overseas; congressional Republicans such as Jacob Javits had advocated a long-term economic development program; and the British government, after conversations with the FOA director, Harold Stassen, had formally told the United States that it "welcomed the conception of using surplus food and feeding stuffs to foster economic development." In addition, a study undertaken by the Department of State during the first half of 1955 had indicated opportunities for using agricultural surpluses to finance up to half the costs of development projects in selected countries.[4]

The Department of Agriculture, however, had been cautious. In a view shared by most USDA officials, Butz had told Benson that "often the Technical Cooperation Program had encouraged production of agricultural products abroad that ultimately come in direct competition ·with our own agricultural production, when they could have encouraged something else just as well." Benson, in turn, had "strongly" urged Stassen that the FOA place "greatest emphasis . . . on agricultural commodities of a complimentary nature, rather than stimulating production of commodities already in surplus throughout the world or in direct competition with the United States farmer."[5] And in working out general instructions to PL 480 negotiators, Agriculture had insisted on a provision specifying that "none of the loan funds would be used to foster production of commodities which compete in international trade with U.S. agricultural commodities." FOA and Commerce had both questioned the clause, but for opposite reasons: FOA hoping to relax the prohibition, citing the difficulty of policing it, and suggesting that nations probably could not legally prohibit the production of such crops, and Commerce seeking to apply it not only to agricultural crops but to industrial products as well! Agriculture, however, had warned that "Congress is protesting the use of these funds to build up agricultural production in other areas" or to undertake "economic development programs," and such arguments had managed to keep the clause intact.[6]

Shortly before the Baughman report was released, Benson told Eisenhower that "we have all been waiting for the magic day when the nationalistic urges which impelled many foreign producers to expand their farm production would diminish and foreign marketing opportunities for our farm commodities would improve." Simply put, Agriculture saw a threat in any economic development plan that had as its goal a self-sufficient foreign agriculture. Nor did the USDA want anything to do with the administration of "overseas economic aid activities relating to agriculture."[7]

In the face of this opposition, it is surprising that the Council on Foreign Economic Policy was able to approve the principal Baughman recommendation, "that programs to raise consumption levels and accelerate capital development receive primary emphasis," in a single meeting on November 8, 1955. One can only speculate that the council perceived the recommendation as one to improve markets for United States products rather than as one that might produce more competition for United States agricultural and industrial goods. The council also asked the Office of Defense Mobilization to reconsider the stockpile objectives with an eye to any possible increases that might be filled by barter, and the council agreed that Congress should be asked to remove the fifty-fifty shipping requirement for MSA and PL 480 deliveries.[8]

It was now the end of 1955, and the surplus situation was grim. CCC storage costs were running over a million dollars a day; cotton on hand was up a million bales over the preceding year, and while the year-end PL 480 report showed total programming at $1,692 million, title I sales represented only $679 million of this, and only 71 percent of the programmed commodities had actually been shipped, including barely half of the projected cotton. Nor was sales promotion having much discernible effect. Although the USDA had begun participating in international trade fairs, the CCC had hired a sales manager, and the department had signed its first agreement with a private trade group (the National Cotton Council) for cooperative market promotion, nearly a third of the commodities shipped under PL 480 ($539 million) had been donated rather than sold.[9]

Another disquieting thought for the Eisenhower officials was that the surplus had mounted despite all their efforts and the use of all their levers to control it. Import quotas and export subsidies, PL 480 and MSA, all had been used in the attempt to dispose of the overage. And they had failed. Baughman's report really suggested that the administration's original concept of a one-shot surplus disposal program was faulty, that the problem was a continuing one to be met by long-term programs.

Support for PL 480 as a surplus-disposal measure remained strong, especially in Congress. In 1956 the lawmakers raised the title I authority to $3 billion, and it seemed clear that they would extend its 1957 deadline. The administration, however, was not convinced of PL 480's success.

Shortly after the Baughman study was completed, the Council on Foreign Economic Policy decided that it had been based on an "insufficient backlog of experience." The council commissioned a second report, written by economist Edward Hall during the spring and summer of 1956 and presented to the CFEP in November. In the report, Hall had little quarrel with title II or the MSA programs. In these, he felt, there was too much interagency competition between ICA and Agriculture and a somewhat unhealthy tendency for nations to become "habitually dependent" on the free food, but on the whole they were operating satisfactorily and had "seldom" excited "audible resentment" from export competitors, probably because "nobody wants to find fault with generosity." Barter, on the other hand, seemed to be working badly. More than 98 percent of the stockpiling contracts had been for low-priority materials, and these "to a large extent" had displaced dollar sales. And title I, Hall concluded, was not preventing a further growth of surpluses. In its two years of operation, commodities costing $2.2 billion had been sold for local currencies totaling $1.46 billion, only about half of which had been collected. Yet at the end of fiscal year 1957 CCC obligations from price support programs were $8,501 million, compared with $6,006 million at the end of fiscal 1955.

On the positive side, Hall conceded, title I had prevented even larger surplus accumulations "by some unmeasurable amount." It had also helped to ease dollar shortages, to expand foreign aid resources (both military and economic), to generate goodwill in the purchasing countries, and to achieve some "broadening of agricultural markets." Yet in doing these things it had involved the nation in "state trading on a big scale," thereby violating "the principles of trade we urge on other countries." It had hurt "some of our best friends." It had meant "troublesome" and "unbusinesslike" transactions in soft currencies, offering "limitless opportunity for misunderstandings and resentments." And, instead of attacking the surplus problem at its root, it had probably helped to delay any real solution. The benefits, he thought, could be obtained "in other, more direct ways," and for this reason the law should be allowed to expire on June 30, 1957. Or, if politics made this "impractical or inadvisable," actions should at least be taken to limit title I authority to a half-billion dollars a year for each of the next two years, limit programming to government-owned commodities, and announce publicly that the measures were temporary expedients "in opposition to the foreign trade policy of the Administration and to the Administration's policy of removing the government from business."

Clarence Randall, who had now replaced Joseph Dodge as CFEP chairman, was sympathetic to this critique but was convinced that Congress would not tolerate a termination of title I. Randall therefore lent his support to Hall's second option—a two-year extension of title I, another half-billion dollars for title II, a reconsideration of barter practices, and repeal of limitations on trade with the Soviet bloc. He wanted to sell only government-owned commodities, but he thought this could be accomplished by administrative action rather than by legislation.[10]

Although the CFEP had "a rather solid block of opposition to further extension" of PL 480, it ultimately endorsed a modified version of Hall's proposals, limiting the title I extension to a one-year, one-billion-dollar program. Earl Butz came away "perturbed"; he warned his colleagues in Agriculture that any further extension "would run into real opposition in the Executive Branch of Government."[11]

Secretary of the Treasury George Humphrey was one of the leaders of the opposition. He complained to Clarence Randall that "no Department in Government came anywhere near exceeding its budget estimates last year by as wide a margin as the Department of Agriculture." "It is absolutely necessary that we get some better control," he thundered, and "until we have exhausted every possible alternate means of doing a better job with these farm surpluses than we have done in the past, I think it is a mistake to hurry to a decision for the record rather than to try to develop some aid toward a solution for the problem." He requested a broad new survey, but Randall, doubtful that "any man, however wise or ingenious," could devise anything new, resisted the request as likely to "greatly embarrass the Administration." As a compromise, Randall finally agreed to ask Francis for an "objective second look at all known alternates" with a "careful listing of the arguments *pro* and *con*," and Francis, in turn, once again persuaded Ernest Baughman to undertake the thankless job.[12]

In his study, Baughman considered eight alternatives to PL 480 title I, labeling four of these (increased export sales for dollars, industrial uses, direct distribution, and increased foreign grants of surplus commodities) alternate disposal methods and four of them (food stamps, direct payments to producers, two-price plans, and rigid or flexible price supports) alternate programs for price and income support. None of these, he concluded, was a satisfactory replacement for title I "at the present time." Disposal must continue to be a multisided program utilizing a number of tools, he said, and for the present title I should be extended for another year, with "every effort made" to insure that transactions under it did not displace dollar sales or "opportunities for gainful barter" and with safeguards to prevent it from taking on "the characteristics of a permanent Government program."[13]

Baughman's endorsement of "gainful" barter highlighted the problems inherent in the barter program. In his report two years before, Baughman had warned that barter should not displace dollar sales, but a year later Hall had found that displacement had occurred. The problem of barter under PL 480 had been complicated by an amendment to the 1956 Defense Department appropriations act that authorized the secretary of defense to dispose of $100 million worth of surplus agricultural commodities in return for military housing. The first use of this authority had been to ship wheat to France in return for housing construction, and, as it turned out, this became a barter program that probably displaced dollar sales, both United States and Canadian.[14] Now, with Baughman's report in hand, the CFEP considered whether barter transactions should include "usual marketing" (additionality) safeguards.

The CFEP knew that some members of Congress were strong proponents of barter; yet they also knew that the volume of metals and minerals needed for the United

States stockpile was small in comparison to the quantities of agricultural commodities available for barter and that the countries producing such defense materials were not always those that would want imports of agricultural commodities in surplus in the United States. At the CFEP meeting on January 31, 1957, a faction led by State argued that barter should be curtailed because it was bilateral trade inconsistent with the multilateral trade policy of the United States and because there often was "no pressing need for the kinds and quantities of minerals accepted in exchange." The result, the faction claimed, was merely a change in the kind of surplus held by the government "without any real reduction in total governmental holdings or obligations." At the very least, State thought, usual marketing safeguards were essential. Assistant Secretary Earl Butz, speaking for Agriculture, pointed out that a barter agreement was made between the government and a private trader, the government agreeing to supply a quantity of surplus commodities and the trader promising to supply the government with a stated amount of strategic material. It was then up to the trader to make the international contracts to fulfill the agreement. Therefore, Butz claimed, it would be "virtually impossible to do any barter business" if usual marketing guarantees were required, because "neither the destination of the farm produce, nor the kind of commodity to be shipped, nor the price are known at the time the Government enters into a firm contract to acquire strategic materials." Far from being unilateral, he argued, barter was actually multilateral in nature, nonrestrictive, and a contribution to the "volume of free international trade and the convertibility of currencies." He urged the CFEP not to waste its time worrying about barter, because as stockpile goals were nearing fulfillment and marketing conditions were strengthening, the barter volume would, he thought, inexorably decrease. After debate, the council decided that barter would not be subjected to usual marketing restrictions.[15]

Despite Butz's brave words, however, the USDA itself was far from fully satisfied with the barter programs. In mid-April it undertook an extensive barter review, and the results clearly showed that bartered agricultural commodities, including those exported for the French housing contract, were not only replacing cash sales but also encouraging a system of deferred payments that placed the burden of financing on the CCC and had already reduced its borrowing authority by some $600 million. Alarmed by the report, the department suspended all barter contracts, then announced program revisions on May 28, 1957. The USDA ordered barter contractors to certify that the proposed transaction would result in a net increase in United States exports of the commodity (there were exceptions to these "certificates of additionality" for cotton, wheat, and feedgrains if shipped to certain countries), to designate the specific commodity to be acquired and the country in which it originated, and to provide "satisfactory" assurances that United States commodites would not be transshipped from the approved destination.[16] The USDA projected that these limitations (which ruled out any further military housing projects similar to the French barter arrangement) would reduce barter operations by more than 50 percent, and this brought protests from the Department of the Interior[17] and from interested congressmen.[18] In spite of these, however, the decision stood. The USDA had prevailed in the CFEP on the additionality issue, only to adopt the opposition's stand four months later. Barter transactions fell to one-fourth the previous level and ceased to be a major part of United States agricultural trade (see table 1).

Throughout the spring of 1957, Earl Butz worried about the future course of PL 480. He believed that the troublesome wheat and cotton surpluses could be eliminated by mid-1960 and that disposal programs might be discontinued as early as June 30, 1958, and he thought some planning for these eventualities was in order. In a letter to Clarence Randall, Butz outlined the dimensions of the problem.

Over the past three years, Butz wrote, 80 percent of the $3 billion programmed under title I had gone to underdeveloped countries with balance-of-payments difficulties,

Table 1

Exports of United States Farm Products under Public Law 480 Compared with Total Exports of United States Farm Products by Fiscal Years (in Millions of Dollars)

	1954–55 and 1955–56	1956–57	1957–58	1958–59	1959–60	1954–55 through 1959–60
Public Law 480						
Title I	512	909	659	725	825	3,630
Title II	174	88	92	56	65	475
Title III						
Barter	423	401	100	132	153	1,209
Donations	319	165	173	131	104	892
Total	1,428	1,563	1,024	1,044	1,147	6,206
Other exports	5,212	3,165	2,979	2,675	3,380	17,411
Total exports	6,640	4,728	4,003	3,719	4,527	23,617
PL 480 exports as % of total exports	22	33	26	28	25	26

with more than $1 billion going to just five "key foreign aid countries" (Yugoslavia, Turkey, Pakistan, Korea, and Spain) and another $1 billion to "countries on the rim of communism" (Austria, Burma, Egypt, Finland, Greece, Indonesia, India, and Iran). Such countries, moreover, were expected to have a continuing need for $500 to $600 million worth of agricultural imports per year until at least 1962. Hence it seemed likely that the abandonment of surplus disposal would have "a shocking impact on sensitive foreign policy areas," particularly as "many" countries used title I to meet "minimum consumption needs" and "several" used PL 480 financing to "support their governments and/or military forces." "If they were told to shift for themselves after 1958," said Butz, such governments as those in Spain, Turkey, Korea, and Pakistan "might change and adversely affect U.S. national security."

The question, then, became one of how to use the putatively diminishing surpluses and minimize the shock of their passing. Would it be necessary, Butz wondered, to offset the abandonment of title I with increased foreign aid appropriations, and, if so, how large an increase would be needed? Would it be desirable to utilize the bargaining power inherent in a diminishing supply of surpluses to improve the structure of currency uses, exchange rates, and usual marketing provisions? Would it be helpful if the large foreign currency accumulations in some countries were used to finance exports of nonagricultural aid to others? And, finally, should more of the surpluses be used as weapons in the cold war? Should the type of grain deal that had helped to achieve "Yugoslavia's degree of western orientation" be extended to Poland, and should Soviet shipments to such countries as Egypt be countered with "greater use" of American farm products?

Randall referred the letter to the State Department, and in May 1957 Under Secretary Christian Herter replied at length. He urged a "tapering off" of the PL 480 program over a period of years, with a few countries receiving additional allocations of direct aid in the "painful" process of "weaning" them. This, Herter argued, would be better than trying to continue "the indirect route which causes us so much trouble with other countries." As for financing third-country aid with title I currencies and negotiating arrangements with fewer "concessions," he believed that both would be helpful in reducing costs and bettering relations with "friendly" countries. But when it came to the suggestion that more surpluses could be used to counteract Soviet penetration, he offered objections rather than encouragement. In Asia, he pointed out, PL 480 agreements had alienated rice suppliers, afforded "free ammunition to Communist propagandists," and allowed the Soviet Union to gain "political capital" by buying rice. On the whole, they had been counterproductive as cold war weapons, and the State Department was inclined "to feel that we would be better off without PL 480 than with it."[19]

In the summer of 1957, the Bureau of the Budget also closely examined the workings of PL 480. On the whole, it thought, the United States had "gone much too far" in developing tentative programs, urging countries to accept them, and then continuing them at that level whether or not the original justification remained. In "many countries" aid could not be justified on either military or economic grounds, the Bureau said, and "to a large degree" the economic aid had been utilized to support local military forces "far beyond what the local economy could support," making the United States vulnerable to propaganda claims that United States aid "is all pointed to war, not peace." Furthermore, said Budget, recent developments in Eastern Europe suggested that East-West trade controls may be "just the opposite of what we need." "A major objective" of United States policy should be to help satellite nations obtain alternative sources of supply, not to lock them into Soviet bloc trade.[20]

Butz's facile assumption that the surplus would soon disappear was wrong. The thoughtful analyses of spring and summer 1957 were based on inaccurate assumptions; nonetheless, they showed the administration's sensitivity to the foreign policy implications of PL 480. Butz worried principally about direct importers and how their import needs would be met; in other words, where the money would come from to continue to purchase American foodstuffs. State's concern diverged from Agriculture's over the issue of third parties—those countries whose exports were adversely affected by the increased flow of American commodities. Budget argued for a constriction and a rationalization of all aid programs. The positions were entirely predictable, but they caused continuing conflicts over policy direction.

Unlike the questioning administration, Congress easily passed the PL 480 extension in the summer of 1957, largely along lines agreeable to the administration. And as a new round of programming got under way in August 1957, no discernible redirection of title I programming came from the numerous PL 480 reviews of the previous years. The ISC designated seven countries "first priority," five of them (Pakistan, Israel, Korea, Yugoslavia, and Spain) because of "urgent and paramount" foreign policy considerations, and two (Mexico and the United Kingdom) because they provided opportunities for market development.[21] Even a special study of Middle East programming by a Foreign Agricultural Service official critical of previous disposal policies there had little effect on the decisions.[22] In the Mideast only Greece, Turkey, and Israel got title I agreements, the first two without much debate and the third with "a *minimum* of publicity" and reduced commodity amounts because of State's concern about "the attitude of the Arab World." Title I requests from Morocco and Iran were rejected, Morocco because of its trade agreements with the Soviet bloc and Iran because its needs could be met without special currency arrangements. One important action in the Middle East involved title II. In that case the United States decided to deliver some 20,000 tons of wheat to the French authorities in Tunisia, officially helping them to "relieve the critical unemployment situation" and unofficially strengthening the hand of the French authorities against the Tunisian rebels.[23]

Meanwhile, throughout late 1957 and early 1958, the administration struggled to translate the results of the

various policy reviews into legislative proposals for the
1958 congressional session. Despite earlier predictions, it
now appeared that surplus disposal would have to be continued. While the CCC investment in surplus commodities
on June 30, 1957, was about a billion dollars less than a
year before, it still totaled more than $7.3 billion and was
not expected to drop significantly during the coming year.
It seemed unlikely, moreover, that the new Soil Bank program and the flexible price support mechanism could reduce
surpluses fast enough to make it possible to terminate
foreign currency sales; besides, as Don Paarlberg told
White House staff member Jack Z. Anderson, it was "less
costly and more humanitarian and better public relations to
move the stuff abroad than . . . to try to buy the farmers off
from producing it under the Acreage Reserve." In these circumstances, Agriculture suggested a $2 billion, one-year
extension of PL 480. State, exhibiting the hint of a positive
attitude toward title I, urged an increase to $1.5 billion for
one year and additional authority to sell in Eastern
Europe. And the International Cooperation Administration, hoping to integrate responsibilities, wanted broader
provisions allowing title II to provide the "agricultural
products component" in assistance programs for "aid" countries.[24]

Opposition came from Treasury, Commerce, and Budget,
each of whom disliked the apparent permanence of PL 480.
Commerce urged divorcing such disposal from the calculation of price support levels, increasing title II at the expense of title I, and selling for foreign currency only when
a nation had "serious dollar exchange problems" and when
the commodities were held by the CCC. Treasury, however,
did not like Commerce's proposed shift to dollar sales, arguing that such credits would reduce the credit standing of
foreign countries and thereby reduce their eligibility for
economic development loans and ultimately create serious
balance-of-payment problems.[25] Eventually the administration compromised and recommended to Congress a one-
year extension of PL 480 with $1.5 billion for title I. Con-

gress, however, provided $2.25 billion for eighteen months of title I, and the administration accepted it.[26]

But the surplus continued to grow. By 1958 most Eisenhower administration officials recognized that the surplus disposal problem could not be solved by a "one shotter," and this admission made them eager to make additional adjustments in the ongoing programs. In particular, the rapid accumulation of foreign currencies argued for a reconsideration of soft currency loan policies and assistance techniques, and the increasingly stringent congressional restrictions on regular foreign aid appropriations encouraged another look at food aid as a substitute for dollar aid. And through it all, the administration desperately desired some favorable publicity on the surplus disposal operations, for, as ICA complained, "perhaps never before has so much benevolence been acclaimed by so few and despised by so many." To solve any of these problems, Ezra Taft Benson realized, it was "pretty close to now . . . or never."[27]

The foreign currency problem was pressing. Soft currencies were accumulating both from PL 480 sales and from other loan programs, a reflection of the administration's second-term turn toward a soft loan policy. In 1957 the administration had moved to replace foreign aid grants with repayable development loans, which, Eisenhower believed, would help to better the fiscal position of the United States, save "the self-respect of everybody," and enlist "greater local concern" in seeing that the funds were "spent efficiently and properly."[28] Such loans, however, might be repaid in inconvertible foreign currencies, and the accumulation of soft currencies multiplied.

Accordingly, ICA hired a trio of financial consultants to study the question, and they found that the soft currency holdings of the United States had already become excessive in some currencies and could become a much more widespread problem. Although important as tools in the cold war, the consultants agreed, soft currencies could not "do the work of dollars," and since accumulations of them could leave the United States open to charges of manipulating a foreign nation by controlling great chunks of its currency, it was desirable that steps be taken to prevent such accumulations. In particular, the consultants suggested, it would be wise to dispose of some of the currencies through grants, to reduce interest rates and maintenance-of-value requirements on loans, to encourage more loan repayment in dollars, and to eliminate the 25 percent Cooley reserve and the Cooley limitation to projects that would not increase competitive exports to the United States. "Foreign countries should not be restrained from encouraging dollar-earning projects," they argued, and restraints should not be placed on the use of already accumulated currencies to finance a variety of new technical assistance and nonprofit development projects.[29]

The ICASD could not agree on these recommendations. State and ICA supported them. Commerce was not wholly opposed if they would create more dollar sales and reduce the risk of foreign inflation. But Agriculture was worried that financing economic development projects with foreign currencies would mean increased competition and fewer markets for American farmers and that without maintenance-of-value requirements loans would be repaid in inflated currencies, making the program more costly, giving the United States no "credit" for the increased aid, and tending "to discourage stabilization of currencies in some countries." Eventually the matter was referred to the National Advisory Council on International Monetary and Financial Problems, and in 1960, after long deliberation, the council decided to eliminate the maintenance-of-value requirement and allow 4 percent loans of local currencies to foreign governments.[30]

A second major issue late in the administration was the continuing problem of how to make foreign aid both a balance wheel for the domestic economy and an effective weapon in the cold war. Early in 1958 Paarlberg reviewed a proposal for increased aid in the form of food rather than dollars and decided that this could not fulfill "a major purpose" of the foreign aid program—namely, enabling the recipient nation to purchase capital goods for economic development. It would be better, he thought, "to give our assistance in a form which can help build up these underdeveloped countries than to continue carrying them along on a subsidized sub-par basis."[31]

At about the same time, the State Department hired the former assistant secretary of agriculture, John H. Davis, to review PL 480 and other agricultural programs as they related to foreign economic policy. In his review Davis expressed great concern about the "casual manner" in which the United States decided to "feed the people in low income countries at a level better than they could feed themselves, without clearly facing the fact that should we suddenly stop such feeding, the repercussions, both economic and political, might be far-reaching—even to the point of undermining the strength of the free world." To correct matters, Davis recommended a comprehensive five-year program "integrating" efforts on "the four basic fronts of (1) domestic market development, (2) foreign commercial market expansion, (3) P.L. 480 type distribution, and (4) accelerated adjustments in domestic agriculture." He was especially eager to see PL 480 planned on a multiyear basis (as was the Marshall Plan), and he hoped that it could be made "an integral part of a comprehensive food-fiber program, which might be called the *Food for Peace Program,* to be announced by the President and designed to utilize and adapt our agricultural productive capacity for the benefit of the United States and the advancement of peace in the free world." As Davis saw it, this program would initially increase assistance to low-income countries, but during its latter stages, as local production developed, there would be systematic reductions in the size of foreign currency sales accompanied by more assistance to make purchases in the world marketplace, thus helping to "avoid the danger of countries becoming overly dependent on an uncertain source of food and fiber, such as P.L. 480."[32]

The Davis plan, however, quickly ran into opposition in the ICASD. Some members argued that rather than giving impetus to corrective domestic farm policies, five-year programming would be another excuse to postpone changes in farm legislation. Others maintained that the Marshall Plan analogy was a false one, that the problems of restoring productivity in Western Europe were not really comparable to those of increasing production "faster than population" in the underdeveloped world. And within the USDA doubts were expressed both about the administration's ability to secure the necessary legislation and about the economic and political risks involved in such a program. Benson feared that if local production failed to develop the United States "would have created a group of more or less permanent relief clients," and he warned that if the administration adopted the Food for Peace idea, it "might be accused of embracing a proposal favored by Senator [Hubert] Humphrey and others from the opposition camp."[33]

Once again the ICASD rejected a consultant's report. During the deliberations, ICA argued that a multiyear program would allow better planning, but Commerce thought a multiyear Food for Peace program "would seem to promise more than we can or should deliver," State doubted that recipients would really regard it as "FOOD FOR PEACE," and Budget was fearful that endorsement of the plan would "justify continuation" of the whole array of "costly" farm subsidies. Longer-range planning of surplus disposal, the ICASD concluded, would give better "perspective," but under the conditions it was best that surpluses be used only for selective purposes and that special export programs "not be extensively publicized" for fear of making "needed legislative changes" even more difficult and further discouraging production in recipient countries.[34]

By this time, though, Benson was changing his mind. Initially he had told Sherman Adams that the USDA was "not now ready" to advocate the Davis program but that if Eisenhower favored it it could be launched either by a series of speeches or by a presidential call for an international conference. The latter, as he envisioned it, would invite "those nations from the free world which either export or import farm products" to "consider the volume of supply which is likely to be available for export during the years immediately ahead," "the needs of importing countries," the proportion of those needs that "could be met on a commercial basis with the help of vigorous programs of market development," and what share could "appropriately be met, on a tapering-off basis, by special programs." As time passed, Benson found the conference idea ever more attractive, and on July 8, 1958, he presented it to the members of the CFEP. They had "considerable doubt" as to the "wisdom" of such a venture, and Clarence Randall believed that by the close of the meeting Benson had "accepted the unfavorable comment" and withdrawn the suggestion. He was wrong: Benson was only biding his time.[35]

Late in 1958 the USDA developed a special agricultural message that the president sent to Congress on January 29, 1959. And in it, alongside such routine recommendations as flexible price supports, elimination of acreage allotments and marketing quotas, and extension of the conservation reserve, Benson inserted a "Food for Peace" section in which Eisenhower announced he was "setting steps in motion to explore anew with other surplus-producing nations all practical means of utilizing the various agricultural surpluses of each in the interest of reinforcing peace and the well-being of friendly peoples throughout the world—in short, using food for peace." Randall, who had not been consulted in advance, was furious. The CFEP, he correctly believed, had been outmaneuvered.[36]

After the president's message, Benson lost no time in setting Food for Peace plans in motion. In April the United States officially invited the governments of Canada, Australia, Argentina, and France and the director-general of the FAO (UN Food and Agriculture Organization) to participate in a cabinet-level meeting on wheat exportation. Australia was frankly fearful that Food for Peace disposals would severely disturb commercial marketings, but all agreed to attend.[37]

Neither Clarence Randall nor Clarence Francis liked the plans. Randall complained that the USDA conference proposals made him "catch [his] breath at a few places" because they suggested "very bold and daring concepts" and dealt with "subjects which are not the responsibility of that

Department," and which were, in fact, "as broad as the whole concept of foreign economic assistance." Randall was only partially mollified when Paarlberg, now a White House staff member, assured him that if the conference seemed to be moving beyond established United States foreign policy, he would ask that the discussion be referred to the CFEP. Francis, on the other hand, felt that the scope of the conference proposal was too narrow. "If ways and means were found to distribute the full quota of surpluses which exist today," he argued, "only temporary good could result," and "what would happen" afterward was "not pleasant to contemplate." The real need was for "a sound long-term practical program of self-help," not for "another means of disposing of surpluses, disguised in a somewhat nicer but still a very transparent dress." "It's difficult for me to believe," he naively complained, "that the President had a surplus disposal plan in mind when he made his statement."[38]

All these fears were groundless. The conference, although well publicized and well attended, had no substantial results. The conferees merely issued a statement of humanitarian platitudes and established a "high level standing committee" that would "explore methods of attaining agreed objectives and . . . consult on wheat export policies and programs" but whose powers were limited to consultation. Eisenhower felt the conference was "well conceived and effective," and Francis, taking his cue from his superior, grudgingly agreed, although he still believed that unless the program was broadened to include economic development "a great opportunity" would be missed.[39]

Meanwhile, the ICASD, preparing for congressional hearings on PL 480, was making yet another evaluation of the program. Agreeing for once, State and Agriculture thought current PL 480 operations were "generally satisfactory," although the USDA suggested amendments to the legislation to permit dollar sales to the Soviet bloc, two- and three-year agreements, expanded foreign school lunch programs, overseas payment of wages in kind, encouragement of overseas livestock production and meat consumption to utilize American feed grains, and establishment of foreign national reserves of agricultural commodities under strict limitations. ICA disagreed. There should, it argued, be a complete restructuring of the law and a shift "from a Disposal Program to a Foreign Operating Program." As it stood, ICA said, PL 480 focused "negative" attention on the United States because of the disposal aspects while allowing the benefits of the program to go "largely unsung." In particular, the ICA wanted a change from sales to grants, "with foreign policy, rather than disposal objectives in mind." It was "a most undignified spectacle," it maintained, "for a great power like the U.S. to have to press other countries to accept 'loans' of the proceeds of these 'sales' in order to perpetuate the fiction that they were really 'sales.' " Besides, said ICA, the whole procedure led to excessive accumulations of foreign currency, which left the United States open to charges of imperialism, "however false," and also made it more difficult to secure appropriations from congressmen who tended to equate foreign currency balances with dollar purchasing power. It would be better, the agency thought, if PL 480 titles I and II and the MSA disposal section could all be replaced with a simple authorization allowing the president to draw upon $2 billion worth of CCC stocks annually for foreign aid.

However, neither Budget nor Commerce approved these proposals. Budget promptly announced that it opposed "every recommendation in the [ICA] memorandum," and Commerce grumbled that the first problem was to "attack and eliminate the causes of surplus production" at home, not to modify PL 480 as a "continuing means of disposal of agricultural products." Commerce was also concerned that currency grants or loans for economic development might "result in the recipient country postponing badly needed adjustments in its internal economy," upsetting its economic balance, or at best "merely transfer[ring] from individuals to the government claims on these resources," thereby undermining private enterprise.[40]

Characteristically, discussion of these various positions was referred to an ICASD subcommittee, and it was still considering them when, on April 16, 1959, Hubert

Humphrey introduced a PL 480 bill. In his proposal, titles I and II would be extended for five years, long-term credits for special sales would be authorized, grants of CCC commodities would be used to establish food reserves abroad, and a new post of peace food administrator would be created to administer PL 480 and the disposal section of MSA. With Congress considering this measure, Benson moved to regain the initiative for the executive branch. At a White House meeting of legislative leaders on May 19, he suggested that PL 480 be extended for three years, and the next day (probably with Paarlberg's connivance) the administration sent to the Hill a bill providing for a three-year renewal.

This was the ultimate encroachment on Clarence Randall's bureaucratic territory, and he resented it bitterly. "I have been hanging on to my chair for the past hour, trying to keep from blowing my top in a manner unseemly for a cardiac," he scribbled to General Wilton Persons. "This action is in direct contradiction to existing policy as established by the Council on Foreign Economic Policy, and I was given no chance either to express my personal views or submit it to the Council." The CFEP, he added, either had "a function to fulfill" or it did not, and if not he would resign and the council should be abolished. For the present, though, he hastily called a CFEP session to meet June 4 and attempt to shut the door to the empty PL 480 legislative barn.

At the meeting, State, Agriculture, and Clarence Francis all favored a three-year extension; and, given this alignment, the CFEP concluded that although a one-year extension was preferable, three years was acceptable "if the political situation urgently required it." It also decided that the administration should request $1.5 billion for title I and $300 million for title II, that Congress should be asked to authorize grants of surplus commodities for national reserves (with repayment in local currency "if and when the commodity is sold internally"), and that commodity grants for economic development purposes "not practical to administer under Title I" should be authorized under title II.[41]

The administration bill, adjusted accordingly, was introduced as S. 1748 and quickly precipitated a three-cornered struggle, with one group of congressmen interested mainly in efficient surplus disposal, a second group (led by Humphrey) hoping to transform the program into a major instrument of foreign policy, and the administration backing its own compromise. Because the first of these factions controlled the legislative machinery, the Senate Agriculture Committee was able to kill the Humphrey proposal by taking up the administration version first. In these the circumstances, Humphrey was forced to submit his provisions a section at a time, for consideration first by the committee, then by the Senate as a whole.

As sent to the president, the PL 480 or "Food for Peace" bill was an amalgam of factional compromises. Titles I and II were extended for two years—not one as the CFEP had wished or five as Humphrey had proposed, but in line with the personal proclivities of Benson and the surplus disposal advocates. The administration had managed to quash an amendment that would have given barter priority over foreign currency sales, would have required $350 million in annual barter transactions, and would have prohibited additionality criteria for barter contracts, but it was unable to obtain authorization to build national food reserves abroad or to make grants of commodities to further economic development. And while Humphrey's version was largely scrapped, there was a new title IV authorizing ten-year supply contracts to friendly nations with payment in dollars to be spread over as long as twenty years. In addition, a federal food stamp plan, which the administration had successfully opposed since 1954, was now written into law. The final bill was something Eisenhower could sign, but when he did so he carefully pointed out its shortcomings.[42]

As one might expect, the administration was not disposed to implement the programs Congress had "forced on" it. The new title IV was especially repugnant to the Republican policy-makers. The State Department agreed with foreign complainants that the long-term contracts were actually concessional transactions in violation of FAO principles, and Agriculture was not much more enthusiastic. Its Commodity Stabilization Service (CSS) suggested using the new title only in hard-currency countries, where the credit could be tied to "the development of some facility or project which offers real possibilities for expanded purchases of surplus agricultural commodities." Eventually the ICASD did agree to a plan for carefully selected pilot programs, but fears that the contracts would displace cash sales and private credits, make outstanding Export-Import loans more difficult to collect, alter credit terms to the disadvantage of the United States, or involve the nation in "frightful" banking practices meant that no effort was made to push the programs during the remainder of Eisenhower's presidency.[43]

Even the appointment of a Food for Peace coordinator was controversial. Republican party leaders argued that a coordinator would heighten the "public awareness of things being accomplished under this program." Administration officials, however, were generally unenthusiastic. Clarence Randall, still piqued that Food for Peace had gone forward without his approval, thought appointment of a White House coordinator would be a "dangerous" and "dramatic" step that would "involve an implied commitment to the under-nourished countries for their permanent nutritional support." Clarence Francis believed that Food for Peace should be built around an expanded technical assistance program, not the movement of agricultural surpluses. Budget, pointing out that the administration had opposed the coordinator provision in the Humphrey bill, doubted the wisdom of augmenting "a program which serves to bail out and thereby perpetuate unwise farm legislation." And Benson, while agreeing with those who argued that a White House coordinator would have high visibility, tended to see the proposal as an implied rebuke to USDA efforts to publicize Food for Peace. As a compromise, Benson suggested that Paarlberg, who had already been working on the program at the White House, merely have "Food for Peace administrator" tacked onto his current title. The other agencies agreed, and on April 13, 1960, Eisenhower officially designated him Food for Peace coordinator.[44]

By the middle of 1960, then, few of the problems that had bedeviled the administration from the beginning had been settled. The donation program was still in disarray, and to it had been added the burden of establishing a domestic food stamp program. The delicate balance between aid in food and aid in dollars had not been achieved. Only a beginning had been made on what later administations would call a "public relations offensive." The long-term programs to reduce soft currency accumulations and to provide five-year scheduled disposals had been established, but the details had yet to be worked out.

It was clear that in the brief time remaining to the administration, no substantial changes could be made. No basic PL 480 legislation would again confront the Eisenhower team, although appropriations for the titles would be made, giving the administration one last opportunity to present its case to Congress. The administration did want Congress to amend title II to allow these commodities to be used for economic development, and this it got, but it failed to win support for its twin requests for special administrative funds for title II and fewer ICA funds tied up in surplus disposal.

Consequently, Paarlberg devoted much of his brief time as Food for Peace coordinator to publicity ventures designed to gain plaudits for the administration's disposal program. Chief among these was the effort to tie the American Food for Peace program into a larger United Nations operation. This idea, it seems, originally came from Vice-President Richard Nixon, who, in the spring of 1960, suggested that the surplus food stocks of the agricultural exporting countries be pooled and distributed to the needy nations through a multilateral operation under United Nations auspices. In early July, in a conversation with Benson and Paarlberg, Eisenhower indicated that he was considering proposing this to the United Nations at its September meeting. Before doing so, however, he wanted the USDA, State, and the White House staff to "check this out very carefully."

In private, administration officials acknowledged that the proposal's "major purpose" was the "impact" it would have "at home and abroad," and since "impact" was desired, it was finally decided that Eisenhower would request a concurrent resolution from the two houses of Congress assuring the president of congressional support for such a program. On August 8, 1960, Eisenhower sent a special message to the Hill requesting such action, and on August 27 the resolution passed the Senate, though the House adjourned without taking it up.[45]

The Senate resolution was enough. Next the United States gathered Canada, Haiti, Liberia, Pakistan, and Venezuela as cosponsors, and on September 22 Eisenhower set forth the surplus stocks proposal in an address to the United Nations General Assembly. It was referred to the United Nations' Economic and Financial Committee, which reported it favorably. The chief opposition came from the Soviet Union, which argued that the proposal was "not new, not urgent," and that there was "no need to give it priority." On October 27 the General Assembly adopted the resolution and asked the FAO to establish "without delay" procedures by which the "largest practicable quantities of surplus food may be made available on mutually agreeable terms as a transitional measure against hunger." But these procedures, as Paarlberg frankly admitted, showed "no disposition to be operational." The FAO would serve mostly as "a clearing house or broker," which would "interfere in no way" with America's "current unilateral and multilateral operations."[46] As a public relations spectacular, the United Nations offensive was at least moderately successful, and its launching did indicate something of a change in view from a time when the administration had strongly opposed proposals for world food banks, world food capital funds, or "Free the World from Hunger" years.[47] But the change was mostly cosmetic. The new operation was to be dominated and controlled by the United States, and nothing new of real substance was accomplished.

Indeed, the whole Food for Peace operation represented less a change in substance than a recognition that existing programs needed a better image and better and more stable coordination. It began at a time when old problems were reasserting themselves and when there was growing recognition that the ICASD was a "weak vehicle" for settling them. Too often, the assistant secretaries who were the official ICASD members did not attend the meetings, and their substitutes were not qualified to make decisions for their departments; consequently, decisions were delayed while checks of agency positions were made. Too often the ICASD met at irregular intervals, and its rulings were delayed by cumbersome appeals to the CFEP. And, too often, Francis had turned the routine administration over to his assistant, traveling to Washington for only a few meetings and refusing to stay in close touch with day-to-day operations. For those concerned with this situation, the appointment of a White House coordinator, a person familiar with the problems and consistently accessible, represented a new try at better coordination.

In another sense, too, the Food for Peace actions represented a final admission by the administration that surplus disposal was not a short-term, easily solved problem. By 1959 it acknowledged that surpluses would be around for some time to come and that continuing disposal would require continuing domestic support. It thought a base of support might be created by stressing the "constructive" role that such programs could play in building "world peace" and improving American relations "with the uncommitted countries of the world."[48] In the future, it hoped, Food for Peace would secure support for United States foreign aid from the domestic agricultural constituency while securing support for domestic agricultural programs from the internationalists. But whether these optimistic predictions could be fulfilled would become the concern of another administration.

Yet better coordination, more positive publicity, and a recognition of the nature of the problem did not reach to the heart of the issue. Through the surplus disposal programs, the administration wanted to achieve a delicate equilibrium between private commercial sales and spurting domestic production. It believed that the government programs could be designed so as not to undermine the commercial ventures of the private sector, and some in the administration hoped to protect the commercial trade of friendly nations as well. Moreover, some officials thought the disposal program could be a vehicle for market development that, instead of harming the commercial trade, would actually help it. As if all these expectations were not enough, the Eisenhower men also hoped to use surplus disposal as an instrument of international politics, rewarding some nations, enticing others, punishing still others for their stance on international issues of concern to Americans. If missionaries could save souls through donated foods, they reasoned, why could not the United States government use food to save souls for capitalism? In addition, there was genuine humanitarian concern over world hunger, and some visionaries even believed that food could be used as a means of stimulating economic development in Third World nations. These conflicting aspirations were all too much for the slender vehicles of PL 480 and MSA. Humanitarianism was one thing, foreign policy another, a balance wheel for domestic agriculture yet a third. It was an unholy alliance, an impossible ideal, and mere tinkering with the mechanism was not going to make it either blessed or possible.

Chapter 6

The Politics of Trade

Our entire marketing system, including exports of grains from the United States, is conducted through private enterprise. Government employees with order books do not fit into such a marketing system.

—True D. Morse, Under Secretary of Agriculture, 1960

DURING THE EISENHOWER ADMINISTRATION, PL 480 shipments annually accounted for a quarter to a third of all United States exports of agricultural products (see table 1). Fiscal year 1960 found nearly three-fourths of all wheat exports leaving in PL 480 shipments, along with nearly two-thirds of all milled rice and nearly half of the cottonseed oil and soybean oil (see table 2). Small amounts of commodities were shipped under other aid programs as well.

But the agricultural trade policy of the Eisenhower administration was much more than surplus disposal, and surplus disposal was much more than PL 480. The surplus gave a peculiar urgency to the search for greater markets, and it inevitably required greater government involvement in day-to-day routine of trade. Given a choice, however, Ezra Taft Benson and his associates would have placed less emphasis on the government export programs and more on indirect assistance for private export trade. As it was, the Department of Agriculture administered PL 480 and also

99

Table 2

Exports under Public Law 480 Compared with Total United States Exports of Specified Commodities, Fiscal Year 1960

Programs	Wheat (million bushels)	Corn (million bushels)	Milled Rice (million cwt.)	Cotton (thousand bales)	Cottonseed Oil and Soybean Oil (million lbs.)
Public Law 480					
Title I	303	21	10.0	705	752
Title II	11	1	0.6	10	—
Title III					
Barter	26	27	0.7	112	—
Donations	25	11	1.4		—
Total	365	60	12.7	827	752
Other exports	146	167	7.5	5,809	849
Total exports	511	227	20.2	6,636	1,601
Total Public Law 480 exports as % of total exports	71	26	63	12	47

developed a series of stimulants to the commercial trade, sought to dispose of the accumulated commodity backlog and also to find markets for future production, tried to avoid statist controls and also to adapt them to congenial goals. In view of the magnitude of the surplus and the favorable weather conditions throughout the decade, the administration realized that it was essential to use every available export tool.

The preceding two chapters have considered surplus disposal in terms of the government export programs of PL 480 and the Mutual Security Act. This chapter examines the administration's vigorous pursuit of commercial sales and the variety of tools and levers, inherited and initiated, that they used. These included the search for alternative sales procedures, the support of new products, the use of import controls to protect the domestic market, and the manipulation of the General Agreement on Tariffs and Trade to provide the United States with as much latitude as possible in establishing its agricultural trade policy.

The search for alternative sales procedures was an effort by the department to move government-held commodities quickly and efficiently into the hands of the commercial trade and to give that trade some assistance in moving the commodities competitively onto the world market. Several programs were initiated, as the administration responded to pressures from commodity groups and political partisans. Just as the noncommercial PL 480 trade was extremely susceptible to the administration's anticipation of foreign reaction, the commercial export programs were equally susceptible to domestic demands.

The first of these new sales-promotion devices was competitive bid sales. In a bid sale, the government offers to sell a certain amount of a product, and prospective buyers submit bids to purchase some or all of that quantity at a buyer-suggested price, with the government free to accept or reject bids. Agriculture began selling cottonseed oil and linseed oil through bids in the spring of 1954, and that fall—in response to low prices, large stocks, and pressures from dairy farmers—the Agriculture Department proposed

selling surplus stocks of butter by bid. The ICASD split on
the proposal. State and Budget firmly opposed the plan, arguing that since May the USDA had offered butter at
world market prices and had succeeded in moving less than
a million pounds while "earning us wholesale criticism
from otherwise friendly countries"; the USDA, Clarence
Francis, and the Department of Commerce supported it.[1]
The proposal was referred to the cabinet, which on December 17, 1954, gave tentative approval to offering twenty
million pounds of butter in "relatively" small parcels, with
no bids to be accepted below an established price and with
Dulles to discuss the program in advance with "other affected supplying countries."[2] The first offering of ten million pounds brought no "acceptable" bids. A second offering
did result in the sale of 44,416 pounds to Armour and Company for resale in the Philippines and Haiti, and
eventually, despite strong protests from New Zealand,
three more sales were made. In addition, some ten million
pounds of dried milk were sold by bid.[3]

Bid sales were also featured in the 1955 round of the
longstanding debate over an administration cotton program. The cotton question was complicated by the intense
interest taken in the commodity by Southern congressmen
who were now, with a Democratic majority in the new
Eighty-fourth Congress, powerfully represented on the
House and Senate agriculture committees. It was further
complicated by the persistent divisions between cotton
growers and textile manufacturers, one afraid of losing foreign markets if the export price was not reduced, the other
terrified that foreign-produced cheap cotton goods would
ruin the domestic market. Price support law required the
government to sell CCC cotton on the domestic market at
105 percent of parity plus carrying charges, and Benson
declined to sell for export at a lower price. In March 1955
some 56 senators and 129 representatives sent open letters
to Benson, urging that CCC cotton stocks be sold abroad at
"competitive" prices. By late March, groups such as the
Liverpool Cotton Association, the Manchester Cotton Association, and the Le Havre Association Marche Cotons com-

plained that "uncertainties" regarding future American cotton policy were disrupting world markets and bringing the movement of American cotton to a standstill. Domestic exchanges, firms, and associations also complained to Benson, one exporter reporting that he had "received no inquiry from overseas for ten days."[4] To remove some of the uncertainty, Benson announced on March 29 that there would be no export subsidy for the 1954 crop, but this did not quiet the cotton trade. In early April the USDA received requests from cotton interests worldwide to announce policy for the marketing year beginning August 1, 1955.[5]

Benson refused to commit himself, choosing instead to establish a Cotton Export Advisory Committee (consisting of representatives of the Cotton Producers Association and the Farm Bureau, a large cotton producer, and five representatives of large cotton companies) to work with the department to devise a cotton disposal program. By July they developed a two-price proposal under which CCC cotton would be sold for export at "competitive world prices" (as in the butter sale) but at home would continue to command the higher of either the domestic market price or 105 percent of the current support price plus "reasonable" carrying charges. On July 20, however, the Council on Foreign Economic Policy rejected the plan by a vote of eight to one, the USDA representative casting the lone vote for it. CFEP offered a dozen arguments against the two-price proposal, including the probable negative effect on foreign relations and the likelihood that domestic textile producers would respond with a demand for section 22 restriction of foreign-produced cotton textiles. Nor would the president reverse this decision. Meeting with nearly a hundred cotton-state senators and congressmen who tried to enlist his support for a cotton subsidy, he avoided making any firm commitments.

Benson, certain that some sort of a cotton export program was necessary, persuaded Eisenhower to bring up the cotton question at the August 5, 1955, cabinet meeting. There the USDA made an hour's presentation of the department and advisory council proposal, but after another two hours of argument no agreement could be reached. At the next cabinet meeting the USDA proposed that the CCC offer a million bales of "lower quality" surplus cotton for export sale through open competitive bids beginning on January 1, 1956. To this the cabinet reluctantly agreed, and Eisenhower told Benson, "All right, Ezra, you've got your program." It was announced the next day, August 13.[6]

By May 1956 the price of American cotton abroad was eight and a half cents per pound below the January 1 price, with no bottom in sight. One factor in the drop may have been the million-bale program; another may have been the administration's announcement that further sales of CCC stocks would begin August 1. But, whatever the cause, the low prices brought demands for action.[7]

Congress was debating the 1956 farm legislation; so North Carolina's Congressman Harold Cooley introduced a bill requiring the CCC to sell extra-long-staple cotton for export at "competitive world prices" and to create an export program for all cotton that would "reestablish and maintain the fair historical share of the world market" for United States production. To achieve the latter, sales for the coming year were to be made at prices not above the lowest price received under the million-bale program.

Such provisions greatly upset the administration. If signed into law, the officials felt, the provisions would calcify programs that had previously been matters of administrative discretion and would exacerbate the conflict between domestic and foreign policy. In November 1955 Dulles had persuaded the Japanese to voluntarily limit their cotton textile exports to the United States;[8] now, in hopes of forestalling the legislation, the Department of State hastily obtained a note from the Japanese government assuring the United States that the limitations on cotton textile exports would continue through 1957. For its part, the Department of Agriculture announced that the "benefits of the cotton-export program would be extended to exports of cotton textiles, cotton yarns, and spinnable cotton waste manufactured from American upland cotton." Foreign governments protested. But congressional support for cotton growers' relief was strong, and the bill was passed and sent to the president.[9] The administration was uniformly unhappy with the bill, but because he had already vetoed one agricultural bill during that congressional session and because it was an election year, Eisenhower eventually signed it.[10]

The cotton provisions of the 1956 farm bill reflected both the pressures of commodity groups and the politics of the election year. Partisan political concerns led both Democrats and Republicans to try to manipulate the surplus issue to the benefit of their own party, and the cotton provisions were a show of strength by congressional Democrats. Similarly, the Republicans, through the director of the party's farm division, begged Benson to inaugurate programs for "immediate assistance" to agriculture.[11] The administration responded by instituting two more new sales promotion measures: new credit programs and a system of payments in kind.

In the past, the CCC had sold only for cash, but in February 1956 the National Advisory Council on International Monetary and Financial Problems had approved a CCC proposal to extend credit to American exporters of CCC commodities for loans at 3–4 percent for periods up to three years. By September 1956, more than $8.5 million worth of commodities had been moved under these arrangements, and that success led the USDA and the Export-Import Bank to lobby for similar credits for foreign purchasers. Consequently, on September 10, 1956, the administration launched a new credit program whereby the Export-Import Bank would help foreign banks and importers obtain "U.S. agricultural surpluses in situations in which adequate credit is not available from the usual commercial sources." Such loans would normally be extended for six months to a year, but the bank could arrange longer terms in special circumstances. This was very good agricultural news for the immediate preelection period.[12]

One other election year use of credit arrangements involved meat exports. Cattle prices were very low in the summer of 1956, and in July the director of the Republican party's farm division appealed to Benson to begin a cattle purchase program at once. Unless this was done, he warned, "my time is wasted and . . . the Republican National Committee gains very little by setting up the Farm Division." Over the objections of Percival Brundage, Bureau of the Budget chief, who pointed out that meat was not in chronic oversupply, the USDA and the Export-Import Bank worked out a $5 million loan to Mexico that provided $3,750,000 for the purchase of beef cattle (primarily in drought states) and the remainder for dairy stock. This, so they argued, both aided Mexican farmers and strengthened the American market by removing some of the surplus and stimulating a Mexican demand for United States breeds.[13]

The second major election-year measure to move the surplus was known as payment-in-kind. For months, grain dealers had complained strenuously that in its export sales the CCC was "repeatedly" making deals that broke the market, displaced dollar transactions, and brought windfalls to firms that had the terminal warehousing and transportation to take advantage of the situation. Such complaints had taken on added weight when it was revealed that the Continental Grain Company had been manipulating the futures market in order to lower prices, thereby activating "resting orders" to purchase wheat from the CCC at specific prices to fill export commitments. The remedy, so the complaining dealers thought, was to stop CCC sales and instead provide a subsidy (at a rate to be announced daily) for exports of free commercial wheat. The Minneapolis Grain Exchange suggested that the subsidy be in kind; the National Grain Trade Council endorsed the plan; and the USDA's Grain Division, although warned that other nations might view such a program as "dumping," supported the idea. However, Assistant Secretary of Agriculture Marvin McLain pointed out that payment-in-kind conflicted with the congressional mandate to dispose of CCC stocks. The department would favor it, he said, only if the farm organizations and Congress would concur.[14]

Conscious that the spring wheat crop was nearing har-

vest, the USDA quickly began sounding out the farm organizations. The AFBF, the Grange, the NFU, the National Federation of Grain Cooperatives, and the Farmers
Union Grain Terminal Association all endorsed a one-year
payment-in-kind trial run, but by the time their concur-
rences were complete it was July 5, five days after the start
of a new marketing year and well into the wheat harvest.
And by July 13, when the payment-in-kind subsidy was
finally announced, the harvest had been completed
throughout much of the Midwest. Wheat prices rose an
average of seven to nine cents, but, as McLain had feared,
most of the gain "fell into the hands" of the grain trade
rather than the farmers. Charges were now rife that this
effort to correct an "undesirable" concentration of operations in the CCC was actually a program to enrich a few
grain dealer "profiteers."

Realizing this could be a serious campaign charge,
McLain himself drafted a reply to be used by the USDA's
Office of Information. In it he argued that although the
grain trade's proposal admittedly had been made "many"
months ago, the time lag was caused by the Department's
desire for concurrence from the "farm organizations, the exporters, the millers, and others who were to be affected by
the new program." "As soon as the Department was satisfied that this program met with the approval of the *big end*
of those who were to be affected by it," he wrote, it was
promptly put into effect [emphasis mine]. Nor had wheat
farmers been deprived of its advantages, he claimed. Most
southern wheat "had been sold at least at the loan rate or
near to it," and central and northern wheat had been marketed after the program was announced. Such a reply could
hardly have been pleasing to the farmers who were re-
garded as the "small end" of the wheat industry, but apparently it served its political purpose, for the new wheat
program did not become a major campaign issue.[15]

During the next year, payment-in-kind was extended to
feed grains and cotton. The feed grain extension came
about because efforts to dispose of the corn surplus through
competitive bid sales and emergency aid to livestock pro-

ducers had failed, and the grain trade, the Republican National Committee, and the White House all wanted "more freedom" in the grain sales program.[16] In the case of cotton, a sharp drop in the volume of exports in late 1957 and early 1958 led the administration to reconsider what might be done to stimulate the market.[17] Accordingly, on March 31, 1958, after consulting with the American Cotton Producers Association, the Farm Bureau, the Grange, and the NFU, and after severe criticism of the USDA from House and Senate appropriations committees, Eisenhower announced payment-in-kind programs for corn, cotton, and other feed grains.[18] In 1959, after further serious deterioration in cotton prices, the USDA discontinued the competitive bid program and raised the payment-in-kind export subsidies for cotton by one and a half cents a pound. There were vigorous international protests, but the decision remained firm.[19] By December of that year the USDA could see that the new cotton price was creating a "very successful" cotton export year, and early in 1960 the department announced that it was reducing the subsidy rate by about two cents a pound and increasing the resale price on 1959 and older cotton crops.[20]

These three major new sales procedures—bid sales, credit arrangements, and payment-in-kind subsidies—added to the administration's ability to move commodities out of government warehouses and into commercial channels. Like traditional export subsidy programs, these measures did not influence the ultimate use of the commodities. Nor did they necessarily open new markets or find new uses for commodities. However, new markets and new uses were also goals of the administration's disposal plan, and they were the raison d'être for several specialized programs.

Two projects designed to capture new markets in the Far East were undertaken early in the administration. One involved processing CCC wheat into bulgur, with a percentage to be distributed free as samples, the rest to be sold on an experimental basis, and the by-products to go to the corporate agency handling the transaction (the Fisher

Flouring Mills Company). Fisher promoted the product under the brand name ALA, but it failed to break into Japanese and Indian test markets.[21] The second effort involved the processing of ghee, a liquefied butter. In this case the USDA first offered butter to commercial firms on a bid basis for conversion into ghee, and later, when no sales were made, it converted some eighty-one million pounds itself, offering it for donation under title II. Only fifteen million pounds were eventually sold, and these at the depressingly low price of seven cents per pound.

In addition to the Far Eastern projects, some efforts were made to develop new uses and new markets elsewhere. One new process, for example, allowed a half million pounds of butter to be combined with dried milk to form fluid or evaporated milk for sale abroad. Another project permitted domestic chocolate manufacturers to purchase two and a half million pounds of butter at reduced prices and utilize it as a cocoa butter extender. Benson campaigned successfully to have milk offered as a beverage on airlines, and with official encouragement the American Dairy Association undertook a vigorous advertising campaign for dairy products. The latter, however, had little effect. Although United States consumption of dairy products rose 1 percent, this was at a time when per capita income was climbing 3 percent and retail milk prices were falling 5 percent.[22]

In an effort to identify all potential uses for agricultural products, the Agricultural Act of 1956 established a Commission on Increased Industrial Uses of Agricultural Products. The commission eventually made a long report, but it got no immediate results.[23] Surplus disposal and export stimulus through introducing products to new markets was a difficult, lengthy process, the short-term effect was marginal, and the benefits, if any, would be reaped by ensuing administrations.

The search for new markets was inevitably tangled in the problems of import controls, both at home and abroad. The administration devoted considerable energy to reducing foreign tariff barriers against American products, while at home producers and manufacturers demanded protection from influxes of foreign goods. This led to continuing difficulties with the United States' partners in the GATT, difficulties that were smoothed over but never truly resolved. Import controls and GATT manipulation were significant levers in the administration's attempts to expand and protect commercial sales.

New section 22 import quotas were imposed nineteen times during the eight years of the Eisenhower administration (see table 3), but the number would have been even higher were it not for some gentlemen's agreements that the administration negotiated. For example, in 1954 Argentina and Panama agreed to restrict their exports of tung nuts and tung oil to the United States during the

Table 3
Section 22 Invocations, 1953–61

Year	Number	Commodities
1953	5	Dairy products, nuts, oats
1954	4	Rye, rye flour, rye meal, oats, nuts, barley, and barley malt
1955	1	Rye, rye flour, rye meal
1956	0	—
1957	5	Butter substitutes and butter oil, rye, butterfat products, tung oil, nuts
1958	2	Tung nuts, long-staple cotton (modification)
1959	1	Rye, rye flour, rye meal
1960	1	Tung oil and tung nuts
Total	19	

1954–55 marketing year so that no quotas would be imposed.[24] Much more significant than tung oil, however, was cotton, where massive export subsidies gave foreign textile manufacturers a decided cost advantage over domestic firms who paid the higher domestic price for American growths. As noted above, the State Department obtained Japanese assurances that they would limit textile exports, but the congressional cotton interests still succeeded in inserting into the 1956 farm bill a clause that encouraged the president to limit textile imports through gentlemen's agreements. Linked with the strong cotton export requirements of the legislation, it was clear that Congress meant cotton exports to stay exported.

A principal difference between the gentlemen's agreements and the section 22 import controls was that the former were bilateral and the latter were unilateral, which meant that the latter were much more likely to anger trading partners. The GATT intersessional meeting in midsummer 1954, for example, brought demands that the United States accept "some reasonable limitation on its freedom of action" in establishing quotas and subsidies. A United Nations Food and Agriculture Organization regional meeting in Buenos Aires passed resolutions on surplus disposal and stabilization of international price relationships. The economic experts of the Organization for European Economic Cooperation, meeting in Paris, sharply questioned the American delegates on agricultural surplus disposal policies. The British Commonwealth Conference discussed the section 22 import restrictions, leading British Prime Minister Anthony Eden to protest to Dulles the "apparent inability" of the United States to "do anything" to modify section 22.[25]

On October 28, 1954, GATT met for a comprehensive review of all GATT functions, including a survey of the controls over agricultural trade. It quickly became apparent that the United States' only hope for avoiding an undesirable GATT clause on import restrictions was to seek a waiver for section 22. The GATT partners recognized that the internal politics of the United States necessitated the waiver, but they were determined to exact other concessions in return. After the United States refused to cooperate in any new commodity organization, the other partners concentrated their efforts on securing as much United States consultation as possible on surplus disposal and export subsidies.[26]

The American position on these questions was worked out in a storm of cables between Washington and Geneva. The United States finally agreed that consultation was a "mutually applicable principle" the United States would use in the case of title I sales. Before these PL 480 agreements were concluded, competing exporters would be invited to state their trade interests; there would be periodic discussion of general policies with them; specific agreements would be discussed with countries having a "substantial" interest "shortly before execution of an agreement or issuing an announcement"; and there would be unlimited consultation "after the fact." Consultation on section 22 was also declared to be the current "consistent practice" of the United States government, and other nations were informed that the United States would expect them to "consult on particular agricultural transactions which because of size or character are likely to have disrupting effects on U.S. markets." But these were the limits. There would be no consultation on other PL 480 titles, on section 32 export subsidies, on MSA disposals, or on other CCC transactions. These transactions, the ICASD argued, did "not repeat not usually involve potential displacement of third nation markets." Ultimately, given these American assurances, two-thirds of the partners approved an unlimited section 22 waiver.[27]

Just as self-interest dictated manipulating GATT to protect the American import control system, so too it led the United States to use GATT to urge other countries to liberalize their import quotas. For example, during 1957 and the first half of 1958, United States pressures, both unilaterally and through the GATT, led twenty-two countries to liberalize quotas on agricultural commodities,[28] even though the United States did not make equivalent concessions. In fact, the United States terminated only one quota during that period (on short, harsh, or rough cotton, a quota that was usually barely 20 percent filled), while it extended the rye quota for two years, imposed new quotas on tung nuts, butter oil, and butter substitutes, placed a tariff on almonds, and subdivided the long-staple cotton quota for better control (see Table 3).

Yet, despite this liberalization abroad and growing protectionism at home, the outlook at the end of fiscal 1958 was somber. For the first time since the beginning of the administration, the total volume and value of farm exports declined. And since the total harvested acreage remained the same and productivity per acre continued to rise, there had been an increase in domestic stocks and, consequently, a rise in storage costs and a decline in prices.[29] More important, for the first time since World War II the United States balance of payments slid into the red, reflecting in part the general slowdown in the domestic economy but also the decline in agricultural exports.

The balance of payments problem was a grim new development. As recently as 1957, total nonmilitary exports had been nearly one and a half times imports, a difference of more than $6 billion. By 1959 barely a billion dollars separated them, and in the wake of the 1958 recession United States gold stocks were drawing down while foreign and international holdings were rising rapidly.[30]

The Eisenhower administration was particularly concerned about the slumping industrial sales. Agriculture was a lesser concern; in fact, Don Paarlberg and Ezra Taft Benson actually thought agriculture might benefit from the new balance of payments situation. In the past, a number of European countries had justified their trade restrictions on the basis of the dollar shortage, a rationale that the GATT Contracting Parties had accepted. But now, with a greater supply of dollars in Western Europe, it seemed possible to challenge the continuing legitimacy of these restrictions.

In any event, at the GATT session in May 1959, the United States delegation took advantage of recent moves toward greater currency convertibility to argue that "as inconvertibility has given way to convertibility, so discrimination and bilateralism should now give way to nondiscrimination and multilateralism." And the argument was followed by some action. At the conclusion of the session, the United Kingdom liberalized import restrictions on a "wide range" of consumer goods and foodstuffs. West Germany, prodded by an earlier finding of the International Monetary Fund that it was no longer in difficulty over balance of payments, also agreed to remove nontariff restrictions on a number of items and to increase sales "opportunities" for others. And in late 1959, after the International Monetary Fund had called for the removal of all discriminatory restrictions with all feasible speed, the GATT Contracting Parties adopted a report stating that discrimination in trade on balance of payments grounds should be ended quickly. Benson informed Homer Brinkley of the National Council of Farmer Cooperatives that "the GATT served as an effective medium through which to operate." There was, he said, "full push" behind the United States drive for trade liberalization.[31]

For agriculture, moreover, the GATT now became an important counterweight to such multilateral trading blocs as the European Economic Community (EEC), the European Free Trade Association (EFTA), the Latin American Free Trade Association (LAFTA), and the Multilateral Treaty [organization] of Free Trade and Central American Economic Integration. The United States, following Dulles's penchant for organizing the diplomatic world into a series of regional groupings, had encouraged the formation of these organizations. Yet they also brought with them the prospect of a powerful agricultural protectionism operating within each bloc and working to exclude American commodities. The prospect was not a pleasant one, and it was against this potential power that Benson hoped to use GATT "as a positive and moderating influence." GATT article XXIV, the USDA pointed out, prohibited the increase of levels of protection in the formation of a customs union, and Agriculture now urged the State Department to emphasize that support for these organizations was "predicated on compliance by the countries concerned with GATT."[32]

In the spring of 1960 the United States was especially nervous about a set of Common Market agricultural proposals designed to convert the practices of the individual members into a collective policy over a six-year transition period. These practices included variable import fees, export subsidies, and specially administered grain and sugar quotas. With nearly a fourth of its agricultural export market at stake, the United States joined with Canada, Australia, and New Zealand to urge an early review by the GATT Contracting Parties of proposals that might be "detrimental not only to . . . exporters of agricultural products but to the Community itself." And after the GATT session in 1960 joint consultations were held between the EEC countries and the complaining parties, and the American representatives made it clear that the United States was not so anxious to have the Common Market succeed that it would not raise serious objections to such proposals. As a result, the six agreed to GATT review, and American officials privately resolved to press harder for relaxation of agricultural import restrictions, believing that the level of restrictions the countries carried into the EEC agricultural agreement would largely determine the restrictiveness of the Common Market policy. At the same time, it was urged that GATT take a look at the EFTA and LAFTA agreements.[33]

In July 1960 Benson made a special trip to Europe to discuss the Common Market agricultural proposals with his ministerial counterparts and to argue that these proposals differed from United States' practices. As Paarlberg put it in a preparatory memorandum, section 22 was "intended to keep us from pulling farm products out of the normal pattern of international trade" and was therefore "different

from restrictions applied by an importing nation which
keep farm products from the normal trade pattern." Furthermore, restrictive action "in concert" was "more of an
impediment to trade than action by a single country," was
especially difficult for the United States to combat, and was
contrary to GATT principles. Speaking bluntly, Benson
told the Europeans that the United States favored a "lib-
eral agricultural policy" for the Common Market that
would maintain "a reasonable international division of labor" and strengthen the "free world."[34]

Paradoxically, though, even as the USDA moved to
check new forms of protectionism abroad, the pressures for
protectionism at home were growing. As Paarlberg recognized, American farmers now had all the arguments historically used to justify protectionist measures "plus a big
new one, namely, that shutting down on imports will save
dollars and improve our balance of payments position."
And through a series of specific actions, the groups seeking
protection were securing at least a part of what they
wanted. The rye import quota was extended despite Tariff
Commission recommendations against it; the payment-in-
kind program was continued although administration
analysis indicated that it was both costly and ineffective;
there was a special subsidy for wheat exports to Japan. For
the time being, pressures for further restrictions on imports of meat, tung oil, and almonds were successfully
resisted, but whether they could be in the future was prob-
lematical.[35]

Pressure from the dairy industries was especially strong,
and here efforts to hold the line were far from a complete
success. In February 1959, after an extensive review of the
prices charged for exports of surplus butter and nonfat dry
milk, the USDA adopted a new reduced price schedule and
began what New Zealand called a "subsidized invasion" of
overseas markets. For milk, the reduced price was a successful purchasing incentive and surpluses quickly declined, and by late 1959 the USDA not only had raised its
price again but had also been forced to halt sales and cut

off dry milk distribution to the voluntary agencies. Consequently, the administration was able to resist pressures for new import restrictions and even to enlarge the quotas for Edam, Gouda, and Italian-type cheeses, but it was not able to prevent a Senate vote in 1960 to raise the domestic price supports for butter and industrial milk. In Europe this was interpreted as a sign that the United States planned to retain a protected home market.[36]

The other commodity that again became a focus of protectionist pressures was cotton. In line with producer demands, the USDA in early 1959 supported a further reduction in the existing import quota on extra-long-staple cotton. But this proposal ran into strong opposition from the State Department, which thought it likely to damage the economies of Peru and the Sudan and impair the improving "relations with the UAR." And the Tariff Commission, which was called upon to study the quota request, agreed with State's arguments. The USDA, it pointed out, had allowed a doubling of domestic acreage allotments and marketing quotas, thereby creating a surplus that domestic consumption had not been able to absorb, and in these circumstances a twenty-year-old quota should not be reduced merely because of domestic mismanagement. Eisenhower took the commission's advice.[37]

Textile manufacturers, too, now demanded protection. In August 1959, acting on a request of the National Cotton Council, both Clarence Randall and the Department of Agriculture supported a section 22 investigation on cotton textiles. Commerce opposed the inquiry, warning that any import fees or quotas would impair United States relations with other GATT nations, lead to claims for compensation by them, and undermine the United States drive for a general reduction in the use of quantitative restrictions abroad. State also opposed a section 22 investigation, arguing that it was contrary to the "gentlemen's agreement" on textiles with the Japanese and would lead Japan to scrap its voluntary quotas. And, though an investigation was finally ordered, no further actions were taken. The domestic textile industry would have to look elsewhere for relief.[38]

Meanwhile, with protectionists at home only partially satisfied and the strength of their counterparts abroad uncertain, the administration was moving to correct the balance of payments situation. On March 8, 1960, the Council on Foreign Economic Policy requested an ICASD analysis of the possibility of increasing cash dollar sales, and in November Eisenhower issued a directive ordering government agencies to take steps to increase the exports of goods and services, "especially U.S. agricultural products." The USDA then suggested a presidential statement "on making the benefits of the trade agreements program effective" for agriculture, if need be by withdrawing concessions from countries that would not cooperate, and in January 1961 the department's export committee made recommendations in seven major policy areas, ranging from educational and informational programs to payment-in-kind for dairy products. Such proposals, however, came at a time when they could mean little. There was no way that an eleventh-hour administration could make an effective threat to withdraw concessions or implement the USDA's recommendations.[39]

As the Eisenhower administration ended, then, policymakers were confronted with a balance of payments problem and continued high levels of agricultural production. The USDA was deeply worried about the development of trading blocs in the "free" world, blocs that might come to resemble the closed systems of communist countries, and blocs that could certainly lessen the advantages the United States had once enjoyed. If they kept developing, the United States would not be the only free world nation with a large protected market and the power to control access to it.

During the 1950s the Eisenhower administration had tried both export stimulants (new commercial assistance measures, new products, new markets) and import depressants (quotas, gentlemen's agreements) to alleviate the pressure of surplus stock and to guard against future accumulations. It had attacked trade barriers abroad; it had used the GATT to protect domestic import controls and to lay siege to foreign ones. It had responded to the pressures of Congress, political partisans, and commodity groups while minimizing foreign policy considerations in its search for commercial export markets. While these efforts had surely prevented even further accumulations by some immeasurable amount, the stocks on hand in January 1961 showed that the program, judged on its own terms, was at best a partial success.

Yet throughout the 1950s there was one market that remained untapped, a market with an unknown potential. It lay behind the iron curtain.

Chapter 7

The Communist Question

It is impossible to speak seriously of the liquidation of the "cold war" and of the lessening of tensions in international relations unless the existing abnormal situation in international trade is likewise liquidated.

—Nicolai Bulganin, Prime Minister, USSR, 1958

I don't think that there is a great possibility of relieving tensions through trade.

—John Foster Dulles, Secretary of State, 1958

EISENHOWER'S AGRICULTURAL TRADE POLICY relied heavily on special export programs and stiffer import controls; however, some export restrictions remained, particularly on trade with the Sino-Soviet bloc. As the surplus continued to build throughout the decade, tension grew over these controls. On the one hand, some officials hoped to remove these export controls and open new markets behind the iron curtain; on the other hand, some believed that the controls could be weapons in the cold war.

A major constraint on expanding trade with the bloc was the emotional antipathy of both officials and the public toward communism. And, given the rampages of Joseph McCarthy on Capitol Hill and the purges that had just taken place in the State Department, the early years of the Eisenhower administration were a difficult time to argue for trade with the Soviets. It is to the credit of a few admin-

istration officials, including Benson, a few newspapers, a
few homegrown entrepreneurs, and the American Farm
Bureau that the issue received an airing.

Officially, two types of export restrictions were available
to the administration: short-supply and strategic. In the
agricultural field, however, the former by 1953 applied
only to rice and hog bristles (and rice was dropped in 1954),
and the latter had not been applied at all, even though
farm products might technically fall within the Defense
Department's blanket definition of "strategic goods."[1] Instead, agricultural exports to the Sino-Soviet bloc were controlled under the licensing authority of the Department of
Commerce. It had to approve any shipment to the USSR
and Eastern Europe (China and North Korea were under
total blockade), and though the year beginning October 1,
1952, saw the approval of $1,732,590 worth of nonstrategic
exports, the movement of agricultural products was almost
nonexistent. If trade figures for the fourth quarter of 1947
and 1952 are compared, the dollar value of agricultural exports to the bloc dropped by more than 99 percent.[2]

The first clear trade opportunity since the cold war began
with Stalin's death in the spring of 1953. Stalin's succes-
sors, Georgi Malenkov and Nikita Khrushchev, faced massive agricultural shortages. Grain production, traditionally
a Soviet food and export staple, was running below that of
prewar years, making it difficult for the Soviets to supply
feed grains to the grain-short satellites. Cotton and industrial oils were in chronic short supply, and there were serious shortages in meats and dairy products. Total cattle
stocks in 1953 were ten million head below 1928, and the
number of milk cows was 13 percent lower than in prere-
volutionary 1916. The new Kremlin leadership quickly announced its intent to support agricultural development
while at the same time importing some agricultural products, a departure it hoped would give agriculture a
breathing space, provide more food for consumers, and supply raw materials for light agriculture-related industries.[3]

Consequently, early in 1954 the Soviet Union made direct offers to buy surplus butter and cottonseed oil from the

United States, and commercial exporters sought export licenses from the Department of Commerce. Opposition quickly developed. Secretary of Commerce Weeks opposed the licenses. Denmark protested that the sale of butter would invade a normal Danish market, and C. D. Jackson, the White House expert on psychological warfare, concluded darkly that the Soviet offer was "very evidently Russian psychological warfare" designed to divide the United States from its allies. Congressional reaction was also negative.[4]

On January 15 and February 5, 1954, the cabinet considered issuing licenses for the export of butter and cottonseed oil to the Soviet Union. Although butter was in extreme surplus, due to two years of very low exports, the final decision was no. The cabinet feared that there would be "an adverse public reaction" if the sale price was below the domestic retail price, as would be true in an export transaction at the world market price. Following the January cabinet meeting, Secretary Weeks announced that "as a general principle" he would not approve any application "which would permit an exporter to buy butter at considerably lower prices than those paid by the American housewife and then send that butter into Russia."

At this time, too, the Soviet Union was rumored to be willing to barter manganese for butter. Eisenhower was intrigued by this possibility, and on February 5 the cabinet decided there would be no objection to bartering perishable agricultural commodities for minerals. This left the trade door slightly ajar, as did Weeks's subsequent statement that the ban on commercial export licenses applied only to the export of government-owned agricultural products to the Soviet bloc for cash. The ban, he said, did not preclude "study" of license applications from those who acquired the commodities "in the open market and not from the CCC surplus stocks." In fact neither barter nor licenses materialized.[5]

The debate over East-West trade continued through the spring of 1954. The President's Commission on Foreign Economic Policy recommended the liberalization of "peaceful" trade with the Soviet bloc, and the Commodity Credit

Corporation's advisory board strongly recommended sales of surplus agricultural commodities to the bloc.[6] In response to the continuing controversy,[7] the National Security Council (NSC) considered the question at its meeting on April 1, 1954. The NSC reaffirmed the cabinet ban on cash sales of CCC-held commodities to the European Soviet bloc, but it did push the trade door open a bit further by approving the sale of fats to friendly countries that would then be able to release "native fats" for sale behind the iron curtain.[8]

In the ensuing congressional debates over the bill that became PL 480, it was clear that political opposition to transactions with communist nations was not about to disappear. Administration opposition, to be sure, eventually led the conference committee to drop the Dies Amendment (which would have prohibited any commodity transfer that would allow its recipient to continue or increase trade with a Soviet bloc country), but in the measure that finally passed not only were "unfriendly" nations excluded from participation, but the president was also directed to "assist friendly nations to be independent of trade with the USSR or nations dominated or controlled by the USSR" and to "assure that agricultural commodities sold or transferred" under PL 480 did not "result in increased availability of those or like commodities to unfriendly nations." A number of powerful congressional leaders, including George Aiken, chairman of the Senate Agriculture Committee, were interested in United States–Soviet barter, but Congress generally seemed to oppose any other form of East-West trade.[9]

Whether there were actual opportunities to sell agricultural commodities to the Soviet bloc in the summer of 1954 is unclear,[10] but chances to sell butter arose again in the fall. At that time Commerce and Agriculture had a "number of inquiries" from the Netherlands and Sweden and from American firms with business connections in those two countries concerning the possible shipment of five to ten thousand tons of butter for consumption there plus an equal amount either for direct transshipment to the Soviet Union or for industry use in Sweden and the Netherlands with the resulting products shipped to the bloc.[11]

This arrangement seemed to meet the spirit of the April 1 NSC decision, but the administration hesitated. During two long meetings on November 23 and December 7, 1954, the ICASD considered the potential shipments. Agriculture, predictably, argued in favor of the sale, suggesting that it was better to "drain the Soviets' purchasing power in butter than through hard goods." Also as expected, State hesitated, pointing out that this trade would be inconsistent with the PL 480 policy of discouraging other countries from dealing with the bloc. The surprise was Commerce. During the cabinet discussions, Sinclair Weeks had opposed United States–Soviet trade, but he had since changed his mind, and Commerce now announced that it would favor such transactions at world prices. After hours of discussion, the ICASD formulated a two-part proposal and referred it to the cabinet. One part called for direct sales of CCC commodities to the Soviet bloc, the other for sales to friendly countries for transshipment to the bloc, and the ICASD proposed to give both a ninety-day trial.[12]

On December 16, the day before the cabinet was to discuss the ICASD proposal, Benson told a press conference that "we ought to be willing to trade with Iron Curtain countries, whether in butter or anything else, so long as the trade is in our favor." That same day the delegates to the American Farm Bureau Federation's annual convention resolved "that U.S. farm products be offered for sale in world markets without regard to destination whenever it will advance the welfare and freedom of the people of the United States." The *New York Times* put Benson's statement and photo on the front page, and the *New York Herald Tribune* editorialized in favor of Benson's plan. "After all," it argued, "it is butter—not guns—that goes to the Communists."[13]

At the cabinet meeting, advocates of the ICASD plan contended that it would meet the demands for surplus disposal without incurring "ruinous cost," it would take advantage of the only substantial outlet for the butter surplus, it would not enhance Russia's military potential, and it would not incur unfavorable public reaction because a narrower gap now existed between the world price and the

CCC cost than had existed the previous January. Eisenhower said he thought the United States "should engage in any trade with the enemy which is to our net advantage," but State pointed out that the sale might undermine United States efforts to discourage other countries from trading with the Soviet bloc and might violate the express prohibitions on sale and transshipment of agricultural commodities to the Soviet bloc that had been written into title I of PL 480. In the face of this strong objection, the president postponed a decision.[14]

What State actually wanted was a comprehensive legal opinion from the attorney general on PL 480 limitations. In November, the FOA's general counsel had ruled that the Battle Act, which terminated aid to nations that supplied the Soviet bloc with certain military items, applied both to title I sales where the proceeds went for military and economic assistance and to title II donations where they were made on a nation-to-nation basis, and that therefore these types of agreements could not be concluded with a nation that failed "to embargo the shipment of strategic materials to the Soviet Bloc and Communist China." Given this ruling, State and CFEP Chairman Joseph Dodge now wanted to know if the express prohibitions of sales and transshipments to the Soviet bloc written into title I also applied to donations under title II, barter transactions under title III, and dollar sales and transshipments of surplus commodities not acquired under the PL 480 titles. In effect, they were questioning the legality of the previous cabinet and NSC decisions on barter and transshipments, and on January 12 the White House requested an opinion from the Department of Justice.[15]

In the meantime a number of new inquiries about possible export licenses for Soviet destinations arrived at the Department of Commerce, and pressure to authorize the sales continued to build.[16] The *Washington Post* editorialized that the United States "ought to jump at the chance to get something useful for a commodity that is a drug on the market," and the Washington News Syndicate's weekly farm newsletter reported that "most farmers" supported the idea of selling surplus butter and dairy products to the

USSR. Benson mentioned the possibility of Soviet sales at one of his press conferences, and Charles Shuman, the new president of the American Farm Bureau Federation, told the press that he was "a little bit puzzled" about why the State Department was blocking direct sales.[17]

Yet mixed with these favorable comments were signs that opposition to such trade measures was still strong. In particular, a subcommittee of the House Committee on Government Operations was now investigating rumored transshipments of CCC commodities from stated export destinations to Soviet ports, and it expressed vigorous displeasure over possible transgressions.[18]

With confusion mounting, the Department of Justice finally released its opinion on February 21, 1955. Under PL 480, it declared, no government-held surplus agricultural commodities could be traded or bartered, either directly or indirectly, with the Soviet bloc. However, dollar sales of such commodities were within the president's discretion, it said, and although Justice thought it "appropriate" that the president "give consideration" to the congressional attitudes expressed in PL 480, it decided that he could authorize such sales without violating the law. This opinion killed both the pending license requests (which involved CCC stocks) and the ICASD proposal. The Department of Commerce, smarting from congressional criticism of possible transshipments, now issued new export regulations tightening destination controls.[19]

By mid-1955, efforts to bridge the gap between American surpluses and Soviet bloc shortages had made little progress. However, the latter part of the year brought a few encouraging signs. At the 1955 summit conference in Geneva, Anthony Eden suggested that an "expansion of the existing channels of trade between East and West" was a "desirable objective." Eisenhower agreed that increased trade would be a major step toward "normalizing" East-West contacts, and Bulganin expressed the belief that the "broad development" of economic relations "based on the principle of mutual profit would facilitate the strengthening of friendly relations between States and permit an improvement in the welfare of the people." As a result, the final directive instructed the foreign ministers of the conferring nations to study measures that would "bring about progressive elimination of barriers which interfere with free communications and peaceful trade between people."[20] The foreign ministers met in November, and Dulles told Soviet Minister Molotov that there were now good possibilities for normal trade in agricultural surpluses. And in conjunction with the foreign ministers' meeting, Secretary of Commerce Weeks announced that beginning on January 1, 1956, his department would slightly ease trade restrictions with the Soviet bloc.[21]

These official gestures were overmatched by private initiatives. An exchange of agricultural delegations between the United States and the USSR occurred in the summer of 1955, solely because Lauren Soth, an Iowa newspaperman, conceived the idea, which was quickly seized upon by the Soviets. The Soviet delegation was a very high level one headed by the acting minister of Agriculture, Vladimir Matskevitch, and it spent a month touring a wide variety of agricultural institutions and production facilities, especially those related to corn-hog operations. And as it moved about, there was some concern over the results of the exchange. The Office of Strategic Information in the Department of Commerce, for example, worried that the Soviet delegation might wish to purchase purebred livestock or advanced farm machinery and wondered if that might constitute "strategic information." USDA officials, too, thought the "technological trade" would be in favor of the Soviet Union and wondered if the United States would get "commensurate" benefits, "politically, psychologically, or the like." No major diplomatic incidents developed, however, and the Russians were clearly intrigued with the potential of hybrid corn.[22]

After the delegation returned to the Soviet Union, Khrushchev told a group of visiting United States senators that the USSR wanted to import American farm products and equipment, and in the fall of 1955 an Iowa corn dealer, Roswell Garst, sold hybrid seed corn and farm equipment to the Soviet Union and Romania.[23] Also in September, Poland and Hungary expressed an interest in purchasing wheat. The USDA calculated that if trade restrictions were elimi-

nated, the United States could sell the bloc more than two
and a third million tons of dairy and meat products, vegetable oils, grains, cotton, and tobacco. State and Agriculture
jointly recommended to the president that East-West trade
increase, and the ICASD and the Council on Foreign Economic Policy advocated lifting the ban on trade in government-owned surpluses.[24]

By now the administration was determined to liberalize
trade with the bloc. The question was how. The USDA argued that since dollar sales were already discretionary with
the president, the only serious impediment was the prohibition on barter, and that could be solved by a congressional
amendment. But the CFEP decided that the administration
should seek a congressional amendment both permitting
barter and giving the president standby authority to authorize all Soviet trade transactions. And no matter what happened, CFEP said, all Soviet sales should be for dollars.[25]

Consequently, the president's 1956 message on agriculture recommended the sale of CCC stocks to European satellite nations for dollars and the authorization to barter CCC
stocks behind the iron curtain. Republican congressional
leaders warned the White House that the administration
would "have a tough time putting this over," and they were
right. Sentiment against liberalizing East-West trade was
strong, and on July 18 the House, led by Congressman
Walter Judd, eliminated a committee-approved provision
for barter with the Soviet satellites. The only crumb for the
administration was the conference report's statement that
the prohibition on Soviet bloc trade did "not apply to any
transactions beyond the scope of the act and should not be
construed to apply to dollar sales." Congress would not
authorize Soviet bloc trade, perhaps because members opposed such trade in principle, but also perhaps because they
realized that the administration already had authority in
this area that it was reluctant to use. The administration
wanted Congress to assume the burden of approval, and
Congress refused to do so.[26]

Thrown back on its own executive powers, the White
House now asked for another attorney general's opinion on
dollar sales of government-held surpluses to the bloc at

world prices, citing the language of the PL 480 conference report. Justice, in response, reiterated that the president already had the discretionary authority for such sales.[27] But with the 1956 presidential election just weeks away, and with anti-Soviet attitudes evident among voters, the administration delayed.

In one area the administration did move to liberalize trade. During 1956 Poland had settled its lend-lease claims and thereafter sought to purchase United States cotton. In the wake of the Polish riots and in view of a CCC report describing a "widely held opinion" among West Europeans that the United States was "weakening rather than strengthening its position with the people of satellite countries by refusing to trade with them," the administration decided "that it was appropriate to consider that the present [Gomulka] government of Poland" as "not so completely dominated by the Government of the Soviet Union, or by what is called in the legislation 'international communism' as wholly to preclude the possibility of U.S.-Polish trade." On January 5, 1957, the Department of Commerce announced that it would give "favorable consideration" to applications for export of CCC-owned or subsidized commodities to Poland for dollars at world market prices, and over strong Canadian objections the United States sold Poland wheat, cotton, soybeans, fats, and oils.[28] The Export-Import Bank extended $30 million in credit; Poland agreed to purchase $18,900,000 of cotton and fats and oils for Polish currency, which, if the United States had not used it in five years, would be repurchased by Poland for dollars; and a supplemental title I agreement carried a Polish commitment to purchase $46,100,000 worth of wheat and corn. In the wake of the agreement, the Department of Commerce put exports of surplus agricultural commodities to Poland under general license authority, which eliminated the need for individual export licenses. At the USDA, Don Paarlberg applauded the action as "support to a people who have given evidence of a sincere effort to free themselves of Soviet domination," although he warned against "using U.S. Government financing to make food available to countries whose external policies are dictated by the Kremlin."[29]

Although the United States softened its Polish hard line, the second term brought no suggestion of trade relaxation with nations elsewhere in the bloc. Administration officials believed that a Soviet trade offensive had been gathering force since 1955, with special emphasis on trade with countries of the Near East and South Asia, and that, coupled with the uprisings in Poland and Hungary, strained relations between the United States and the USSR. The launch of Sputnik in October 1957 profoundly disturbed American assumptions of scientific and technological superiority, and the uneasiness was reinforced the next month when Khrushchev declared "war upon you . . . in the peaceful field of trade." When Bulganin proposed "normal" trade relations and "peaceful cooperation" in two letters to Eisenhower on December 10, 1957, and January 8, 1958, the administration was suspicious. The State Department and the National Security Council contended that, in view of the expanding Sino-Soviet trade offensive, all Soviet trade was "overwhelmingly political." Eisenhower finally told Bulganin that the United States welcomed "trade that carries no political or warlike implications." Privately, the administration thought no Soviet trade met that criterion.[30]

Undeterred, the Soviets pressed their suit again on June 2, 1958. This time Eisenhower disingenuously replied that Soviet trade organizations were "free right now . . . to develop a larger volume of trade with firms in this country," and that the low level of trade might simply reflect that those organizations were "not taking advantage of all available possibilities."[31]

As discussed above, the fiscal year ending June 30, 1958, was disastrous for agricultural exports, and the USDA intensified its search for overseas markets. But the administration did not seek to solve its export problem by trading with the Soviet bloc. Transshipment controls were applied more rigorously than ever before, partly because a number of firms had been discovered violating the Export Control Act and partly because the new chiefs at Commerce, Lewis Strauss and Frederick Mueller, opposed expanded United States–Soviet trade.[32]

But the Soviets continued to make trade overtures. Dur-

ing a visit to the United States in January 1959, Anastas
Mikoyan talked with Under Secretary of State C. Douglas
Dillon and urged trade expansion, but Dillon, in a chilly
public reply, suggested that if the Soviets were truly
interested in trade, they would settle Soviet debts to the
United States, permit American businesses greater access
to Soviet producers and consumers, publicly announce the
goods they would like to buy and sell, accede to the copy-
right convention, insure "genuine" protection for private
industrial property, and "demonstrate firmer adherence to
business principles, instead of turning trade off and on, as
Soviet leaders so frequently do in the interest of political
expediency." Privately, the State Department believed that
even with trade controls lifted, there would be little trade in
agricultural goods with the Soviet Union. The Soviet supply
situation was adequate without United States supplements,
it thought, and current Soviet consumption levels were
"tolerable."[33]

In July 1959 Khrushchev again expressed Soviet interest
in trade with the United States, this time during an interview with seven United States governors who were visiting
the Soviet Union. "People who want to live in peace,"
Khrushchev said, "trade. When they prepare for war, or
after the beginning of war, there's no trade. Therefore, we
have the right to think, since we've not fought and stopped
trade, you have ulterior motives." In September he visited
the United States, discussed trade relations with Eisenhower at Camp David, agreed to resume negotiations on a
lend-lease settlement, and toured agricultural institutions.
Likewise, Ezra Taft Benson visited agricultural regions in
the Soviet Union that fall, but neither trip led to any expansion of trade. If there was to be any new trade with communist nations, the United States had concluded, it should be
trade that might weaken Russian control over Eastern Europe. Therefore, in March 1959 the United States resumed
diplomatic relations with Bulgaria; in November of that
year it began talks with Romania aimed at settling American claims against that nation; and in December 1960 Poland was accorded most-favored-nation status.[34]

The United States' attitude toward communist China was,

if anything, even more frigid than that toward the Soviet Union. When widespread flooding was reported on the Chinese mainland in 1959, the "appropriate agencies" decided that China might have deliberately inflated the extent of the damage "for internal reasons," that she probably would not accept relief offers, and that "the mere offer of aid . . . might have a deleterious effect upon our foreign policy." Making food available, either directly or indirectly, was held not to be in the nation's "best interests." Seemingly, there was to be not only a suspension of trade but a suspension of humanitarianism as well.[35]

Trade restrictions also became an anticommunist weapon against Fidel Castro's Cuba. And here such a policy came into direct conflict with what Assistant Secretary of State William Macomber, Jr., called the two fixed principles of inter-American relations: "nonintervention" and a "continuity" that implied no "judgment upon the domestic policy" of any government.[36]

At issue was the Cuban sugar import quota of slightly over three million tons annually at preferential prices. The legislation authorizing this quota was scheduled to expire in 1960, and despite strong support for extension from "Sugar Czar" Harold Cooley, the chairman of the House Agriculture Committee, the administration decided that "Cuban developments" made it inadvisable to consider extension in the 1959 congressional session. The administration claimed to be worried that agrarian reform in Cuba might lead to a major shortage of sugar in the United States, but that was clearly a cover story, for, when Castro offered to negotiate a 1961 commitment of eight million tons of sugar at four cents a pound, Benson tartly replied that the United States would not need that much sugar from Cuba. Incredibly, in view of this abundance, the State Department then officially warned Cuba not to go so far with agrarian reform as to "impair or reduce" productivity.[37]

Throughout the remainder of 1959 and the first half of 1960, relations with Cuba steadily deteriorated. One incident followed another, and finally, on May 14, 1960, Eisenhower invoked the Mutual Security Act and officially terminated technical assistance to Cuba, including all agricultural technical aid. Meanwhile Congress considered extension of the sugar legislation, but, unable to reach agreement, finally settled for a law that merely extended it through the first quarter of 1961, thereby throwing the problem into the lap of the next Congress. Under the temporary extension, the president was to determine what Cuban quota would be in "the national interest." The intention, so Cuba's minister of commerce, Cepero Bonilla, told the press, was not to protect the interest of consumers but to impose economic sanctions on Cuba, an action that was in violation of the OAS charter. "The eagle," he declared, "is showing its claws."[38]

Bonilla's deductions were correct. On July 4 and 5 officials from the departments of State and Agriculture met almost continuously on the Cuban sugar issue, and on July 6 Douglas Dillon, Thomas Mann, and Richard Rubottom of State, True Morse of Agriculture, Treasury Secretary Robert Anderson, and White House staff members Wilton Persons, David Kendall, John Eisenhower, James Hagerty, and Don Paarlberg met with Eisenhower in the oval office. There the president learned that Cuba had just canceled sailing permission for a cargo of nickel from a United States–owned plant and that the Cubans had made an arms deal with Czechoslovakia. Enraged, Eisenhower exploded, "What is this madman's final act?" The group speculated that it might be a Cuban treaty with the Soviet Union.

Turning to the sugar question, Anderson and Dillon urged strong action against Cuba so that the United States would not be "merely provocative." There was some fear, Dillon noted, that economic sanctions might endanger the lives of American citizens in Cuba. But this, it was quickly decided, did not justify stalling. As Anderson put it, "We can't hand everything over to the Cubans!" And, as Mann argued, "We shall have to show that irresponsibility doesn't pay." Eisenhower then asked what the next step might be, and Dillon strongly recommended a boycott. A few months of that, he thought, would severely hurt the Cuban economy. Secretary of the Treasury Anderson backed the idea, provided the United States did not act alone. The Canadians, British, Dutch, French, and West Germans, he felt, should be induced to go along, and, when Eisenhower asked how to keep the Latin American countries "in line," Dillon said he thought this could be done by providing an attractive price for Latin American sugar, cooperating with the OAS, and increasing economic assistance to Latin American nations.

The remaining question was what to do if trouble developed, as the ambassador in Havana feared it might. The navy, Dillon suggested, could "get the people out," and, as the president saw it, steps must be taken to ensure "that the Soviet Union doesn't get a base in Cuba." This was unlikely, Rubottom replied, if intelligence reports were to be believed, and in his view the action would constitute "the kind of aggressive leadership that the Latin American people might now respond to." Mann and Paarlberg then redrafted a presidential proclamation cutting the Cuban quota by 700,000 tons, and Eisenhower signed the Sugar Act and issued the proclamation that afternoon.[39]

Now the problem was how to allocate the 700,000 tons to other sugar-producing nations, and it led to another conflict between the State Department and Congress. In the extension of the Sugar Act that Eisenhower had signed, Harold Cooley had succeeded in inserting a provision requiring that a portion of any reallocation go to the Dominican Republic. The State Department, however, disenchanted with the activities of Rafael Trujillo, informed Benson that "foreign policy reasons" made purchase of Dominican sugar inadvisable. The administration then urged a further extension of the act, one that would repeal the Dominican purchase provision and provide for long-range planning. But Congress was unsympathetic and adjourned without action.[40]

Meanwhile the domestic sugar market fluctuated wildly as nations scrambled for pieces of the Cuban share. Purchase authorizations on July 21 and August 2 temporarily decided the matter, but under these conditions supplies remained uncertain. In early September the USDA found only a few sugar cargoes available for October-November import (excluding, of course, cargoes from Cuba and the Dominican

Republic), and some of these suppliers were as much as six sailing weeks away from New York. Something had to be done. Reluctantly, the State Department agreed to the purchase of Dominican sugar provided it paid an entry fee of two cents a pound (nearly a third of the purchase price). Cuban sugar was still out. On December 16, Eisenhower set the Cuban sugar import quota at zero, and both at that time and again on January 17, 1961, he renewed his request for removal of the Dominican purchase requirement.[41]

By this time, too, the United States had imposed export as well as import controls on Cuba. In July 1960 the USDA had provided the White House with an analysis pointing out that Cuba imported about 40 percent of its total food intake, that 90 percent of this came from the United States, and that with the decline of tourism, sugar sales, and available dollars, food supplies per capita were likely to decline. On October 19 the Commerce Department established controls over all exports to Cuba except unsubsidized foodstuffs, medicines, and some other medical supplies. The action, so the Department of Commerce declared, was taken "in order to carry out the responsibility of this Government to defend the legitimate economic interests of the people of this country against the discriminatory, aggressive and injurious economic policies of the Castro regime." In the Department of Agriculture, however, one eye was still on sales. The department told inquirers that as long as they were shipping unsubsidized commodities and were getting paid in dollars, there was "no reason not to export."[42]

It was, then, an intact embargo that the Eisenhower Republicans turned over to the incoming Kennedy administration. During the 1950s there had been repeated trade overtures from the nations of the European Soviet bloc, but for the most part the United States had not responded favorably. The trade issue was far more than a matter of economic self-interest, for it raised questions of philosophy, foreign policy, national defense, strategic psychology, and domestic political strategy. The members of the Eisenhower cabinet favored exploring trade opportunities with the European communist countries, but Benson probably reflected their mixed emotions toward bloc trade when he said, "I believe that communism is the greatest evil in the world, and I knew that the record of payments with Russia wasn't good. They wanted to buy, and we had the stocks, but I wanted to make sure that we would get cash on the barrelhead."[43]

Throughout the first term, the administration searched gingerly for ways to relax the embargo, but congressional and public reaction was so hostile that the administration decided not to press the issue. Then, during the second term, the space race and the trade and aid race chilled the international climate; the adverse balance of payments, the domestic recession, and the advent of Sputnik undermined the public's sense of strength and security that would have been essential to a relaxation of the embargo; and the administration's interest in liberalized trade with the Soviet bloc waned. This diminished interest coincided with the Castro take-over in Cuba, and the United States cut off trade with that nation. With the exception of trade with Poland, the philosophy of economic sanctions against the enemy dominated the United States' trade policy toward communist nations.

Conclusion
The Balance Wheel Elusive

The Eisenhower administration was caught in an agricultural dilemma. It hoped to restore rural prosperity by reducing government controls over production and marketing while simultaneously increasing agricultural exports. Both Eisenhower and Benson believed that trade expansion could dispose of accumulated surpluses, absorb the increasing flow of new production, and provide the key to restoring a healthy rural economy wherein farmers had the "freedom to farm." But the decade of the 1950s was a difficult time to test this belief. Advancing agricultural technology and reviving postwar agricultural production abroad meant that domestic stocks of agricultural products continued to climb throughout the decade. And, as the surpluses mounted, the administration faced demands from Congress and from farmers that they use more import controls, more export stimulants, and support agricultural prices through government action. It was a problem of ideology, of economics, and of politics.

Eisenhower was committed to a policy of expanding trade, and his officials carefully considered what role the government should play in encouraging the expansion.

Like the Republicans who directed the Commerce Department in the 1920s, these modern Republicans decided that the best method of expanding trade was through a partnership in which the federal government would aid private exploitation of trade opportunities. "Both the President and I," Benson reported, "believed there was opportunity to build up exports. We had PL 480 to help dispose of our surpluses for foreign currency by barter and donation. But what we wanted most of all was to sell our farm products for dollars." The job, as he saw it, was "to try to open closed doors, and open wider those that were partly closed, for United States traders and trade organizations." And to do this, he argued, "private trade and government had to work together" because there were some phases of the problem "that could only be handled under close cooperation."[1]

Although these views were shared by most Eisenhower officials, this did not produce a harmonious or consistent administration position on agricultural trade. The struggle to shape a trade policy was marked by interagency conflict and organizational politics, often featuring a struggle between the needs of domestic agriculture, the exigencies of midcentury foreign policy, and the commitment to fiscal conservatism. The difficulty in resolving these disparate viewpoints on agricultural trade issues often reflected the ideological inconsistencies of the particular individuals involved. Eisenhower conservatives tended not only to be trade expansionists, but to be anticommunists, antistatists, protectionists, and humanitarians as well. Ezra Taft Benson, for example, was a committed humanitarian; yet as a trade expansionist he insisted that nations with hungry people purchase normal import quantities of food before receiving PL 480 title I shipments. Likewise, John Foster Dulles, while retaining a deep commitment to free trade, also supported a Soviet trade boycott. The incongruities are striking; yet, because they dealt with issues piecemeal, these policy-makers may have been only marginally aware of the contradictions in their beliefs.

Just as individuals were ideologically or programatically inconsistent, so too were agencies. At any given time an agency's position on an issue might represent a personal belief of one of its officials, a response to a demand from a powerful constituency, a reflection of political realities, a considered judgment of the department's professionals, or a strategic maneuver to protect bureaucratic territory. And, given these possibilities, it is not surprising that agency viewpoints often clashed, especially over a program like agricultural trade, which touched sensitive policy issues in many different agencies.

Yet out of these clashes a trade policy took shape. It emphasized private marketing initiatives, with the government supplying basic marketing information. It supported basic research, and it committed the government to efforts to remove or ease foreign import restrictions. And the administration put it into practice.

However, despite all its efforts, the United States was unable to move agricultural products abroad swiftly enough to suit the Eisenhower officials, Congress, or the representatives of organized agriculture. Surpluses remained, and the accumulated stocks were unsettling to markets, expensive to store (as much as a billion dollars for the 1961 fiscal year—more than $2.5 million every day) and embarrassing in a world of hungry people. Consequently, even as it preached private action, the administration also resorted to surplus disposal through two programs inconsistent with its rhetoric: export subsidies and government aid.

The first of these, export subsidies, took many forms. There were, of course, the classic cash payment programs, but there were also payment-in-kind programs, competitive bid sales, mutual security programs, and, above all, the complex program of sales for foreign currency authorized by PL 480. Unfortunately, such measures tended to work at cross-purposes with some of the principles of United States foreign policy. The purpose of a subsidy, after all, was to sell a product abroad at a competitive price below the United States domestic price, a practice usually called dumping and officially frowned upon by the United States.[2] And, in practice, when the United States sold cotton or rice or dairy products at concessional prices, the world price normally went down, and the lower prices both injured competing suppliers, many of whom were the United States' best friends in the community of nations, and discouraged the development of local sources of these agricultural products.

The State Department repeatedly complained about this disruption of the market, and even the Department of Agriculture worried that severe market distortions, such as those in rice, might "drive those rice-exporting nations into the soft Communist underbelly of Asia."[3] Yet pressured to move the surplus, the Department of Agriculture continued to support and utilize an array of export subsidies as important surplus disposal tools. Agriculture officials rationalized by arguing that "normal" trade was not affected by the subsidized shipments since the United States was merely using the subsidy to recapture its "historical fair share" of the commodity trade.

The government aid programs were equally wracked by conflict. Whether the donation was direct (to a foreign government, a welfare organization, or an individual) or indirect via the acceptance of soft currencies, long-term loans, or other financial concessions, it had the same potential for market disruption as did the export subsidy programs. Furthermore, commodities like nonfat dried milk, flour, corn meal, or bulgur, which were important to the donation program and embodied commercial processing, affected not only the foreign producer but also the foreign processor and manufacturer.[4] These were problems that administration officials tried to handle by requiring recipients to continue the normal levels of commercial imports. However, competing suppliers were far from satisfied that this was being done, and to the extent that it was it limited the effect of food aid by requiring the recipient country to tie up the same amount of capital in food imports, thereby preventing some capital release to promote economic development.

The administration's effort to promote trade expansion through export subsidies and government aid programs is a good example of the government's role as a power broker among agricultural producers and distributors, and also consumers. Under PL 480, for example, the administration could exercise discretion in the choice of commodities to be provided, countries to which they would be delivered, and terms of delivery. In each of these areas the administration favored the vocal, the strong, and the capitalist.

The choice of commodities, for example, determined what producer groups would benefit from the programs. Although by law the administration was locked into a domestic allotment system that meant big subsidies for large commercial farmers, it was not committed to any definite pattern of export subsidies and aids. Yet, as the assistant secretary of agriculture, Marvin McLain, pointed out, "entirely too much of the 480 funds" were "used for the basic commodities" that had "sucked the teat" the most, and far too little of them were "used to take care of emergency situations with our perishable commodities and particularly meats."[5] Cotton, wheat, and dairy producers were well organized to pressure the department and were represented in Congress by key men on the agricultural committees, and their products were repeatedly the subjects of government promotion efforts. Other producer groups were treated much less generously. The administration was anything but even-handed, and this contributed to a lack of movement by producers from commodities in extreme surplus to those in more demand.[6]

Similarly, the administration must bear the responsibility for the unequal distribution of export subsidies to exporters. For example, Anderson, Clayton and Company exported nearly $60 million in cotton under PL 480 title I, $25 million more than the next largest exporter; title I grain exports flowed heavily through three major firms, Continental Grain Company ($358 million), Louis Dreyfus Corporation ($305 million), and Cargill, Incorporated ($264 million). According to Ezra Taft Benson, the department and its advisory committee were aware of the disparities, but they were unable to find a solution. However, the administration apparently made no effort to broaden the exporter base or to require that a percentage of all exports be handled by small firms. The lack of debate over these obvious alternatives suggests that the administration was not seriously concerned about the malapportioned commercial trade.[7]

In its choice of recipient nations, too, the administration deserves criticism, especially for its failure to examine critically the nature of a "friendly" country. With its polar view of the world, it assumed that any noncommunist country was friendly, whether it was a Spanish dictatorship, a repressive French colonial government, or a degenerate hereditary monarch. Consequently, aid flowed to nations to whose governments democracy was repugnant; yet it was by precisely that criterion that PL 480 was denied to communist bloc nations. To be sure, early in the administration some disaster aid was provided for Eastern Europe, and later Yugoslavia and Poland were included in PL 480 programs. But reports of disaster-level need in Communist China were met with firm opposition to providing aid. And when communist forces in a nation seemed to be gaining the upper hand, aid was withdrawn or withheld until the situation righted itself, as in Egypt and Indonesia, or until the unhappy situation and therefore the withdrawal became permanent, as in Cuba.[8] Only at the end of the administration did the United States withdraw assistance from a "free world" dictator (Trujillo of the Dominican Republic), and in that case the reason for the withdrawal was the fear that his rule was so repressive that it would be uprooted by a communist rebellion. Even there, opposition to communism, not adherence to democracy, was the key to the choice of which nations would receive assistance.

The terms of trade that the United States demanded also reflected the continuing conflicts between commercial trade and humanitarianism. American ideology traditionally has placed a high value on humanitarian activities, and the idea of America the beneficent had been raised to a glittering pinnacle during the outpouring of Marshall Plan aid to postwar Europe. Yet during the 1950s, when food aid seemed to impinge on United States commercial sales, humanitarianism invariably lost. Additionality was required; no PL 480 sales proceeds could be used to increase foreign production of a crop that would compete for markets with a United States crop; and no continuing commitments would be made to relief agencies as long as there was a chance that commercial markets would materialize. Nor would the United States consider providing commodities for a multinational relief program under United Nations auspices. Sherman

Adams was interested in the possibility, but John Foster Dulles opposed it, arguing that Congress would not approve of "an anonymous giveaway" of American products and that "the loss of American control over the distribution might raise the question of whether we were giving food to enemy countries."[9] Furthermore, the American opposition to proposals for a world food bank was not an enlightened attitude. The argument was that such stocks would make the world market perpetually unstable, and there was no disposition to see that they might also become tools for dealing with long-term shortages and achieving a larger political stability.

Nor could the humanitarian voices within the administration combat the Agriculture Department's resistance to development assistance for agriculture abroad. Reflecting producers' fears of increased competition, Earl Butz told Clarence Randall that Agriculture would not agree to additional overseas production of those commodities already in surplus "if such increased production were destined for foreign markets," and in the selection of technical assistance projects he felt that "due consideration should be given to the probable future world supply situation of the commodity to be produced and the interest of American agriculture and the U.S. economy generally."[10] This view prevailed, and it helped prevent useful diversification of crops in some nations and the accumulation of foreign exchange earnings that might have enabled nations to purchase more commodities from the United States. By stifling this form of self-sufficiency, the United States helped to create diseconomies and to perpetuate unbalanced agricultural production. A different set of choices might have helped feed the world and stabilize unstable economies.[11]

As the programs operated, then, they tended to generate charges of unfair distribution of benefits, callous disregard for human needs, and injury to the economies of recipient countries and competing suppliers. They also tended to stimulate new protectionist demands at home. Because of these export programs, foreign manufacturers could produce goods from United States materials more cheaply than United States producers could; and, since domestic price levels were held above world market prices, the United States became an extremely attractive market for the foreign exporter. In these circumstances section 22 became a major instrument of protection, and though in 1955 the United States succeeded in obtaining a GATT waiver that allowed section 22 quotas to continue, this could hardly be construed as approval by the GATT partners. Rather, they allowed themselves to be bullied by the United States into accepting the arrangement, probably because each of the partners wished to keep its own protectionist structure intact.

Later, to be sure, the dependence on section 22 lessened, and the last two years of the administration saw fewer impositions of import quotas (see table 3). But, in addition to the section 22 quotas, another weapon was used: the gentlemen's agreement, such as the one with Japan over cotton textiles. This form of international control was not new, but it was in direct contradiction to the stated United States goal of a free world trade ordered by open agreements rather than by sotto voce duets.

The administration's debates over the nature and acceptable limits of protectionism reflected both the demands of producers and processors for assistance and the heat of domestic partisan politics. Sometimes processor demands for protection were a direct result of export subsidies on raw materials; at other times, producers and processors allied to block the entry of foreign manufactures that might drive down prices for both raw and finished domestic products; at still other times, processors and producers joined fervent anticommunists to demand the exclusion of Soviet-bloc products. In addition, vocal though sporadic support for protection came from Republican party officials who thought votes could be influenced in election years by judicious use of protectionist devices. Such varied demands pressured the Department of Agriculture to adopt a protectionist stance that conflicted with its desires for a freer worldwide trading system and its recognition of the necessity for foreign nations to earn dollars in order to promote additional United States exports. The State Department usually opposed the imposition of new section 22 controls, and the result was a varied application of protectionist devices during the Eisenhower years.

The strength of protectionist notions also pointed up the United States' hostility toward international commodity agreements and international regulatory organizations. The administration must be faulted for not giving greater support to such institutions, support that might have made them strong regulatory and development forces capable of bridging the demands of national independence and international cooperation. GATT, for example, was abused by American policy-makers, and when the United States needed it in the late 1950s to deal with a world of nascent trading blocs it was too weak to be effective. The Food and Agriculture Organization received only halfhearted American support; yet, as Clarence Francis finally realized, it might have served as a vehicle for technical assistance in underdeveloped areas. In addition, the United States scuttled proposals for joint producer-consumer commodity agreements, arguing that they stabilized nothing but overproduction, and it opposed the type of commodity agreements that could have aided the exporters of coffee and other tropical products and perhaps stabilized these volatile markets. Yet it could devise no substitute for dealing with the international problems involved. The protectionist arm was very long indeed.[12]

The contradictions characteristic of the debates over export subsidies, humanitarianism, and the protection of the domestic market were acute in the continuing controversy over trade with the Soviet bloc. Here the influence of personal philosophy was particularly powerful, and in many cases an emotional anticommunism struggled with a pragmatic desire for trade expansion.

The idea that trade might make the communists more cooperative and less dangerous was held by a few. Occasionally administration officials would toy with the idea that sales or donation to communist countries might do more to weaken or influence than to strengthen them. But even among those who were interested in developing East-West trade, there was a feeling that congressional and public opinion would not allow it. Clarence Randall, for example, believed that trade opportunities in agricultural products did exist, but that there was a "psychological barrier existing in the minds of businessmen that to engage in such trade is unpatriotic."[13] Then, too, most citizens were unwilling to place much faith in the power of commerce to influence politics. On the contrary, they argued that communists would not trade according to established trading principles, that you could not trade with state traders, that communists would not be open and "fair." The theory of influence through trade could not prevail in the face of such beliefs.

There were also arguments that the Soviet bloc was uninterested in American trade. Yet in view of the postwar trade that had developed before the imposition of the Export Control Act, it seems that the potential was there, and in view of initiatives from the other side it is difficult to argue that the communists were solely responsible for the potential's not being realized. The Soviet Union made several offers to purchase fats and oils from the United States, offers that were brusquely rejected but that might have led to a standing supply relationship. Throughout the period, the continued purchase of agricultural commodities from Western European and Third World countries indicated that the Soviet bloc was interested in supplementing its insufficient agricultural production by importing certain commodities. When trade controls with Poland were lifted, moreover, United States–Polish trade did improve remarkably, an indication of what might have happened had controls been lifted elsewhere.

For the most part, then, anticommunism acted as a restraining influence on trade expansion. As a result, the United States trade in agricultural products with the USSR was negligible, that with Communist China nonexistent, and that with Cuba, a traditional trading partner, suspended after Fidel Castro came to power. The only countervailing trend was in the expanded trade with Poland and some of the other Eastern European nations. Here the desire to wean such countries from the Soviet Union, the protrade pressure from Eastern European ethnic groups in the United States, and the growing recognition that the national communism of these countries was durable combined to produce a departure from the prevailing pattern.

Ultimately, the constant wear of such ideological and organizational conflicts over the wide-ranging fronts of agricultural trade policy discouraged senior officials at the Department of Agriculture. In a poignant letter written toward the end of the administration, Assistant Secretary Marvin McLain lamented, "We recognize that the farm program has not worked as it should. Experience indicates that it not only has failed to adjust production to consumption, but that its costs have been exorbitant." Likewise, looking back on the two terms, another USDA official reflected, "Great strides were made in improving the efficiency of the physical operation of C.S.S. and A.S.C. operations. This is a dubious distinction—in fact we tried to improve the socialistic system and make it work, and at less cost to the taxpayer." Don Paarlberg complained that, in spite of all efforts, the stocks of surplus commodities increased. There was a nagging feeling that the exhausting labors of the past eight years had been in vain.[14]

The Eisenhower administration, like its predecessors, had supported farm income through production and marketing mechanisms, and it had relied heavily on increasing agricultural exports to maintain farm prices. It was therefore extremely vulnerable to changes in the levels of production, and during the administration production increased in astonishing leaps. During the 1950s, farm output per work hour nearly doubled, production per acre was up a third, and although the number of farms decreased from 5.4 to 3.7 million between 1950 and 1960, the number of acres cropped declined barely 10 percent. Whereas one farmer could feed seventeen people in 1950, he could feed twenty-five in 1960, and in the face of such increases it seems doubtful that any program short of direct payments to farmers could have maintained farm income.

Not surprisingly, Benson's program could not do so, and

as prices remained low and surpluses kept mounting it was attacked from all sides. Farmers and farm-state congressmen viewed the continuing low prices as evidence of failure. Egalitarians condemned the program for inequitable distribution of benefits, whether to farmers, agribusiness firms, or foreign consumers. Humanitarians berated trade that prevented the growth of economic self-sufficiency while failing to feed the hungry poor. Fervent anticommunists thought the program a failure because agricultural trade and aid had not prevented the spread of communism or decreased its extent. Some observers believed that the program itself accelerated technological change to the detriment of a stable agriculture by promising a market for all production; others urged that the USDA research emphasis be shifted from production to diversified utilization. Some critics charged that Benson's policies were not stringent enough; others felt they had gone too far in the direction of socialized farming.

Throughout the decade there were, of course, those who suggested alternate means to a healthy rural economy. Most of the proposed solutions were also based on manipulating production and marketing, although it was clear that such solutions disproportionately benefited larger commercial farmers, leaving small producers with marginal income at best. A favorite alternative plan relied on severe production and marketing controls to match production to consumption, thereby driving up farm prices. Yet, given the rapidity of technological change, this plan probably would not have succeeded either, for controls stringent enough to prevent the accumulation of surpluses would have been politically impossible to obtain. Another alternative seemed to be a mass exodus of farmers from the land, leaving a smaller number to share in the profits, but again this solution was pragmatically impossible, for the agrarian myth remained too potent a force to allow a transfer of resources out of agriculture on a scale sufficient to provide a minimum level of income for all who remained. A third option was to reduce production and match it to consumption by taking land out of cultivation.

That was the principle behind the administration's Soil Bank plan; yet, as that program demonstrated, less cropped land did not necessarily mean less produce marketed, at least at levels of land retirement that could win public and political support.

The political realities, then, limited any proposed solution to the United States' agricultural dilemma. Throughout the Eisenhower administration Congress acted as a constraint upon the policies the USDA could adopt. In 1953 and 1954, the Republican Congress showed some sympathy for Benson's plan for lower price supports, fewer acreage controls, and a reduced level of government activity in farming, but even it could not stomach severe cuts in farm supports. The best it could muster was a sliding scale for price supports, and Benson, exhibiting more political sense than he is usually credited with, did not insist that Congress go beyond politically tolerable reforms. He recognized that total elimination of price supports was impossible, and he did not insist on introducing such dead-letter legislation.

With the Democratic Congresses that followed, however, Benson reached an impasse, and Eisenhower was repeatedly forced to veto farm bills.[15] As Don Paarlberg recalled, Benson "continually reiterated the economic case for adjustment" while Congress adhered to "the political discipline" that made adjustment unpalatable, "so the Secretary and the Congressmen sailed majestically past one another, arguing from different postulates."[16]

But beyond the daily political conflicts, both the administration and Congress knew that the aim of agricultural policy was to enable farmers to obtain a level of income that would provide an adequate standard of living for farm families and allow them to continue producing commodities. Income could be maintained in a number of ways, they knew, but the real question was for which farmers income maintenance should be sought. If the object was to keep the farmer on the farm, to maintain a family farm agriculture, and to protect the rural community, then direct income payments would be reasonable means. But if the object was to produce commodites cheaply, copiously, and efficiently, whether for purchase by consumers or for donation here and abroad, then production and marketing programs, in which the most productive farmers benefit most and the least productive are encouraged to move out of agriculture, would be appropriate. The former course would risk a continuing drain on the treasury and the support of a certain number of unproductive farmers in return for the preservation of the familiar rural social structure. The latter course would risk increasing concentration of the means of production, with the possibility of eventual market manipulation to the detriment of the consumer, in return for immediate cheap food. But if the object was both to produce food cheaply and to maintain the rural social structure, then extremely complex income-maintenance programs seemed inevitable. With these, the problem would be one of balancing production incentives with income guarantees and of creating a managerial framework that would still encourage individual initiative.

Modern American agricultural policy has taken the latter, mixed course. The Eisenhower administration inherited such a program but hoped to modify it. Administration officials wanted to encourage individual initiative by reducing statist controls, to maintain production by finding markets for all commodities, and to promote modernization by ensuring a satisfactory return on production. They accepted as inevitable some migration off the farm, but they also encouraged small farmers to raise crops that were not in surplus in an effort to keep these farmers in agriculture. The administration relied on markets for income support and counted on export markets as a balance wheel to absorb production above domestic requirements.

But the export marketing emphasis brought forth political, economic, and social conflicts. Hampered by competing demands from various agricultural constituencies, none of whom could be fully satisfied, by the desires for protection in the domestic market that led to tighter import controls and invited foreign retaliation, and by the shifting demands of the world markets, the trade program could not operate under principles of pure economic advantage, and it was weakened by the shifts necessary to accommodate the interest groups. In addition, nonagricultural interests hoped to use export trade to support social, political, or foreign-policy goals. This complicated the adoption and implementation of particular trade initiatives and did not ultimately lead either to an effective domestic food donation program or a world food program, or to the successful use of food as a cold war weapon. And, in the end, balance was not achieved.

The existence of constraints, however, does not mean that the administration had no options or that criticisms of its performance were unwarranted. As shown above, it did have considerable latitude in trade policy direction, and there were choices and decisions to make in implementing congressional mandates. By its own lights, as well as ours, it failed. The agricultural trade policy of the Eisenhower administration, despite its goal of prosperity and balance through trade expansion and free market revival, remained one characterized by dumping, state trading, anticommunist embargoes, and shortsighted pursuit of commodity sales. And it left American agriculture more concentrated, agricultural incomes more maldistributed, agribusiness receipts more dependent upon government action, and commodity production more skewed than ever before. Once again, the long search for a balance wheel for farm income had ended in frustration.

Notes

To avoid excessively long notes, I have adopted certain abbreviated forms. All personal papers and oral history interviews cited are in the Dwight D. Eisenhower Library at Abilene, Kansas, unless otherwise noted. The General Correspondence records of the Office of the Secretary of Agriculture are filed by year; consequently, they are cited as GC plus the appropriate year. The following abbreviations are also used in the notes:

EP   Dwight D. Eisenhower Presidential Papers
RG   Record Group, National Archives and Records Service
OF   Official File

PREFACE

1. Don Paarlberg to the author, May 18, 1973.

INTRODUCTION

1. *Report of the Commission on Foreign Economic Policy, Staff Papers* (Washington, D.C.: Government Printing Office, February 1954), pp. 150–53 (hereafter *CFEP Report, Staff Papers*).
2. *Hearing before the Senate Committee on Agriculture and*

154   *Notes*

Forestry on Foreign Trade in Agricultural Products, 83d Cong.,
1st sess. (April 9, 1953), p. 6, testimony of Ezra Taft Benson.
    3. Murray R. Benedict and Elizabeth K. Bauer, *Farm
Surpluses: U.S. Burden or World Asset?* (Berkeley: University of
California Press, 1960), pp. 67, 75, 83. The marketing agreements
controlling milk, fruits, vegetables, and nuts limited amounts
reaching the market at any given time. If storage was available
to the producer, however, the product could be held and
marketing staggered, thus evading the law. Acreage controls
could also be nullified, both by more intensive cultivation and by
crop substitution, which potentially could result in a surplus in
another crop.
    4. United States Department of Agriculture, *Yearbook of
Agriculture*, 1963 (Washington, D.C.: Government Printing
Office, 1963).

CHAPTER 1

    1. When asked about Eisenhower's interest, Ezra Taft Benson
said simply, "Eisenhower didn't know very much about agriculture. He had grown up in a rural area, but he hadn't been
involved in agriculture as an adult." Oral interview with the
author, October 7, 1977 (hereafter Benson interview).
    2. Eisenhower's administrative theories are well known. See,
for example, Patrick B. Anderson, *The President's Men* (Garden
City, N.Y.: Doubleday, 1968), pp. 133–93; Robert Keith Gray,
Eighteen Acres under Glass (Garden City, N.Y.: Doubleday,
1962), pp. 256–64; Paul Y. Hammond, "The National Security
Council as a Device for Interdepartmental Coordination: An
Interpretation and Appraisal," *American Political Science Review*
54 (December 1960): 899–910.
    3. Ezra Taft Benson, *Cross Fire: The Eight Years with
Eisenhower* (Garden City, N.Y.: Doubleday, 1962), pp. 266, 255,
600.
    4. Benson may never have understood the extent of rural
poverty, and he seems to have seen the impoverished not as poor
but as lazy. Asked about his opposition to a food stamp program,
he replied, "The greatest helping hand we have is at the end of
our own sleeve" (Benson interview).
    5. Michael A. Guhin, *John Foster Dulles: A Statesman and
His Times* (New York: Columbia University Press, 1972), p. 185;
Hammond, "National Security Council," p. 908; *The Basic Papers*

of George Humphrey, 1953–57, ed. Nathaniel Howard (Cleveland: Western Reserve Historical Society, 1965), pp. 181, 476.

6. Sherman Adams, *Firsthand Report: The Story of the Eisenhower Administration* (New York: Harper and Brothers, 1961), p. 389.

7. Earl Butz, Don Paarlberg, and J. W. Hicks to Benson, December 20, 1952, "International Wheat Agreement—1953," Farm Program, reel 13, Ezra Taft Benson papers, microfilm copy, Dwight D. Eisenhower Library (hereafter Benson film); Paarlberg to Karl D. Butler, December 31, 1952, "Wheat," GC 1953, RG 16; Don Paarlberg, oral history interview, January 17, 1968, p. 5.

8. Don Paarlberg, *American Farm Policy: A Case Study in Centralized Decision-making* (New York: John Wiley, 1964), pp. 351, 159, 216.

9. Clarence Francis, oral history interview, May 18, 1967, pp. 9, 21, 25.

10. Clarence B. Randall, *A Creed for Free Enterprise* (Boston: Little, Brown, 1952), pp. 146–59. Gabriel Hauge, an economist on the White House staff, declared that the chapter "The Businessman and Foreign Policy" more closely approximated Eisenhower's own ideas than anything else he had ever read. Dulles originally opposed the appointment because he thought Randall was a protectionist and "reactionary," but in the end he acquiesced. Clarence B. Randall, *Sixty-five Plus* (Boston: Little, Brown, 1963), pp. 48–56.

11. Clarence B. Randall, *A Foreign Economic Policy for the United States* (Chicago: University of Chicago Press, 1954), pp. 7–8.

12. Richard F. Fenno, Jr., *The Power of the Purse: Appropriations Politics in Congress* (Boston: Little, Brown, 1966), pp. 361–66, 377–81, 457–60.

13. "Agriculture is the field where the distinction between public and private has been almost completely eliminated, not by public expropriation of private domain but by private expropriation of public domain." Grant McConnell, *Private Power and American Democracy* (New York: Knopf, 1966), p. 245. State lacked this forceful external support. Fenno, *Power of the Purse*, p. 459.

14. Stanley Andrews, *The Farmers' Dilemma* (Washington, D.C.: Public Affairs Press, 1961), p. 84.

15. Quotations from Lester W. Milbrath, "Interest Groups and Foreign Policy," in *Domestic Sources of Foreign Policy*, ed. James N. Rosenau (New York: Free Press, 1967), p. 244.

16. The president of the Nebraska Union, which was severely at cross-purposes with the national organization, was chosen as a member of the National Agricultural Advisory Commission. Charles M. Hardin, "The Republican Department of Agriculture—A Political Interpretation," *Journal of Farm Economics* 36 (May 1954): 212.

17. The NFU supported 100 percent parity with government authority to limit acreage and marketing, creation of a "democratic world economic union," foreign sale of exports at or below world price with the difference made up by the United States treasury through parity payments to producers, and a voice in agricultural policy-making for consumers ("we feel that non-farmers as well as farm people have a right and responsibility to help decide these issues"). *Hearings, Foreign Trade in Agricultural Products*, 83d Cong., 1st sess. (April 21, 1953), pp. 214–15, testimony by John A. Baker, assistant to the president, NFU.

18. The Grange supported a "world trade certificate" that worked much like the old export debenture plan the Grange had proposed in the twenties. The certificate was to fill the gap between domestic prices and world prices while United States tariffs, especially those on industrial products, were lowered, allowing trading partners to earn dollars. *Hearings, Foreign Trade in Agricultural Products*, 83d Cong., 1st sess. (April 16, 1953), pp. 136–47, testimony by Herschel Newsom.

19. Ibid. (April 17, 1953), pp. 175–77, testimony by Homer L. Brinkley.

20. Hardin, "Republican Department of Agriculture," pp. 210–13. Two notable exceptions are labor protests over proposals for lowering tariffs on Soviet bloc products (they felt it was unfair competition from "slave labor") and on the Saint Lawrence Seaway (they felt some United States port workers would lose jobs).

21. State and Agriculture did not always inform each other of foreign contacts. For instance, representatives of Holland, Sweden, Denmark, New Zealand, Australia, and Canada met with Agriculture officials on dairy matters for two days in March 1955. At the request of the foreign representatives, the State Department was not invited to attend the meeting, and the USDA did not even notify State that negotiations were planned. Only after the conference was over did the USDA "fix up some sort of a

statement" to tell the State Department that the meeting had taken place. W. G. Lodwick to Earl L. Butz, March 31, 1955, "Dairy Products 5," GC 1955, RG 16.

CHAPTER 2

1. "International Wheat Agreement—1953," Farm Program, reel 13, Benson film; "Wheat," GC 1953, RG 16.
2. Joint United States–Canada communique, March 17, 1954, OF 149–B "1954 (1)," EP.
3. J. A. McConnell told Benson, "It is fair to say that in the case of prices under the Agreement, the level this year was established largely by policy decisions of the three major exporting countries rather than world market forces alone. There has been mutual hesitancy to bring prices to the IWA minimum although the administration in each country had the authority and the power to do so." June 1, 1954, "Wheat," Clarence Francis files.
4. Memorandum of conversation, Department of State, fifth meeting of Interdepartmental Group Studying Problems of Agricultural Surpluses, January 14, 1954, "Legislation (4)," Francis files.
5. Evans to Waugh, December 9, 1953, "Legislation (4)," Francis files.
6. Benson to George Humphrey, March 12, 1953, "Cotton 5," GC 1953, RG 16; *Department of State Bulletin* 28, #724 (May 11, 1953): 681; 29, #751 (November 16, 1953): 676; 30, #759 (January 11, 1954): 57; John H. Davis to Glen B. Edgerton, July 2, 1954, "Cotton," GC 1954, RG 16; Clayton Whipple to John H. Davis, March 25, 1954, "Cotton 5," GC 1954, RG 16.
7. Amendment, C.C.C. Charter Act, sec. 2 (h), 63 *Stat.* 155 (1949). Subsequently, barter was also authorized by section 550 of the Mutual Security Act of 1953.
8. Benson to Eisenhower, December 11, 1953, "Carbon copies of memoranda and letters to the President, 1953–56," Gabriel Hauge records; "Commodities 5," "Wheat," "Wheat 5," and "Grain 5," GC 1954, RG 16; "Staff Meeting Minutes—Jan. 1953–March 1954," March 15, 1954, reel 18, Benson film; memorandum of conversation, Department of State and Canada, February 16, 1954, OF 110–74–5, "Wheat (1)," EP; Samuel W. Anderson to NAC, February 25, 1954, and to Sherman Adams, March 1, 1954, "Legislation (1)," Clarence Francis meeting notes,

March 10, 1954, "Policies and Organization," Clayton Whipple to John H. Davis, May 6, 1954, and Thorsten Kalijarvi to Clarence Francis, June 4, 1954, both in "Wheat," all in Francis files.

9. Agricultural Adjustment Act of 1935, sec. 32, 49 *Stat.* 774 (1935).

10. John M. Leddy, "United States Commercial Policy and the Domestic Farm Program," in *Studies in United States Commercial Policy*, ed. William B. Kelly, Jr. (Chapel Hill: University of North Carolina Press, 1963), pp. 179–83, 185–91; hearing, *Foreign Trade in Agricultural Products*, Benson testimony, p. 8; *CFEP Report, Staff Papers*, pp. 169–70.

11. The USDA's Temporary Wheat Advisory Committee endorsed a two-price plan; H. W. Clutter to Benson, August 14, 1953, "Wheat 5"; Study NC–1, draft, "Multiple Price Plans for Wheat and Cotton," August 21, 1953, "Committees 5," both in GC 1953, RG 16.

12. John Foster Dulles to Benson, August 28, 1953, and Dulles to Gabriel Hauge, August 28, 1953, both in OF 106, "Agriculture—Farming," EP.

13. Report to the secretary of state by the chairman of the United States delegation to the eighth session of the GATT, September 17–October 24, 1953, *First Annual Report on the Operation of the Trade Agreement Program*, appendix A, 85th Cong., 1st sess., H. Doc. 93, February 11, 1957.

14. "Dairy Products 5," GC 1954, RG 16; John H. Davis to Clarence Francis, March 23, 1954, "General Dairy Information"; Francis to L. N. Hoopes, April 28, 1954, "Chronological—March thru July 1954"; Clarence Francis to Gabriel Hauge and reply, April 27 and 28, 1954; and Hauge to Sherman Adams, April 27, 1954, "Butter," all in Francis files.

15. Agricultural Act of 1949, secs. 407 and 416, 63 *Stat.* 1055 and 1058 (1949). Leddy, "United States Commercial Policy," p. 193; *CFEP Report, Staff Papers*, pp. 170–71.

16. Eisenhower message to Congress, June 10, 1953, and statement by John Foster Dulles before the Senate Committee on Agriculture and Forestry, June 12, 1953, *Department of State Bulletin* 28, #730 (June 22, 1953): 889–91.

17. J. Earl Coke to Benson, July 15, 1953, "Wheat," GC 1953, RG 16; *Department of State Bulletin* 29, #755 (December 15, 1953): 822–23.

18. Homer E. Capehart to Benson, January 20, 1954, OF 116–J "Latin America (2)," EP.

19. "Special Message to the Congress Requesting General Legislation Authorizing the Use of Agricultural Commodities for Foreign Emergency Relief," June 30, 1953, *Public Papers, Eisenhower*, 1953, p. 461; hearings, Senate Committee on Agriculture and Forestry, *Emergency Famine Assistance Authority*, 83d Cong., 1st sess. (July 16, 1953), pp. 1–58; Roger Flemming to Sherman Adams, June 18, 1953; resolution, Executive Committee of the Full Board of Directors of the NFU, July 25, 1953, both in OF 116–B "Foreign Aid—Foreign Relief (1)," EP.

20. Famine Emergency Relief Act, 67 *Stat.* 476, August 7, 1953; *Department of State Bulletin* 29, #747 (October 19, 1953): 518; 30, #755 (December 14, 1953): 822; 31, #759 (January 11, 1954): 55–56; Harold Stassen to Eisenhower, March 15, 1954, and Eisenhower to secretaries of state and agriculture and directors of Bureau of the Budget and Foreign Operations Administration, March 15, 1954, "Commodities 5," GC 1954, RG 16. John Cabot, assistant secretary of state for inter-American affairs, pointed out that the grant to Bolivia was made in spite of the Bolivian government's "attitude toward American interests." He noted that the shipments followed preliminary agreements on compensation to the former owners of recently nationalized tin mines, and he said that in view of the "mathematical certainty" of famine in Bolivia, "a swing to communism [seemed] probable if we sat on our hands." *Department of State Bulletin* 29, #748 (October 26, 1953): 554.

21. *Public Papers*, Eisenhower, 1953, pp. 491–94, 497–98, 516–20, 601–2; Eisenhower to Alexander Wiley and Robert B. Chipperfield, July 17, 1953, and excerpt, Foreign Service dispatch, "The East German Food Program," November 3, 1953, both in OF 182–A, "Food to East Germany," EP. Between July 21 and October 10, 1953, 5,559,782 packages were distributed to about one-sixth of the East German population.

22. Benson to Charlie Wilson, May 8, 1953, OF 149–B, "Foreign Trade 1953 (2)," EP; Wilton Persons to Gerald Morgan, March 31, 1953, and Robert M. Macy to Robert Cutler, May 8, 1953, "Agriculture Department (Legislation)," Gerald Morgan files; Benson to Cutler, April 28, 1953, Macy to Cutler, May 7, 1953, Cutler to Sherman Adams, May 9, 1953, all in OF 106–I "Agricultural Surpluses (1)," EP; Don Paarlberg to True D. Morse and Benson, June 9, 1953, "Foreign Relations 3," GC 1953, RG 16.

23. John H. Ohly, "Conference strategy with respect to the dif-

ferences between the Senate and House versions of the Mutual Security Act of 1953," June 29, 1953, OF 133–L, "Mutual Defense and Security 1953 (2)," EP. The amendment had bipartisan support and strong rural backing.

24. Mutual Security Act of 1953, 67 *Stat.* 152. Transshipment guarantees are agreements in which the recipient country agrees not to reship the incoming commodities to another nation.

25. *American Farm Bureau Federation Newsletter,* vol. 32, June 1 and 8, 1953; Romeo Short to Karl Loos, August 21, 1953, "Opinions 3—Solicitor 1," GC 1953, RG 16.

26. R. S. Nelson to H. O. Belknap, December 28, 1953, Belknap to Benson, December 31, 1953, John H. Davis to Belknap, January 5, 1954, Clayton E. Whipple to Davis, January 6, 1954, all in "Commodities 5," GC 1954, RG 16.

27. Fred Rossiter to John H. Davis, January 8, 1954, "Commodities 5," GC 1954, RG 16.

28. Memorandum of conversation, J. G. Crawford, Willis Armstrong, and George Alexander, March 15, 1954, Francis files; Thruston Morton to Walt Horan, March 31, 1954, "Commodities 5," GC 1954, RG 16.

29. Clayton Whipple to John H. Davis, March 8, 1954, John H. Davis to Bill Lodwick, April 9, 1954, both in "Commodities 5," GC 1954, RG 16; *Department of State Bulletin* 30, #771 (April 5, 1954): 518; #772 (April 12, 1954): 566; #774 (April 26, 1954): 641.

30. Agricultural Adjustment Act, sec. 22, 49 *Stat.* 773 (1935); Agricultural Act of 1948, sec. 3, 62 *Stat.* 1247 (1948); Defense Production Act of 1950, amendments, sec. 104, 65 *Stat.* 132 (1951).

31. John M. Leddy to Gabriel Hauge, December 11, 1953; Department of State [Leddy] to Hauge, n.d., but ca. December 11, 1953; Hauge to Eisenhower, February 17, 1954, all in "Subject File—Cotton—Long Staple," Phillip Areeda papers.

32. Gabriel Hauge to Eisenhower, December 7, 1953, "Subject File—Tr. Sec. 22 Cases, N–Z," Areeda papers; Walter B. Smith to Paul Martin and reply, December 14, 1953, OF 8, EP; Clayton Whipple to John Davis, ca. January 1, 1954, and W. C. Hopper to John H. Davis, May 27, 1954, both in "Grain," GC 1954, RG 16.

33. State recommended a section 22 rye import quota. Gabriel Hauge to Eisenhower, March 30, 1954; Eisenhower to Louis St. Laurent, March 31, 1954, and reply, April 8, 1954, all in OF 149–B-2, EP; Clayton Whipple to John H. Davis, March 25, 1954, "Grain 5," GC 1954, RG 16.

34. "Farmers and the State Department," *Farm Journal* 78 (April 1954): 190; Thruston Morton to Walt Horan, March 13, 1954; Horan to John H. Davis, April 2, 1954; Davis to Horan, April 9, 1954, all in "Commodities 5," GC 1954, RG 16.

35. Benson to John Foster Dulles, March 29, 1954, "Committees 4," GC 1954, RG 16.

36. Clarence Francis meeting notes, National Security Council, April 1, 1954, "Policies and Organization (2)," Francis files.

37. Ibid; John Foster Dulles to Benson, April 19, 1954, Benson to Dulles, May 3, 1954, Dulles to Benson, May 17, 1954, all in "Meetings 2–3," GC 1954, RG 16.

38. John H. Davis to Glen B. Edgerton, July 2, 1954, "Cotton," GC 1954, RG 16; William Lodwick to Clarence Francis, August 6, 1954, "H," Francis files.

39. James Lambie, Jr., to Interagency Committee on Agricultural Surplus Disposal, December 10, 1954, "Barter with Soviet Bloc," Francis files.

40. In fiscal year 1954, MSA shipments, including section 550, barter, and famine relief, accounted for 17 percent of total United States exports of farm products. FOA, "How Do Mutual Security Programs Effect [sic] U.S. Business?" ca. January 22, 1955, OF 246 "1955 (1)," EP.

41. Clayton Whipple to John H. Davis, January 19, 1954, "Commodities 5," D. A. FitzGerald to Davis, June 3, 1954, "Committees 4," GC 1954, RG 16.

42. Telegram, American Embassy, Bogota, Colombia, to State, June 17, 1954, "Disposal of U.S. Surpluses Abroad," Francis files; digest of report, Foreign Agricultural Trade Missions, Egypt, May 10, 1954, "Foreign Relations 3," GC 1954, RG 16.

CHAPTER 3

1. Gabriel Hauge, oral history interview, April 24, 1957, pp. 29–31.

2. By setting "trade and aid" in opposition, the USDA intentionally colored the discussion of export policy. Benson to AFBF, NFU, and Grange, June 5, 1953, in AFBF *Official Newsletter,* vol. 32, June 15, 1953.

3. Benson said that the federal government had no obligation to support farm income; however, if urban industries were getting support from the government, agriculture should get an equivalent amount of support. Benson interview. Neil Jacoby says Eisenhower wanted a direct income-support plan for low-in-

come farmers but felt "it was too tough a political battle to fight."
Neil Jacoby, oral history interview, November–December 1970,
pp. 49, 122–28.

4. It was inevitable, Benson said, that some small farmers
would move out of agriculture; the charges that the administration was not looking out for the small farmers were largely "political"—the department had a unit specifically assigned to help
small farmers make adjustments. He agreed with the complaints
that subsidies held up domestic consumer prices and said that the
subsidy-induced higher prices prevented agriculture from making
full use of the domestic demand that existed. Benson interview.

5. Senate Committee on Agriculture and Forestry, *Hearings
on Foreign Trade in Agricultural Products,* 83d Cong., 1st sess.,
pp. 84–177, 214–15.

6. Howard H. Gordon to Benson, February 1, 1954, "Commodities 5," GC 1954, RG 16; "Committees 5," GC 1953 and 1954,
RG 16; Percival Brundage, oral history interview, April 28, 1967,
pp. 9–10; Neil Jacoby, oral history interview, November–December 1970, pp. 126–27.

7. Members of the CFEP were: Randall, Fleming, David J.
McDonald, Cola G. Parker, Jesse W. Tapp, John Hay Whitney,
John H. Williams, Eugene D. Millikin (Sen., R-Colo.), Bourke B.
Hickenlooper (Sen., R-Iowa), Prescott Bush (Sen., R-Conn.), Walter F. George (Sen., D-Ga.), Harry F. Byrd (Sen., D-Va.), Daniel
A. Reed (Rep., R-N.Y.), Richard M. Simpson (Rep., R-Pa.), John
M. Varys (Rep., R-Ohio), Jere Cooper (Rep., D-Tenn.), and Laurie
C. Battle (Rep., D-Ala.). *CFEP Report,* commissioners, p. iv; staff,
p. 90.

8. Witnesses included representatives of the American Farm
Bureau Federation, the Grange, and the National Farmers Union
but none from commodity groups, consumers, or foreign nations.

9. *CFEP Report,* pp. 28–34, 37–38, 77–89.

10. "Public Attitudes toward the Report of the Commission on
Foreign Economic Policy," Department of State, February 12,
1954, "Foreign Economic Policy Commission," series 2, Morgan
files; "Randall Report Disappoints Europe," Moscow, Soviet Home
Service, January 27, 1954; "Randall Report Seeks One-sided
Trade," TASS, January 27, 1954; and "Randall Commission's Report Analyzed," TASS, January 24, 1954, all in OF 116–M, EP.

11. Benson to Clarence Randall, March 12, 1954, "Foreign Relations 3," GC 1954, RG 16. The report's recommendations on
East-West trade will be reviewed in chapter 7.

12. George Humphrey to Benson, November 19, 1953, True D. Morse to Gabriel Hauge, November 24, 1953, both in "Committees 3," GC 1953, RG 16; John H. Davis to Benson, April 19, 1954, "Commodities 5," GC 1954, RG 16.

13. *Congressional Record,* Senate, July 24, 1953, 9723–4, July 28, 1953, 10077–88; S. Rep. 642, 83d Cong., 1st sess. (1953); AFBF *Official Newsletter,* vol. 32, June 1 and 8, 1953; William D. Anderson, "The Intersection of Foreign and Domestic Policy: The Examples in Public Law 480," (Ph.D. diss. University of Illinois, 1970), pp. 104–5.

14. Memorandum of conversation, Department of State, first meeting of Interdepartmental Group Studying Problem of Surplus Agricultural Commodities, November 30, 1953; "Index," interdepartmental group meetings; Jack D. Corbett to Samuel Waugh, December 14, 1953, all in "Legislation (4)," Francis files.

15. William V. Turnage to Samuel Waugh, January 13, 1954, Fred Rossiter to John H. Davis, January 14, 1954, Davis to True D. Morse, January 14, 1954, all in "Commodities 5," GC 1954, RG 16; "Unresolved Issues Posed in Draft bill Dated 2/25/54," March 4, 1954, "Legislation (4)"; Clarence Francis notes, "Meeting— March 1, 1954," "Policy and Organization (2)"; and Donald R. Belcher to Francis, March 29, 1954, "Disposal of U.S. Surpluses Abroad," all in Francis files.

16. Joseph Dodge to Sherman Adams and Bernard M. Shanley, March 1, 1954, OF 106, EP.

17. Excerpt from resolutions on "International Affairs" adopted at Annual Meeting of AFBF, December 17, 1953, "Legislation (1)"; minutes, interdepartmental meeting, February 16, 1954, "Legislation (4)"; James C. Foster to Loring K. Macy, April 29, 1954, "Legislation (3)"; John C. Lynn to "all State Farm Bureaus," April 29, 1954, "Legislation (1)"; notes, interdepartmental meeting, April 21, 1954, "Policies and Organization (2)," all in Francis files; Karl D. Loos to True D. Morse, March 10, 1954, "Commodities 5," GC 1954, RG 16.

18. James C. Foster to Loring K. Macy, April 29, 1954, "Legislation (3)"; R. L. Farrington to Clarence Francis et al., May 26, 1954, Guy Noyes to Gerald Morgan, May 27, 1954, unsigned, "Summary of discussions at House Agriculture Committee, June 3, on the Hill Bill, H.R. 9389," June 7, 1954, "Legislation (2)," all in Francis files; *Congressional Record,* House, June 9, 1954, p. 7981; June 15, 1954, pp. 8268–301; June 16, 1954, pp. 8361–80; June 22, 1954, p. 8686; June 30, 1954, p. 9358; *Congressional Rec-*

ord, Senate, June 22, 1954, pp. 8596–9; June 30, 1954, pp.
9258–59; H. Rep. 1776, 83d Cong., 2d sess. (1954); Conf. Rep.
1947, 83d Cong., 2d sess. (1954).

19. Agricultural Trade Development and Assistance Act, 68
Stat. 454 (1954). Although the USDA had studied the opportunities for domestic disposal of surpluses at the request of the interagency committee, it had not identified many. The USDA
strongly opposed any type of federal food stamp plan. Most of the
domestic programs of title III were restatements of programs already authorized by the New Deal agricultural legislation.

20. Samuel Waugh to Clarence Francis, July 6, 1954; Francis
to William Lodwick, July 13, 1954; Sinclair Weeks to Francis,
July 16, 1954; Thruston Morton to Rowland Hughes, n.d.; Harold
Stassen to Roger Jones, July 23, 1954; memo, Francis conversation with William Lodwick, n.d.; Francis to "members of the
Committee," August 9, 1954; all in "Policies and Organization
(2)," Francis files. It was during this time that Eisenhower, "im-
pressed with the fact . . . the Executive Branch lacks an orderly
way of identifying and reconciling conflicting points of view and
interests in the development of long-range international economic objectives," asked the advisory committee on Government organization and the Director of the Bureau of the Budget to study
the problem. Eisenhower to Nelson Rockefeller and Rowland
Hughes, July 12, 1954, OF 116–EE, EP.

21. Clarence Francis to Gabriel Hauge, August 17, 1954, "H";
Francis to Hauge, August 17, 1954, reporting (falsely) agreement
between FOA and Agriculture, "Policy and Organization (2)";
memorandum of understanding, FOA and Agriculture, August
23, 1954, "ICASD—Legislation," all in Francis files; Earl Butz to
John H. Davis, August 31, 1954, reporting (correctly) agreement
between FOA and Agriculture; Harold Stassen to Benson, August
30, 1954; Benson to Stassen, September 15, 1954, all in "Commodities 5," GC 1954, RG 16.

22. U.S., President, Executive Order 10560, "Administration of
the Agricultural Trade Development and Assistance Act of 1954,"
Federal Register 19 no. 178, September 14, 1954, 5927–29; *Public
Papers,* Eisenhower, 1954, pp. 841–46.

23. Samuel Anderson to Clarence Francis, August 5, 1954,
"Policy and Organization (2)," Francis files; Anderson to Francis,
October 8, 1954, "Agricultural Surplus Disposal—Committee Re-
port—Miscellaneous 1955," James Lambie, Jr., files.

24. E.O. 10560, "Administration of the Agricultural Trade Development and Assistance Act"; *Public Papers,* Eisenhower, 1954,

pp. 841–46; John H. Davis to Benson, July 20, 1954, "Commodities 5," GC 1954, RG 16.

25. John H. Davis to Gabriel Hauge, May 19, 1954, Clarence Francis to Davis, June 1, 1954, Samuel Waugh to Francis, June 3, 1954, James Lambie to Clarence Randall, August 20, 1954, all in "Policy and Organization (3)," Francis files.

26. John H. Davis to Gabriel Hauge, May 19, 1954, "Policy and Organization (3)," Francis files; Dennis A. FitzGerald to Clarence Francis, June 15, 1954, Davis to P. V. Cardon, March 11, 1954, Francis to Davis, June 2, 1954, all in "Commodities 5," GC 1954, RG 16; Don Paarlberg to True D. Morse, June 9, 1953, "Foreign Relations 3," GC 1953, RG 16.

27. *Public Papers*, Eisenhower, 1954, pp. 841–43; Thorsten Kalijarvi to Clarence Francis, July 7, 1954, James Lambie to Francis, July 9, 1954, Samuel Waugh to Francis, August 31, 1954, Francis to Waugh, September 7, 1954, all in "State, Department of," Francis files; Lambie to Randall, August 20, 1954, "Policy and Organization (3)," Francis files; W. G. Lodwick to Earl Butz, August 27, 1954, "Agricultural Surplus Disposal Correspondence (2)," Lambie papers.

28. Agricultural Act, 68 *Stat.* 897 (1954).

CHAPTER 4

1. William Lodwick to Earl Butz, September 14, 1954, "Agricultural Surplus Disposal Correspondence (2)," Lambie papers; Butz to Benson, October 4 and 8, 1954, "Commodities 5," GC 1954, RG 16; minutes, ICASD, September 20, October 5 and 12, 1954, "Minutes of ICASD Meeting—1954, 1955, 1956, 1957," and minutes, ICASD, September 28, 1954, "Barter with the Soviet Bloc," all in Francis files; minutes, ISC, September 24 and October 8, 1954, "Interagency Committee on Agricultural Surplus Disposal—Minutes (1) 1954–55," Lambie records.

2. Sinclair Weeks to Benson, January 3, 1956, "Meetings 2–3 Secretary," GC 1956, RG 16; press release, USDA, February 6, 1956, OF 1, EP; Francis to Percival Brundage, April 10, 1956, Brundage to Francis, April 10, 1956, Brundage to Benson, April 23, 1956, Bartlett Harvey to Gordon Fraser, May 23, 1956, all in "Bureau of the Budget—1956," Francis files; True Morse to Brundage, April 24, 1956, Earl Butz to Gwynn Garnett, May 15, 1956, Garnett to Benson, June 13, 1956, all in "Commodities 5," GC 1956, RG 16.

3. James Lambie, Jr., to Clarence Randall, January 31, 1957,

and Paul Cullen to CFEP, January 24, 1957, CFEP 543/1, both in "Committee—Misc—1957," Francis files; Jack Z. Anderson diary, January 29 and 31, 1957, Jack Z. Anderson papers; Butz to Anderson, March 7, 1957, "Agriculture—Grain," Anderson records; minutes, ISC, February 7, 1957, "ISC Minutes—1955, 1956, 1957 (2)," Francis files.

4. Minutes, ICASD, November 4, 1954, "Minutes of ICASD meetings—1954, 1955, 1956, 1957," Francis files; minutes, ICASD, November 16, 1954, "Agricultural Surplus Disposal Program—General 1954," Lambie papers.

5. Although there were twenty-two accredited agencies, three (Catholic Relief Services, Church World Service, and CARE) handled 91 percent of the quantities moved. William H. McCahon to James Lambie, Jr., February 12, 1958, "Lambie, James," Francis files.

6. Earl Butz to D. W. Woodward, December 8, 1955, "Dairy Products 5," GC 1955, RG 16.

7. In June of 1956 the USDA restricted wheat and corn donations to programs "where agencies will distribute them directly to needy persons for home preparation and use." Since flour and cornmeal were still freely available for shipment, the ICA program officer in Rome believed the decision "was primarily intended to assist U.S. commercial milling interests." Alexis Lachman to Don Paarlberg, August 26, 1958, "Commodities 5," GC 1958, RG 16.

8. ICA paper, "Grants of U.S. Surplus Agricultural Commodities under P.L. 480, as Amended," September 17, 1956, "ICA—1958," Francis files; Earl Butz to L. H. Fountain, November 15, 1956, "Commodities 5," GC 1956, RG 16. Sales continued to be a problem. See Don Paarlberg, "Observations and Comments," September 19, 1958, following review of voluntary agency programs in eight countries in 1958, OF 116–CC, EP, and the problem in Colombia reviewed by ICASD, August 5, 1958, "Commodities 5," GC 1958, RG 16.

9. Roy W. Lennartson to Butz, October 1, 1956, "Dairy Products 5," GC 1956, RG 16; oral history interview, True D. Morse, October 9, 1967; minutes, ICASD, October 15, 1959, "Minutes of the ICASD Committee—1959," Francis files.

10. The voluntary agencies had begun asking for an interagency review of coordination and supervision a year earlier; see "Appraisal of U.S. Surplus Sharing Programs (Submitted April 1, 1957, by Overseas Voluntary Agency Representatives)," "Agri-

culture—Grain," Jack Z. Anderson records.

11. ICA to ICASD, January 6, 1956, and ICA paper, "Grants of U.S. Surplus Agricultural Commodities under P.L. 480, as Amended," February 10, 1958, both in "Reports and Papers on the Various Sections of P.L. 480," Francis files; Clarence Francis to ICASD, February 12, 1958, Francis to C. Douglas Dillon, February 12, 1958, both in "State—1958," Francis files; William H. McCahon to James Lambie, February 12, 1958, and Lambie to Francis, April 24, 1958, both in "Lambie, James M., Jr.," Francis files; staff notes, meeting of ICASD and voluntary agency representatives, April 29, 1958, "Commodities 5," GC 1958, RG 16.

12. Minutes, ICASD, June 10, July 1 and 7, August 5, 1958, "Commodities 5," GC 1958, RG 16; J. H. Smith, Jr., to Benson, August 11, 1958, Morse to Paarlberg, August 19, 1958, Nathan Koenig to Paarlberg, September 22, 1958, O. V. Wells to Paarlberg, September 25, 1958, all in OF 116–CC, EP. This unclear situation delayed programming; see complaint by CARE (Richard W. Reuter) to Clarence Francis, September 8, 1958, E. D. White to Francis, October 28, 1958, and Lambie to Francis, October 28, 1958, all in "Lambie, James M., Jr.," Francis files.

13. Benson to J. H. Smith, Jr., January 16, 1959, "Clarence Francis—1959"; D. A. FitzGerald to Francis, February 19, 1959, "Agriculture," both in Francis files.

14. Mutual Security Act of 1960, 70 *Stat.* 134 (1960); E. K. Fox to Ralph Reid, August 26, 1960, "PL 480—General," L. J. Saccio to C. Douglas Dillon, September 14, 1960, "Title III—PL 480—p to p donations—barter," Don Paarlberg to C. Douglas Dillon, September 14, 1960, "State Department," all in Paarlberg papers.

15. Minutes, ISC, September 17 and 28, 1954, "Interagency Committee on Agricultural Surplus Disposal—Minutes (1) 1954–55," Lambie records; minutes, ICASD, September 28, 1954, "Barter with Soviet Bloc," Francis files.

16. Minutes, ICASD, October 12 and November 4, 1954, "Minutes of ICASD Meetings—1954, 1955, 1956, 1957," Francis files.

17. William Lodwick to Clarence Francis, October 27, 1954, "L Miscellaneous—1956," Francis files.

18. James Lambie to Clarence Francis, December 4, 1954, "Agricultural Surplus Disposal Programs—Trade Development and Assistance Act 1954," Lambie papers.

19. Minutes, ICASD, December 7, 1954, "Agricultural Surplus Disposal Program—General 1954," Lambie papers. The approved lists were:

Title I (in millions of CCC cost)

Japan	$100	Norway	$ 2
Pakistan	31	Finland	4
Spain	26	Thailand	2
Turkey	30.3	Italy	30
United Kingdom	53.5	France	15
Yugoslavia	60	Brazil	30
Chile	8	Austria	5
Peru	6	India	40
Denmark	10	Reserve	.2
			$453.0

Title II

Austria, East and		Bolivia	$ 9.9
West Germany	$ 3.6	Japan	15
Italy	20	Haiti	1.9
Yugoslavia	34.2	Hungary	2.7
Libya	3.25	Czechoslovakia	1.7
Pakistan	14.8	Christmas package	16.7
Nepal	.2	program	
			$123.95

20. Cabinet paper CP-8, "Review of P.L. 480 decisions taken by the Interagency Committee on Agricultural Surplus Disposal," December 15, 1954, and "The Cabinet: Record of Action RA-6 of meeting December 17, 1954," December 20, 1954, both in "Barter with Soviet Bloc," Francis files.

21. During the life of the administration, title I programs were eventually developed for all of these except Belgium, Sweden, and Switzerland. Officially, no programming was possible for Belgium because "dollar imports into Belgium are relatively unrestricted, therefore, it is impossible to meet the usual marketing conditions required under PL 480." Minutes, ISC, January 24, 1955, "ISC Minutes—1955, 1956, 1957 (1)," Francis files. This suggests a preference for negotiating title I agreements with governments that had import monopolies or strict controls.

22. Minutes, ICASD, October 12, 1954, "Minutes of ICASD Meetings—1954, 1955, 1956, 1957," and Robert Murphey to Clarence Francis, November 23, 1954, "State, Department of,"

both in Francis files. Two examples of the cold war reasoning behind European preference are the discussion of a title I program for Finland (minutes, ISC, January 21, 1955, "Interagency Committee on Agricultural Surplus Disposal—Minutes [1] 1954–55," Lambie records), and for Denmark (minutes, ISC, January 24, 1955, "ISC minutes—1955, 1956, 1957 [1],") both in Francis files.

23. W. Randolph Burgess to Clarence Francis, November 30, 1954, "State, Department of," Francis files; James Lambie, Jr., to members of the ICASD, December 6, 1954, "Agricultural Surplus Disposal Program—General 1954," Lambie papers; minutes, ISC, December 1, 1954, "ISC minutes—1955, 1956, 1957 (1)," Francis files.

24. Minutes, ISC, December 1, 1954, ibid.

25. This procedure refers only to title I shipments. "Participation of U.S. Private Trade Title I—PL 480," February 8, 1955, "Agricultural Surplus Disposal—General 1955," Lambie papers.

26. United States Congress, House, *Semi-annual Report #1, PL 480,* H. Doc. 62, 84th Cong., 1st sess., 1955. The report inaccurately lists Turkey's as the first signed program; actually Japan's was signed first, but implementation was delayed because it needed ratification by the Japanese diet.

27. See, for example, minutes, ISC, January 31, February 14, March 25, April 18, April 20, 1955, all in "ISC minutes—1955, 1956, 1957 (1)," Francis files; minutes, ISC, January 13, 1955, "Interagency Committee on Agricultural Surplus Disposal—Minutes (1) 1954–55," Lambie records; minutes, ICASD, February 1, 1955, "Minutes of ICASD meetings—1954, 1955, 1956, 1957," and minutes, ICASD, February 25, 1955, "Agricultural Surplus Disposal, Interagency Committee on—General," both in Francis files. At the February 14 meeting the State Department reported that the Pakistan PL 480 agreement was basically an aid program and "in Pakistan we were pressing them to use more and more of their budget for military expenditures."

28. Minutes, ISC, January 11, 1955, "Agriculture, Department of (2)"; minutes, ISC, January 14, 1955, "L Miscellaneous—1956," both in Francis files; minutes, ISC, January 21, 1955, "Interagency Committee on Agricultural Surplus Disposal—Minutes (1) 1954–55," Lambie records.

29. Avraham Salmon to Maxwell Rabb, January 27, 1955, "Commodities 5," GC 1955, RG 16; Eduardo Buleta-Angel to John Foster Dulles, February 15, 1955, "Colombia," minutes, ICASD, February 8 and 15, 1955, "Minutes of ICASD meetings—

1954, 1955, 1956, 1957," minutes, ISC, February 14, 1955, "ISC Minutes—1955, 1956, 1957 (1)," all in Francis files.

30. Minutes, ISC, March 29, April 1, April 7, April 25, and June 10, 1955, "ISC Meetings—1955, 1956, 1957 (1)," Francis files. After some delay, the objections to the Israeli sale were withdrawn.

31. Earl Butz to Hubert Humphrey, May 10, 1955, and "Status Report of Title I, PL 480 Programs," May 17, 1955, both in "Commodities 5," GC 1955, RG 16.

32. Minutes, ICASD, January 25 and February 8, 1955, "Minutes of ICASD meetings—1954, 1955, 1956, 1957," Samuel Waugh to Clarence Francis, January 27, 1954 [*sic*, 1955], "State, Department of," James Lambie, Jr., to Francis, February 26, 1955, "Lambie, James M., Jr.," all in Francis files.

33. Samuel Waugh to E. C. Gathings, April 8, 1955, and Waugh to Clarence Francis, April 12, 1955, both in "CFEP Rice to Asia," Francis to James Lambie, Jr., April 4 and 11, 1955, Lambie to Francis, April 18, 1955, all in "Agricultural Surplus Disposal, Interagency Committee on—General," Lambie to Waugh, April 19, 1955, Waugh to Lambie, April 20, 1955, Lambie to Waugh, May 11, 1955, all in "Security within the ICASD," Lodwick to Francis, June 7, 1955, "L Miscellaneous—1956," all above in Francis files.

34. Amendment to PL 480 "To re-emphasize trade development as the primary purpose of Title I of 68 *Stat.* 456," 69 *Stat.* 721 (1955).

35. Minutes, ISC, August 25 and September 6, 1955, "ISC Minutes—1955, 1956, 1957 (2)," Francis files.

36. Dulles news conference, January 11, 1956, *Department of State Bulletin* 34, #864 (January 23, 1956): 117–18, and #871 (March 5, 1956): 365; State to Gabriel Hauge, ca. March 22, 1956, OF 116-B, "Foreign Aid—Foreign Relief (2)," EP; speech, Joseph Dodge, "The New Turn in the Cold War," April 20, 1956, "Dodge Speeches and Releases (1955–56)," Joseph M. Dodge files; United States International Cooperation Administration, *8th Report to Congress*, "Survey of East-West Trade in 1955," by John B. Hollister (Washington, D.C.: Government Printing Office, October 10, 1956), pp. 26–29.

37. Press release, ICA, September 21, 1956, OF 133-L "1956 (2)," EP; minutes, ISC, January 20, 1956, Richard Roberts papers, USDA History Group files; minutes, ISC, February 2 and 10, 1956, "ISC minutes—1955, 1956, 1957 (2)," Francis files.

38. Robert Anderson to Benson, April 21, 1956, C. R. Eskildsen

to Gwynn Garnett, May 16, 1956, Earl Butz to Benson, May 18, 1956, Butz to Benson, June 1, 1956, Garnett to Milan Smith, August 16, 1956, all in "Commodities 5," GC 1956, RG 16; Henry Roemer McPhee to Sherman Adams, May 11, 1956, OF 149-B, EP; *Department of State Bulletin* 35, #899 (September 17, 1956): 454.

39. Press release, ICA, September 21, 1956, OF 133-L, EP; minutes, ISC, April 25, 1956, "ISC Minutes—1955, 1956, 1957 (2)," Francis files; background briefing paper, Mutual Security legislation, June 11, 1956, "ICA 1956 #1," Harlow papers.

40. Howard Davis to Edmund Pendleton, Jr., October 30, 1956, "Commodities 5," GC 1956, RG 16; Earl Butz to Verne J. Barbre, April 5, 1957, "Wheat 5," GC 1957, RG 16; Graham L. Rees, *Britain's Commodity Markets* (London: Paul Elek Books, 1972), p. 117; Dulles press conferences, September 26 and October 2, 1956, *Department of State Bulletin* 25, #902 and #903 (October 8 and 15, 1956): 548, 576. Egypt subsequently purchased wheat from the USSR, amid great fanfare. Hubert Humphrey, *The Middle East and Southern Europe, a Report*, 85th Cong., 1st sess. (1957).

41. AFBF *Official Newsletter*, vol. 35, February 13, 1956; Earl Butz to Herbert C. Bonner, January 27, 1956, Butz to R. C. Patterson, February 20, 1956, Benson to R. G. Smith, June 27, 1956, all in "Commodities 5," GC 1956, RG 16; minutes, ISC, February 10 and April 25, 1956, "ISC Minutes—1955, 1956, 1957 (2)," minutes, ICASD, June 5, 1956, "Minutes of ICASD meetings—1954, 1955, 1956, 1957," National Advisory Council, document no. 88, July 9, 1956, and Walter Schaefer to Dennis FitzGerald, July 20, 1956, "Department of Commerce—1956," all in Francis files.

42. "Memorandum on the Use of P.L. 480 Foreign Currencies for Loans to Private Enterprise in General and U.S. Business in Particular," [CFEP?] August 31, 1957, "PL 480, 83d Cong., Amended (1)," Joseph Rand records.

43. Agricultural Trade Development and Assistance Act, 71 *Stat.* 345 (1957); entire file, "Appr. 8/13/57 S. 1314," Bill File, White House Records Office; Edmund Pendleton, Jr., "Foreign Currency Loans to Private Business," *Journal of the Bar Association of the District of Columbia*, vol. 25, March 1958.

44. Minutes, ISC, August 15 and October 31, 1957, "ISC Minutes—1955, 1956, 1957 (2)," minutes, ICASD, October 1, 1957, "Minutes of ICASD Meetings—1954, 1955, 1956, 1957," all in Francis files.

45. The Battle Act terminated aid to nations that supplied the

Soviet bloc with certain military items; Poland and Yugoslavia
were Battle Act "problems," and the Burmese government was
"unreceptive" to Cooley loans, which State argued was an
"overriding political reason" not to insist on the provision. Ex-Im
and ODM were unhappy about the Burmese exemption but went
along. Gwynn Garnett to Morse, January 24, 1958, Raymond
Ioanes to Morse, February 21, 1958, Ioanes to Paarlberg, March
5, 1958, all in "Commodities 5," Ioanes to Morse, February 28,
1958, "Cotton 5," Ioanes to Morse, February 4, 1958, "Grain 5,"
minutes, ISC, March 27, 1958, "Meetings," all in GC 1958, RG
16; transcript, question-and-answer session on Cooley loans at
the Business International Conference, June 19–21, 1958, "Committee Correspondence—1958," Francis files.
   46. "Status of Work on 104(e) Loan Program," July 2, 1958,
"Committee Correspondence—1958," Francis files.
   47. Paarlberg to Samuel Waugh, April 11, 1958, April 14, 1958,
July 9, 1958, October 6, 1958, all in "Commodities 5," Paarlberg
to Waugh, June 18, 1958, July 7, 1958, Waugh to Paarlberg,
September 8, 1958, Paarlberg to Waugh, September 25, 1958, all
in "Tobacco 5," minutes, ISC, June 19, 1958, "Meetings," all in
GC 1958, RG 16.

CHAPTER 5

   1. "Status Report of Title I, PL 480 Programs," May 17, 1955,
"Commodities 5," GC 1955, RG 16; Eisenhower to Dodge,
December 1, 1954, *Public Papers,* Eisenhower, 1954, pp. 1097–98;
Joseph Dodge to Clarence Francis, June 21, 1955, and Francis to
Samuel Waugh, July 19, 1955, "CFEP—Baughman Report,"
Francis files.
   2. In millions of dollars, Baughman's figures were:

Exports for dollars, unaided		$1,800
Barter	$125	
Title I sale for foreign currency	63	
MS sale for foreign currency	281	
Grants and donations, MS, title II, title III (section 416)	388	
Exports under section 32 subsidies	36	
Exports under other subsidies	450	
		1,343
		$3,143

The $1,800 million for unaided dollar exports included $70 million in exports via government loans, mostly cotton sales to Japan.

3. Clarence Francis to Joseph Dodge, October 22, 1955, "CFEP—Baughman Report," Francis to Dodge, October 31, 1955, "CFEP Miscellaneous (2)," both in Francis files; "Prospects for Foreign Disposal of Domestic Agricultural Surpluses," "Commodities 5," GC 1956, RG 16. Baughman was instructed *not* to make recommendations on domestic agricultural programs, which gave the report an air of unreality, since Baughman personally believed that foreign disposal was not the ultimate answer.

4. Joseph Dodge to Nelson Rockefeller, November 15, 1954, OF 116-AA, EP; Maxwell Rabb to the cabinet, CP-4, December 14, 1954, "Cabinet Meetings," series 2, Morgan files; Samuel Waugh to Gabriel Hauge, December 21, 1954, OF 116-B, "Foreign Aid—Foreign Relief (2)," EP; J. K. Javits to Eisenhower, December 27, 1954, OF 116 "1955 (1)," EP; Department of State Intelligence Report no. 6809, "The Current and Potential Use of Agricultural Surpluses to Promote Economic Development in Underdeveloped Countries," June 29, 1955, "Interagency Committee on Agricultural Surplus Disposal, Misc. 1954–60 (2)," Lambie records.

5. Earl Butz to Ezra Taft Benson, December 28, 1954, and Benson to Harold Stassen, December 31, 1954, both in "Foreign Relations 2," GC 1954, RG 16.

6. Minutes, ISC, January 13, 1955, "ICASD—Minutes (1) 1954–55," Lambie papers; minutes, ISC, February 9, 1955, "ISC Minutes—1955, 1956, 1957 (1)," Francis files.

7. Benson, "The Expansion of Agricultural Exports," November 14, 1955, "Commodities 5," GC 1955, RG 16; Jerry Kieffer to Meyer Kestnbaum, December 9, 1955, "87. USDA—Hoover Commission," Meyer Kestnbaum records.

8. The fate of the recommendation on Soviet trade will be covered in chapter 7. Arthur M. McGlauflin, November 7, 1955, and Paul H. Cullen to CFEP, November 19, 1955, both in "CFEP Miscellaneous (1)," minutes, CFEP, November 30, 1955, "CFEP minutes," all in Francis files; Earl Butz to Ezra Taft Benson, November 30, 1955, "Commodities 5," GC 1955, RG 16. In 1956 the administration tried to get Congress to repeal the fifty-fifty shipping requirement, but it failed.

9. R. S. Nelson to Richard Thruelson, May 2, 1955, "Wheat," GC 1955, RG 16; "Major Steps in Export Promotion," n.d.,

"Committees 5–1 Agricultural Exports Case File," GC 1961, RG 16; United States Congress, House, *Semi-Annual Report #4,* PL *480,* H. Doc. 294, 84th Cong. 2d sess., 1956.

10. Joseph Davis to CFEP, April 25, 1956, Edward B. Hall to Clarence Randall, November 9, 1956, Randall to CFEP, November 13, 1956, CFEP 542/1, all in "CFEP Misc (1)," "Memorandum for Mr. Dodge," probably from Paul Cullen, May 4, 1956, "CFEP Misc (2)," all in Francis files. Of the total United States agricultural exports during 1955–56, 12.4 percent moved under title I, 8.5 percent barter, 9.8 percent MSA, 8.1 percent famine and relief. In value terms, $1.4 billion of the $3.5 billion in agricultural commodities exported during 1955–56 (40.6 percent) moved under a government program. These figures do not, however, include exports using section 32 export subsidies and other indirect means of government support as exports moving under a "government program."

11. State wanted the CFEP to propose amendments to PL 480 to repeal section 304, eliminate barter, finance international exchanges, extend usual marketing provisions of title I to "friendly third countries," limit title I to commodities owned or committed to the CCC, and require title I sales to increase consumption. These positions were clearly at odds with Congress's intent in PL 480. Thorsten Kalijarvi to Randall, November 23, 1956, Randall to Kalijarvi, November 27, 1956, Kalijarvi to Randall, December 1, 1956, all in OF 116-CC (1), EP; Clayton Whipple to Butz, November 19, 1956, "Foreign Relations 3," Butz to Garnett, December 5, 1956, Garnett to Benson, December 20, 1956, both in "Commodities 5," all in GC 1956, RG 16; paper, "Export Disposals and P.L. 480," December 20, 1956, "Pending—Next Meeting," Francis files.

12. George Humphrey to Clarence Randall, November 21, 1956, Randall to Francis, November 27, 1956, and Randall to Humphrey, December 3, 1956, all in "Commodities 5," Earl Butz to Ernest Baughman, December 12, 1956, "Committees," GC 1956, RG 16.

13. Francis to Randall, January 22, 1957, "Commodities 5," GC 1957, RG 16.

14. True Morse to Rowland Hughes, January 13, 1956, "Housing Appropriations," Gwynn Garnett to Earl Butz, June 15, 1956, and Butz notation, June 16, 1956, "Meetings 2–3," Butz to Herbert Prochnow, July 10, 1956, and Morse to Prochnow, July 23, 1956, "Wheat 5," Dulles to Amemb Paris, October 20, 1955,

Prochnow to True Morse, November 2, 1956, Morse to Prochnow, November 27, 1956, "Commodites 5," all in GC 1956, RG 16; minutes, ISC, June 27, 1956, "ISC Minutes—1955, 1956, 1957 (2)," Francis files.

15. James Lambie, Jr., to Clarence Randall, January 31, 1957, "Committee—Misc—1957," and minutes, ISC, February 7, 1957, "ISC Minutes—1955, 1956, 1957 (2)," both in Francis files; Jack Z. Anderson diary, January 29 and 31, 1957, Anderson papers; Butz to Anderson, March 7, 1957, "Agriculture—Grain," Anderson records.

16. James H. Douglas to Benson, April 13, 1957, Morse to Douglas, April 22, 1957, McLain to Morse and Benson to Miller Shurtleff, April 24, 1957, paper, "Barter Policy Problems," n.d., paper, "CCC Barter Policy," April 24, 1957, all in "Commodities 5," GC 1957, RG 16; Earl Butz to Gabriel Hauge, May 1, 1957, OF 110-M "Wool (1)," EP; USDA press release, May 28, 1957, "Clarence Francis files 1957," Lambie papers.

17. Morse to Floyd S. Bryant, June 7, 1957, Ray Ioanes to Paarlberg, October 8, 1957, Royce Hardy to Randall, November 27, 1957, all in "Commodities 5," GC 1957, RG 16; McLain to Phillip Areeda, May 10, 1957, OF 106-I-3, "Barter Program," EP.

18. Congress expressed its displeasure with the changes by amending PL 480 in 1958 to set limits on the restrictions that could be placed on barter. Thereafter the USDA dropped the certificates of additionality and substituted a control mechanism designating commodities as available for "open-end," "multilateral," or "bilateral" barter, depending upon the recipient and the circumstances. USDA press release, November 14, 1958, OF 106-I (14), EP.

19. Earl Butz to Clarence Randall, April 8, 1957, and Christian Herter, Jr., to Randall, May 15, 1957, "Commodities 5," GC 1957, RG 16.

20. Budget wanted PL 480 folded into the Mutual Security Act and the ICA more closely integrated into the State Department for better coordination and direction of all economic aid programs. Robert Macy to Meyer Kestnbaum, July 12, 1957, "57. International Affairs and Foreign Aid 1955–60," Meyer Kestnbaum records.

21. Minutes, ISC, August 15, 1957, "ISC Minutes—1955, 1956, 1957 (2)," Francis files; Gwynn Garnett to Morse, August 14, 1957, "Commodities 5," GC 1957, RG 16. Second-priority countries were Burma, Chile, Formosa, Colombia, Finland, France, Greece,

Indonesia, Italy, Peru, Thailand, and Turkey; funds for a Polish program had already been reserved, in effect making it higher than a "first priority."

22. Paul Overholtzer, Jr., "U.S. Foreign Agricultural Policy with Special Reference to the Middle East," January 25, 1957, "Foreign Relations 2," GC 1957, RG 16.

23. Greece was unable to use all the agreement commodities in fiscal 1958, and the FAS wanted the program discontinued but was prevailed upon to go ahead for another year to avoid "unfortunate political repercussions." Turkey's program was justified by the "desperate foreign exchange position," even after the bombing of a building on United States embassy property in Ankara and an attempt to bomb the United States Information Service library. Paarlberg to Morse, November 27, 1957, Morse to Paarlberg, November 27, 1957, unsigned note attached with memo, Gwynn Garnett to Morse, April 30, 1958, Raymond Ioanes to Paarlberg, June 13, 1958, "Analysis of Requests, Proposals and Program—Fiscal 1958," July 16–18, 1958, all in "Commodities 5," GC 1958, RG 16; *Department of State Bulletin* 38, #973 (February 17, 1958): 257, and #983 (April 28, 1958): 691.

24. The Soil Bank program was part of the Agricultural Act of 1956. FAS to Clarence Randall, August 14, 1957, Raymond Ioanes to Paarlberg, October 30, 1957, both in "Commodities 5," Garnett to Paarlberg, September 13, 1957, "Committees," all in GC 1957, RG 16; Gwynn Garnett to ICASD, August 15, 1957, "Clarence Francis files 1957," Lambie papers; Benson to Sherman Adams, September 1957, OF 1, EP; Paarlberg to Jack Z. Anderson, October 24, 1957, OF 106, EP. Paarlberg's cost estimate was probably wrong, for independent assessments by the CFEP staff and the Bureau of the Budget indicated that the cost of title I was roughly equal to the storage charges and the additional dollar appropriations for foreign aid that would have had to be paid without it. Cost accounting supported no argument. Joseph Rand to Clarence Randall, November 5, 1957, "Rand, Joseph—General," Rand records.

25. "Department of Commerce Position in Regard to P.L. 480 Extension beyond Fiscal 1958," August 30, 1957, and Nathaniel Knowles to Marshall M. Smith, September 20, 1957, both in "Clarence Francis—P.L. 480," Francis files; Raymond Ioanes to Paarlberg, October 30, 1957, "Commodities 5," GC 1957, RG 16.

26. Clyde Wheeler, Jr., to True D. Morse, November 12, 1957, OF 1, EP; Maxwell Rabb to the cabinet, November 14, 1957, and

draft, Francis to Sherman Adams, November 22, 1957, "Clarence Francis—Agriculture Department Correspondence," both in Francis files; Arthur Burns to Eisenhower, November 27, 1957, and Benson to Eisenhower, December 6, 1957, both in "President," reel 11, Benson film; Special Message to the Congress on Agriculture, January 16, 1958, *Public Papers*, Eisenhower, 1958, pp. 100–113.

27. J. H. Smith, Jr., to C. Douglas Dillon, January 20, 1959, "Clarence Francis—1958," Francis files; Benson, *Cross Fire*, p. 429.

28. *Public Papers*, Eisenhower, 1957, pp. 185, 197, 392.

29. Robert L. Berenson, William M. Bristol, and Ralph I. Straus to James H. Smith, Jr., August 5, 1958, "ICA—1958," Francis files; C. Edward Galbreath to Clarence Randall, September 16, 1958, "International Committee on Agricultural Surplus Disposal—Misc (4) 1954–60," Lambie papers.

30. Minutes, ICASD, October 14, 1958, "Committee Meeting Minutes—1958," Marshall M. Smith to Clarence Francis, October 13, 1958, and State-ICA paper, "Recommendations on Davis and Local Currency Reports," n.d., both in "Commerce—1958," all in Francis files; Max Myers to Benson, September 2, 1958, "Foreign Relations 3," and E. L. Peterson to James H. Smith, Jr., November 6, 1958, Myers to True D. Morse, December 24, and Morse to Lawrence B. Robbins, December 30, 1958, "Commodities 5," all in GC 1958, RG 16; Report of the National Advisory Committee on International Monetary and Financial Problems, H. Doc. 380, 86th Cong., 2d sess. (1960), p. 31.

31. Don Paarlberg and Martin Sorkin to Benson, March 31, 1958, "Foreign Relations 2," GC 1958, RG 16.

32. Douglas Dillon to Sherman Adams, January 6, 1958, OF 8, "January 1958," EP; Davis to Benson, March 17, 1958, and Davis to Francis, March 19, 1958, both in "State—1958," John H. Davis, "Utilization of U.S. Agricultural Surpluses as a Tool for Peace," March 26, 1958, "Foreign Disposal of Domestic Agricultural Surpluses (1)," all in Francis files; Davis to Dillon, March 26, 1958, "Interagency Committee on Agricultural Surplus Disposal—Misc (4) 1954–60," Lambie papers.

33. Ralph Reid to Francis, May 13, 1958, "Lambie, James," James Lambie to State and Agriculture, May 29, 1958, Agriculture paper, "Comments to the Francis Committee regarding questions on the Davis Report raised by the Budget Bureau," n.d., State paper, "Utilization of U.S. Agricultural Surpluses as a Tool for Peace," March 26, 1958, all in "Foreign Disposal of

Domestic Agricultural Surpluses (1)," Francis files; O. V. Wells to
Don Paarlberg, n.d., Marvin McLain to Paarlberg, April 16, 1958,
Benson to Sherman Adams, April 29, 1958, all in "Commodities
5, Davis Report," GC 1958, RG 16.

34. Minutes, ICASD, July 1, 1958, and Paarlberg to Benson,
July 2, 1958, both in "Commodities 5," GC 1958, RG 16.

35. Benson to Adams, April 29, 1958, "Commodities 5, Davis
Report," GC 1958, RG 16; Clarence Randall to Gerald Morgan,
February 5, 1959, "Agriculture," Morgan files; Paarlberg to
Benson, October 8, 1958, OF 106-I (10), EP.

36. Benson, *Cross Fire*, pp. 429–33; *Public Papers*, Eisenhower,
1959, "Special Message to the Congress on Agriculture," January
29, 1959, pp. 149–51; Clarence Randall to Gerald Morgan,
February 5, 1959, "Agriculture," Morgan files.

37. Paarlberg to Bryce Harlow, February 24, 1959, "Food for
Peace—White House staff memos," Paarlberg papers; Benson to
Christian Herter, Jr., March 23, 1959, "Commodities 5," and
John McEwen to Benson, April 13, 1959, "Meetings 2–3," both in
GC 1959, RG 16.

38. Clarence Randall to Wilton Persons, April 27, 1959,
"Council on Foreign Economic Policy," Morgan files; Francis to
Benson, May 5, 1959, "Food for Peace—White House staff
memos," Paarlberg papers.

39. *Department of State Bulletin* 40, #1040 (June 1, 1959):
793–94; transcript, Benson news conference, May 6, 1959, "Food
for Peace," reel 6, Benson film; Francis to Bryce Harlow, May 19,
1959, "White House Correspondence—1959," Francis files.

40. James Lambie to ICASD, December 31, 1958, OF 106-I (10),
EP; "Department of State Evaluation of Public Law 480
Programs to Date," February 25, 1959, "U.S.D.A. Material for
Meeting of Francis Committee, February 10, 1959," February 9,
1959, Marshall Smith to Clarence Francis, February 9, 1959, all
in OF 1-Q "Foreign Agricultural Service," EP; J. H. Smith, Jr., to
C. Douglas Dillon, January 30, 1959, "Clarence Francis—1959,"
memo, "Telephone calls with Secretary Douglas Dillon," February 10, 1959, "State Department," minutes, ICASD, February 26,
1959, and Max Myers to ICASD, May 21, 1959, "Minutes of the
ICASD Committee—1959," Subcommittee on Review of Public
Law 480 Operations to Francis, March 27, 1959, "Agriculture," all
in Francis files.

41. Memo for the record, Joseph Rand, May 19, 1959, "Rand,
Joseph—General," Rand records; Clarence Randall to Wilton
Persons, May 20 and June 8, 1959, "Council on Foreign Economic

Policy," Morgan files; Clarence Francis to James Lambie, June 1, 1959, "Correspondence with JML—1959," Paul Cullen to CFEP, June 3, 1959, and minutes, ICASD, June 9, 1959, "Minutes of ICASD Committee—1959," all in Francis files.
42. Agricultural Trade Development and Assistance Act, 73 *Stat.* 606 (1959); *Public Papers*, Eisenhower, 1959, pp. 677–78.
43. Thomas Mann to Clarence Miller, September 28, 1959, and CSS paper, "Analysis of Title IV," October 13, 1959, "Commodities 5," GC 1959 RG 16; John Dean to Clarence Francis, January 6, 1960, Francis to Mann, January 12, 1960, and CSS paper, "Implementation of Title IV, Public Law 480," January 28, 1960, "Title IV—Policy Papers—1960," minutes, ISC, August 4 and 25, 1960, "Interagency Staff Committee Meeting Minutes—1960," all in Francis files; S. J. Meyers to Walter Berger, February 12, 1960, "Agricultural Surplus Disposal—Interagency Committee on, 1960," Lambie papers; Joseph Rand to Clarence Randall, August 22, 1960, "PL 480, 83d Congress, Am. (1)," Rand records.
44. Minutes, meeting on Food for Peace, March 15, 1960, "Food for Peace," Paarlberg papers; Clarence Randall to Wilton Persons, March 2, 1960, "Council on Foreign Economic Policy," Morgan files; Clarence Francis to Randall, March 3, 1960, "Agricultural Surplus Disposal—Interagency Committee on, 1960," Lambie papers; *Department of State Bulletin* 42, #1089 (May 9, 1959): 743.
45. Nixon, campaigning in North Dakota on June 20, said Eisenhower had considered proposing the plan at the Paris summit conference but the collapse of the summit had precluded it. Paarlberg, "Memorandum for the staff secretary," July 5, 1960, OF 106, EP; True Morse to Paarlberg, August 11, 1960, "Commodities 5," GC 1960, RG 16; *Public Papers*, Eisenhower, 1959, pp. 615–16; Senate Con. Res. 116, 110 *Cong. Record*, pp. 18054–55 (August 20, 1960).
46. Dispatch, USIA to overseas branches, November 1, 1960, "United Nations—FFP," minutes, ICASD, November 22, 1960, "Francis Committee," both in Paarlberg papers.
47. See, for instance, Gwynn Garnett to Earl Butz on the proposed United Nations world food capital fund, February 14, 1957, "Commodities 5," GC 1957, RG 16; Benson, "Memorandum on World Food Reserve," March 4, 1957, "Memos to Secretary—by ETB," reel 7, Benson film; Christian Herter to True Morse, December 4, 1958, congratulating him "for having achieved [an FAO] resolution which omits specific endorsement of the title 'Free the World from Hunger'" in line with the CFEP

decision of October 23, 1958, "August—1958," Francis files.
48. Minutes, ICASD, February 26, 1959, "Minutes of the ICASD Committee—1959," Francis files.

CHAPTER 6

1. Thorsten Kalijarvi to Clarence Francis, October 12, 1954, "Agricultural Surplus Disposal 1953-54, Title I—P.L. 480 Policy Problems," minutes, ICASD, November 16, 1954, "Agriculture Surplus Disposal Program—General 1954," both in Lambie papers; Kalijarvi to Francis, December 1, 1954, "Dairy," Francis files.

2. Benson to Eisenhower, December 17, 1954, "Dairy Products 5," GC 1954, RG 16; Gabriel Hauge to Eisenhower, December 21, 1954, "Memos and letters to the President," Gabriel Hauge records; The Cabinet: Record of Action on December 17, 1954, "Barter with Soviet Bloc," Francis files.

3. USDA press releases, February 2 and 9, 1955, "Commodities 5," GC 1955, RG 16; Robert C. Hendrickson to State, dispatch #536, June 10, 1955, "New Zealand," Francis files.

4. Ezra Taft Benson to Don Paarlberg, February 1, 1955, F. Marion Rhodes to Milan D. Smith, August 11, 1955, "Cotton 5," GC 1955, RG 16; *New York Times*, March 18, 1955, 20:5; Clarence Francis to Earl Butz, February 16, 1955, "Agriculture, Department of (2)," Francis files; Graham L. Rees, *Britain's Commodity Markets* (London: Paul Elek Books, 1972), p. 115; Liverpool Cotton Association to Benson, March 22, 1955, Manchester Cotton Association to Benson, March 28, 1955, Association Marche Cotons to Benson, March 26, 1955, Hannay Brothers to Benson, March 28, 1955, Dallas Cotton Exchange and Dallas Cotton Shippers Association to Benson, March 25, 1955, all in "Cotton," GC 1955, RG 16.

5. USDA press release, March 29, 1955, Centro Algodonero Nacional to Benson, April 7, 1955, "Cotton," GC 1955, RG 16; August Taevernier to Benson, April 6, 1955, Butz to Taevernier, April 6, 1955, and aide memoires, British Embassy, April 6 and April 16, 1955, "Cotton 5," GC 1955, RG 16.

6. USDA press release, May 19, 1955, "Committees," Wesley D'Ewart to Benson, August 11, 1955, F. Marion Rhodes to Milan D. Smith, August 11, 1955, "Cotton 5," all in GC 1955, RG 16; minutes, CFEP, July 20, 1955, "CFEP Minutes," Maxwell Rabb to the cabinet, August 15, 1955, "Cabinet CP-8," both in Francis

files; Gabriel Hauge to Eisenhower, July 30, 1955, OF 149-B-2 "Cotton (1)," EP; Benson, *Cross Fire*, pp. 247-49.

7. USDA press release, February 28, 1956, "Subject File—Cotton Textiles—Vol. Agreement, 1956-57," Areeda papers; United States Department of Agriculture, Foreign Agricultural Service, *The Problem of Maintaining High Level Agricultural Exports* (Washington, D.C.: Government Printing Office, November 1957), p. 28.

8. *Department of State Bulletin* 23, #842 (August 15, 1955): 263; #861 (December 26, 1955): 1064-65; *New York Times*, November 25, 1955, 44:5; Preston Richards to J. A. McConnell, November 18, 1955, "Commodities 5," GC 1955, RG 16.

9. Herbert Prochnow to Gabriel Hauge, May 1, 1956, OF 106, EP; Paul Cullen to Hauge, May 21, 1956, Manuel Tello to John Foster Dulles, May 24, 1956, both in OF 149-B-2 "Cotton (3)", EP; Statement to the press by the representative of Uruguay in the Inter-American Economic and Social Council," May 23, 1956, OF 149-B-2 "Cotton (4)," EP; Marvin McLain to Thorsten Kalijarvi, June 22, 1956, "Cotton 5," GC 1956, RG 16.

10. Other provisions in the bill provided a modified soil bank, revised marketing quotas and acreage allotments, required the USDA to develop a food stamp program for submission to the Congress, and established a commission to study increased industrial uses of agricultural products. Sinclair Weeks to Percival Brundage, May 25, 1956, Robert C. Hill to Brundage, May 25, 1956, Arthur Burns to Roger Jones, May 28, 1956, Roger Jones to Eisenhower, May 28, 1956, all in "Appr. 5/28/56 H.R. 10875," White House Bill File, EP.

11. The Republican National Committee wanted Benson to raise dairy supports to 80 or 82.5 percent of parity, place soybeans on the title I PL 480 export list, discontinue offering CCC wheat and corn to the private trade for export so that commercial stocks would move first, and pressure ICA to program agricultural products "aggressively." Rollis Nelson to Benson, January 12, 1956, Marvin McLain to Benson, January 16, 1956, and Benson to Nelson, January 23, 1956, all in "Republican Party Material—Republican—1956-58," reel 22, Benson film.

12. Report to the National Advisory Committee on International Monetary and Financial Problems, H. Doc. 54, 85th Cong., 1st sess. (1957), p. 25; USDA press release, September 10, 1956, and memo, "Information requested by Mr. Richard A. Miller . . . ," October 10, 1956, both in "Agriculture, Department of—Sale

of CCC Commodities (Clarence Francis Materials), 1957," Lambie papers; Benson to Herbert Prochnow, August 31, 1956, "Commodities 5," GC 1956, RG 16.

13. Dan Thornton to Benson, July 12, 1956, "Republican (Nat'l Comm. Other Gen. Inf.) 1953–55," reel 22, Benson film; Benson, *Cross Fire*, pp. 297–99; Jack Z. Anderson diary, June 28, 1956, Anderson papers; Samuel Waugh to Benson, "Animals 2-1-1 Cattle Price Support," Gwynn Garnett to Earl Butz, April 8, 1957, and Butz to Benson, June 3, 1957, "Animals 2-1 Cattle," all in GC 1957, RG 16.

14. Joseph Davis to council, March 14, 1956, "Agriculture—CCC Holdings, Loans, Etc.," Records of the Council of Economic Advisors; Marvin McLain to Earl Butz, March 16, 1956, "Marketing," Marvin McLain to Policy Staff, June 21, 1956, and "Actions of National Grain Trade Council directors at meeting, Wednesday, May 23, 1956," both in "Wheat 5," all in GC 1956, RG 16; Clarence Palmby to Preston Richards, June 5, 1956, OF 110-N-5 "Wheat (1)," EP.

15. Gwynn Garnett to Earl Butz, June 15, 1956, "Meetings 2–3," Charles Shuman to Benson, June 29, 1956, Roy Hendrickson to Marvin McLain, July 5, 1956, Herschel Newsom to McLain, July 10, 1956, Arthur Haelig to R. L. Webster, September 26, 1956, Bob McMillan to Lyle Webster, October 1, 1956, McLain to Haelig, October 4, 1956, all in "Wheat 5," McLain to Policy Staff and CCC board members, July 5, 1956, "Grain 5," all above in GC 1956, RG 16; Dan Thornton to Benson, July 12, 1956, "Republican (Nat'l Comm. Other Gen. Inf.) 1953–55," reel 22, Benson film; USDA, press release, July 13, 1956, OF 1, EP.

16. Cargill, ostensibly speaking for "those in the grain trade," complained to Clarence Francis in the fall of 1957 that continued market activity by the CCC was fostering "a gradual process of socialization in the distribution of farm products." John H. MacMillan, Jr., to Clarence Francis, October 31, 1957, "Clarence Francis—Department of State, Misc. Correspondence," Paarlberg to Francis, April 17, 1958, "Agriculture—1958," both in Francis files; True D. Morse to Gabriel Hauge, April 18, 1957, "Agriculture—Grain," Jack Z. Anderson records; deputy general sales manager, CSS, to Walter Berger, February 20, 1958, "Corn 5," McLain to Morse, Paarlberg, E. L. Peterson, March 14, 1958, Morse to Frank M. Karsten, April 14, 1958, McLain to E. B. Evans, April 16, 1958, "Grain 5," all in GC 1958, RG 16.

17. United States, Department of Agriculture, Foreign Agricul-

tural Service, *Foreign Agricultural Trade Outlook Charts* (Washington, D.C.: Government Printing Office, November 1959), pp. 26–27.

18. This announcement was made in Eisenhower's veto message on the first agricultural bill of 1958, the "freeze bill." *Public Papers*, Eisenhower, 1958, pp. 250–54; CCC docket #ZCK 137a, April 25, 1958, "Grain 5," press release, American Farm Bureau Federation, January 23, 1958, form letter, USDA to AFBF, NFU, Grange, and American Cotton Producer Associates, March 14, 1958, Jack J. Stoneham to McLain, April 3, 1958, McLain to Stoneham, April 8, 1958, McLain to Lamar Fleming, Jr., April 30, 1958, "Cotton 5," all in GC 1958, RG 16.

19. Marvin McLain to Thomas Mann, September 11, 1958, "Cotton 5," GC 1958, RG 16; Clarence Palmby to True D. Morse, n.d., but ca. February 5, 1959, Clarence Miller to Mann, March 10, 1959, Mann to Miller, February 13, 1959, F. Marion Rhodes to Marvin McLain, March 6, 1959, all in "Cotton 5," GC 1959, RG 16; Mann to Miller, February 13, 1959, OF 149-B-2 "Cotton (7)," EP; Don Paarlberg to General Goodpaster, February 26, 1959, "White House Staff (Members—General)," Paarlberg papers.

20. Marvin McLain to H. Roemer McPhee, December 1, 1959, "Cotton 5," GC 1959, RG 16; F. Marion Rhodes to McLain, et al., June 7, 1960, "Cotton 5," GC 1960, RG 16. Near the end of the administration the CCC voted to offer its long-staple cotton stocks for export sale by competitive bids once again. Paarlberg to Elmer Staats, December 24, 1960, OF 149-B-2 "Cotton (12)," EP.

21. Contract, CCC and Fisher Flouring Mills Company, September 8, 1954, and John L. Locke to Milan D. Smith, November 8, 1955, both in "Wheat 5," GC 1955, RG 16; report on meeting on Japanese promotion, September 29, 1955, "Meetings," GC 1955, RG 16.

22. Gustave Burmeister to Edmund E. Pendleton, Jr., May 27, 1955, "ICASD Materials—James Lambie 1955 (2)," Lambie papers; N. R. Clark to James McConnell, July 15, 1954, McConnell to Clark, July 21, 1954, Clark to McConnell, July 28, 1954, "Dairy Products," Clark to McConnell and William Lodwick, August 11, 1954, "Dairy Products 5," all in GC 1954, RG 16; Dale Hathaway to Joseph S. Davis, December 6, 1955, "Agriculture—Policies and Reports (Hathaway File), 1955–56," Arthur E. Burns papers.

23. Entire file, "President's Committee on Increased Industrial

Uses of Agricultural Surpluses, 1956," Francis files.

24. White House press release, November 22, 1954, OF
149-B-2, "Tung Oil (1)," EP.

25. Report on GATT intersessional meeting, August 18, 1954,
OF 147-B-2, EP; "Report of U.S. Delegation to Third FAO
Regional Meeting on Food and Agricultural Programs and
Outlook in Latin America," *Department of State Bulletin* 32, #816
(February 14, 1955): 278–79; "OEEC Examination of the United
States: Record of Dr. Jacoby's comments," September 13, 1954,
"OEEC Economic Experts Meeting, Paris, 9/10/54," Neil Jacoby
papers; minutes, Steering Group on the Foreign Economic
Program, October 27, 1954, "General Agreement on Tariffs and
Trade," series 2, Morgan files.

26. Minutes, Steering Group on the Foreign Economic Program, November 17, 1954, and telegram, State to Amconsul,
Geneva, GATT, ca. November 17, 1954, both in "General Agreement on Tariffs and Trade," series 2, Morgan files. In spite of the
United States refusal, the partners did draft a Special Agreement
on Commodity Arrangements, but it was stillborn.

27. Minutes, ICASD, November 30 and December 2, 1954,
"Minutes of ICASD meetings—1954, 1955, 1956, 1957," Francis
files; James Lambie, Jr., to Sherman Adams, December 2, 1954,
John Foster Dulles to Amconsul, Geneva, GATT, TAGG 107,
December 2, 1954, State to Geneva, GATT, #4234, December 10,
1954, all in OF 149-B-2, "July–December 1954 (2)," EP; minutes,
White House meeting on GATT, February 15, 1955, "Defense,
Department of, Reorganization of (H.R. 1)," Morgan files; C.
Edward Galbreath to Gabriel Hauge, February 18, 1955, OF
149-B-2, "February 1955," EP; minutes, White House meeting on
GATT, March 15, 1955, OF 149-B-2 "H.R. 1—Trade Agreements
Extension Act (1)," EP.

28. "List of Agricultural Items for Which the Import Policies
Were Liberalized for the Dollar Area during 1957 and up to May
1, 1958, by Those Countries with Whom the United States Has
Trade Agreements," "Commodities 5," GC 1958, RG 16.

29. United States, Department of Agriculture, Foreign Agricultural Service, *Foreign Agricultural Trade Outlook Charts* (Washington, D.C.: Government Printing Office, November 1959), pp.
6–10, 45–48. Again, USDA "dollar export" statistics actually
include CCC credit sales, exports under Ex-Im Bank loans, CCC
sales at or below domestic market prices, and exports "assisted by
payments in cash and in kind outside the specified Government
programs," making actual government contribution to export

nearly impossible to determine. It is probably fair to say that commercial sales without any form of government assistance declined even more during fiscal 1958 than did all USDA-defined "dollar sales."

30. United States, Congress, House, *Fourth Annual Report on the Operation of the Trade Agreements Program,* H. Doc. 447, 86th Cong., 2d sess., 1960; Don Paarlberg, "Foreign Economic Policy Issues," November 10, 1959, OF 116–EE (2), EP.

31. Max Myers to Benson, March 24, 1960, "Exports—U.S.," Paarlberg papers; Paarlberg to Benson, August 7, 1959, "Commodities 5," GC 1959, RG 16; Benson to Homer Brinkley, May 9, 1960, "Commodities 5," GC 1960, RG 16; *Fourth Annual Report* (cited in note 30).

32. Benson to Brinkley, May 9, 1960, Clarence Miller to Thomas Mann, May 17, 1960, "Foreign Relations 3," GC 1960, RG 16.

33. Minutes, National Agricultural Advisory Commission, June 6–7, 1960, "NAAC 1960, Committees 4," J. H. Richter to Max Myers, June 24, 1960, "Foreign Relations 5," both in GC 1960, RG 16; Ray Ioanes to Myers, July 7, 1960, "Agriculture Department—File No. 2," Paarlberg papers.

34. Paarlberg to Miller Shurtleff, July 26, 1960, "Agriculture Department—File No. 2," Paarlberg papers; Clarence Miller to Walter W. Goeppinger, December 5, 1960, "Grain 5," GC 1960, RG 16; Benson, *Cross Fire,* pp. 534–36.

35. Paarlberg to Benson, August 7, 1959, "Commodities 5," GC 1959, RG 16; OF 149-B-2, "Rye (4)," EP; Robinson to the director, March 13, 1959, "Agriculture Department," Paarlberg papers; resolution of Board of Directors, Commodity Credit Corporation, October 26, 1960, "Wheat 5," GC 1960, RG 16; White House press release, February 5, 1960, OF 149-B-2, EP; entire file, "Meat," GC 1959, RG 16. The tung nut situation had a Byzantine flavor: "We grow about 30 million lbs. price supported. We import 26 million by quota, chiefly Argentine. This gives us too much oil, so we subsidize the export of about 12 million. In other words, we knowingly let in oil when we know this gives us too much and when we know that imports of this volume make necessary the subsidizing of exports." Memo, unsigned but surely by Paarlberg, "Tung Nuts," August 5, 1960, Paarlberg papers.

36. Ray Ioanes to True Morse, October 21, 1958, "Dairy Products 5," GC 1958, RG 16; entire file, "Dairy Products 5," GC 1959, RG 16; presidential proclamation, May 11, 1960, OF 149-B-2 "Cheese (2)," EP; Oscar Zaglits to Martin Sorkin, Sep-

tember 2, 1960, "Agriculture (General)," Paarlberg papers.
37. Thomas Mann to Clarence Miller, March 3, 1959, and William B. Macomber, Jr., to Maurice Stans, July 23, 1959, both in "Subject File—Cotton—Long Staple," Areeda papers; Phillip Areeda to General Persons, July 28, 1959, OF 149-B-2 "1959 (1)," EP; Don Paarlberg to Eisenhower, September 21, 1959, OF 149-B-2 "Cotton (2)," EP; White House press release, September 22, 1959, *Department of State Bulletin* 41, #1059 (October 12, 1959): 516.
38. Henry Kearns to Areeda, August 31, 1959, "Subject File—Cotton Textiles, sec. 22," Areeda papers; memo, "Cotton Textiles," n.d., Thomas Mann to Paarlberg, October 9, 1959, telegram, State to American Embassy, Tokyo, November 10, 1959, telegram, American Embassy, Tokyo, to State, November 13, 1959, all in "Cotton Textiles," Paarlberg papers; Clarence Randall to Wilton Persons, November 2, 1959, "Agriculture, Department of #1," Morgan files; James Lambie, Jr., to Clarence Francis, November 12, 1959, "Correspondence with JML—1959," Francis files.
39. Memo no. 1441, Ezra Taft Benson to heads of agencies, May 31, 1960, and Benson to True Morse, Clarence Miller, and Clarence Ferguson, January 16, 1961, both in "Committees 2," GC 1961, RG 16; "Summary of the Report of the FAS Committee on Export Problems," June 28, 1960, OF 149-B "1960," EP; Clarence Francis to ICASD, March 8, 1960, Max Myers to Francis, March 31, 1960, and James Lambie, Jr., to Myers, October 10, 1960, all in "CFEP—1960," Francis files; Clarence Miller to Eisenhower, December 16, 1960, and Miller to Francis, December 23, 1960, "Commodities 5," GC 1960, RG 16; minutes, ICASD, April 5, 1960, "Agricultural Surplus Disposal—Interagency Committee on, 1960," Lambie papers.

CHAPTER 7

1. United States Department of Commerce, *23d Quarterly Report under Export Control,* by Sinclair Weeks (Washington, D.C.: Government Printing Offiice, May 15, 1953), p. 7; *26th Quarterly Report* (February 15, 1954), p. 12; N. E. Halaby to Commission on Foreign Economic Policy, November 15, 1953, "Studies—Matteson—State Department Documents," Records of the Commission on Foreign Economic Policy. The Defense Department's definition of a strategic good included items that might not have "any direct military use" but which, if procured by the bloc,

would "release that much bloc productive capacity to devote to its war production."

2. United States Department of Commerce, *25th Quarterly Report under Export Control*, by Sinclair Weeks (Washington, D.C.: Government Printing Office, December 1, 1953), pp. 5, 21–23, 64, tables. Excluding East Germany in both cases (separate statistics were not kept for that country until 1952) and excluding United Nations Relief and Rehabilitation Administration shipments, in 1947 United States agricultural exports to the bloc totaled $144,061,000 and in 1952 they totaled $319,000, a reduction of 99.7 percent.

3. United States Foreign Operations Administration, *4th Report to Congress, Mutual Defense Assistance Control Act of 1951* by Harold Stassen (Washington, D.C.: Government Printing Office, May 17, 1954), pp. 14–15; Leonard Shapiro, *The Communist Party of the Soviet Union*, 2d ed. (New York: Vintage Books, 1971), pp. 518–19; Basil Dmytryshyn, USSR: *A Concise History*, 2d ed. (New York: Charles Scribner's Sons, 1971), pp. 276–79; Sidney D. Ploss, *Conflict and Decision-making in Soviet Russia: A Case Study of Agricultural Policy, 1953–1963* (Princeton: Princeton University Press, 1965), pp. 72–80.

4. Edna Kelly to Eisenhower, January 14, 1954, W. S. Delany to Kelly, January 18, 1954, Thruston B. Morton to Kelly, January 25, 1954, all in OF 149-B "1954 (1)," EP; C. D. Jackson to Samuel Anderson, January 15, 1954, OF 225 "1954," EP.

5. James Lambie, Jr., to members of the ICASD, December 10, 1954 (gives excerpts of the aide memoire of the cabinet meetings of January 15 and February 5, 1954), "Barter with Soviet Bloc," press releases, Department of Commerce, January 15 and February 10, 1954, "Commerce, Department of," all in Francis files; Adams, *Firsthand Report*, p. 391.

6. The Department of Commerce's *31st Quarterly Report under Export Control* (July 1, 1955) says that in the first quarter of 1954, applications for export of butter to the Soviet bloc valued at $31,640,000 and of cottonseed oil valued at $6,464,864 were denied (pp. 7–8). Memo, unsigned, "Major Recommendations of the Commission on Foreign Economic Policy, with Arguments for and against the Recommendations," January 21, 1954, transcript, press briefing on the Randall Report by James Hagerty and Clarence Randall, March 29, 1954, both in OF 116-M "1954 (3)," EP; William Rhea Blake to Lionel E. Holm, March 24, 1954, "Commodites 5," GC 1954, RG 16.

7. A curious part of the controversy involves the Operations

Coordinating Board, which in February 1954 began studying the possibility of distributing surplus commodities either to "Soviet bloc peoples" or to countries bordering the Soviet bloc, the latter to make "Soviet bloc peoples aware of the comparatively more adequate supplies which may become available to their non–Soviet bloc neighbors through association with the Free World" (this was called the "Green Grass" plan). A small working group of CIA and USDA officials analyzed the principal agricultural commodities that "could be made available, if desired, in sufficient quantities to be potentially important economic or psychological factors in the struggle between the Soviet Bloc and the Free World." The bloc, it estimated, would be self-sufficient in wheat and would not be interested in dried milk because of "rather limited consumer acceptance," but there were possibilities in butter, cotton, and such items as cottonseed oil and linseed oil, and in the bordering countries there was a great need for wheat, cotton, and rice. The interagency group that became ICASD discussed the proposal, but it was apparently scuttled. Operations Coordinating Board, "Background," March 25, 1954, and Economic Intelligence Committee, EIC-WP-3, March 19, 1954, both in "O.C.B.," Economic Intelligence Committee, EIC-P-9, March 17, 1954, "Disposal of U.S. Surpluses Abroad," Francis meeting notes, April 21, 1954, "Policies and Organization (2)," all in Francis files.

8. Meeting notes, Francis, National Security Council, April 1, 1954, "Policies and Organization (2)," Francis files.

9. D. A. FitzGerald to Clarence Francis, March 9, 1954, and Lawrence F. Ebb to Francis and Guy Noyes, June 21, 1954, both in "Legislation (1)," administration memo to conference committee on Dies amendment, June 17, 1954, "Legislation (2)," Francis notes, meeting with George Aiken, March 9, 1954, "Policies and Organization (2)," all in Francis files; Christian A. Herter, Jr., to Kenneth R. Hansen, "Agricultural Surplus Disposal Program— General 1954," Lambie papers.

10. J. A. McConnell to Charles Shuman, February 21, 1955, "Dairy Products 5," GC 1955, RG 16. McConnell said that the USDA had sent a "trader" to Europe and he had reported that the Soviets claimed to have "a large increase in their oilseeds and didn't need to import butter or vegetable oils."

11. Minutes, ISC, October 14, 1954, "Interagency Committee on Agricultural Surplus Disposal—Minutes (1) 1954–55," Francis to Lambie, November 19, 1954, "Agricultural Surplus Disposal— Correspondence 1954 (1)," both in Lambie papers; unsigned

[Lambie] to Francis, December 4, 1954, "Barter—Cobalt," Francis files.

12. Minutes, ICASD, November 23 and December 7, 1954, memo, unsigned, "Export Policy on Butter," December 14, 1954 [probably by USDA], both in "Agricultural Surplus Disposal Program—General 1954," Lambie papers.

13. *New York Times,* December 16, 1954, 1:5; *New York Herald Tribune,* December 17, 1954, 1:20; American Farm Bureau Federation resolution, December 21, 1954, "Cabinet Papers—Misc—1956," Francis files.

14. During the discussion the cabinet reaffirmed their previous support for United States–USSR barter. Memo, James M. Lambie, Jr., December 22, 1954, "Cabinet Papers—Misc—1956," Francis files.

15. Christian A. Herter, Jr., to Kenneth R. Hansen, November 8, 1954, "Agricultural Surplus Disposal Program—General 1954," Lambie papers; J. Lee Rankin to Gerald Morgan, February 21 and 28, 1955, "Barter with Soviet Bloc," Francis files.

16. Marshall Smith to Clarence Francis, January 4, 1955, and J. Vandervoort to Francis, January 20, 1955, both in "Barter with Soviet Bloc," Francis files. In late December, the Department of Commerce reported that in the past eight months there had been "approximately" fifty inquiries about shipping surplus agricultural commodities to the bloc, seven of which involved barter. Given the policies in effect, it declared, there was a real possibility that these inquiries were "only a partial measurement of the trader interest." Samuel W. Anderson to Clarence Francis, December 17, 1954, "Barter with Soviet Bloc," Francis files.

17. *Washington Post* editorial, December 18, 1954; Washington News Syndicate, "The Lowdown on Farm Affairs from Washington," vol. 1, #27, December 27, 1954; "New Farm Bureau Chief Urges Surplus Butter Sales to Russia," *Washington Post,* February 16, 1955.

18. Entire file, OF 149-B "1956 (2)," EP; L. H. Fountain to Benson, February 28, 1955, "Commodities 5," GC 1955, RG 16.

19. J. Lee Rankin to Gerald Morgan, February 21 and 28, 1955, Department of Commerce press release, June 23, 1955, all in "Barter with Soviet Bloc," Francis files.

20. USSR draft directive, statements by Eden and Eisenhower on July 22, 1955, "Geneva Conference—Friday, July 22, 1955," Bulganin statement on July 23, 1955, all in Hagerty papers; "Directive to Foreign Ministers," July 23, 1955, OF 116-GG "Big

Four Conference (1)," EP.

21. *New York Times,* December 8, 1955, 1:2; clipping, "Surplus Sale to Reds Seen," by William E. Zimmerman, unidentified San Francisco newspaper, November 10, 1955, "Commodities 5," GC 1955, RG 16. Unfortunately, the proposed liberalization was delayed until April 26, 1956, and then included only such peripheral agricultural products as beverages, hides, and skins. United States Department of Commerce, *35th Quarterly Report under Export Control,* by Sinclair Weeks (Washington, D.C.: Government Printing Office, May 15, 1956), p. 10.

22. Lauren Soth papers (especially box 2), Iowa State University Library; entire file, "Foreign Relations 5," GC 1955, RG 16; Theodore S. Gold to Earl Butz, August 26, 1955, "Animals 2," GC 1955, RG 16.

23. During 1956 the United States sold $1,157,000 worth of seed corn to the Soviet Union, $207,000 to Romania, $173,000 to Poland, $22,000 to Czechoslovakia, and $21,000 to Hungary. The Soviet delegation also purchased sixty-four head of cattle. United States International Cooperation Administration, *8th Report to Congress, Mutual Defense Assistance Control Act of 1951,* by John B. Hollister (Washington, D.C.: Government Printing Office, October 10, 1956), pp. 12–13; *9th Report* (June 28, 1957), p. 109; United States Department of Commerce, *32d Quarterly Report under Export Control,* by Sinclair Weeks (Washington, D.C.: Government Printing Office, November 1, 1955), p. 6.

24. Paul E. Quintus to Ernest Baughman, September 23, 1955, "Agriculture, Department of (1)," Clarence Francis to Joseph Dodge, October 22, 1955, "CFEP—Baughman Report," both in Francis files; Benson to John Foster Dulles, October 24, 1955, "Commodities 5," GC 1955, RG 16; memo, unsigned [Benson], October 26, 1955, "Farm Program—1955," reel 13, and Benson to James McConnell, November 3, 1955, "Mc—General," reel 6, Benson film.

25. Edmund Pendleton, Jr., to True Morse, October 24, 1955, "Foreign Relations 3," Preston Richards to Earl Hughes, November 18, 1955, and Earl Butz to Herbert Hoover, Jr., November 28, 1955, "Commodities 5," all in GC 1955, RG 16; Paul H. Cullen to CFEP, CFEP 528/4, November 19, 1955, "CFEP Misc (1)," and minutes, CFEP meeting, November 30, 1955, "CFEP minutes," both in Francis files. Agriculture's position was technically correct—Justice had never asserted that sales for dollars were illegal, though it considered them inadvisable, and thus administrative action could change the policy.

26. Edmund Pendleton to James Lambie, Jr., July 23, 1956, "CFEP Misc (2)", Gerald Morgan to Herbert Brownell, Jr., August 7, 1956, "CFEP Misc (1)," both in Francis files; Agricultural Trade Development and Assistance Act, 70 *Stat.* 988 (1956).

27. Gerald Morgan to Herbert Brownell, Jr., August 7, 1956, and Frederick W. Ford to Morgan, August 13, 1956, both in "Agricultural Trade Development and Assistance Act of 1954, PL 480," Morgan files.

28. Frank G. Daniels, "Highlights on Report of European Trip, August 31–October 15, 1956," "Foreign Relations 3," Daniels to Marvin McLain, November 27, 1956, "Commodities 5," both in GC 1956, RG 16; Paul Cullen to Clarence Randall, December 3, 1956, Randall to I. Jack Martin, December 3, 1956, both in "Foreign Economic Policy, Council on," I. Jack Martin records; press release, June 28, 1956, *Department of State Bulletin* 35, #890 (July 16, 1956): 113; Dulles press conference, March 26, 1957, *Bulletin* 36, #929 (April 15, 1957): 599; United States International Cooperation Administration, *10th Report to Congress, Mutual Defense Assistance Control Act of 1951,* by James H. Smith, Jr. (Washington, D.C.: Government Printing Office, January 24, 1958), p. 7.

29. Press release, June 7, 1957, *Department of State Bulletin* 36, #939 (June 24, 1957): 1003; press release, August 14, 1957, *Bulletin* 37, #950 (September 9, 1957): 444; United States Department of Commerce, *41st Quarterly Report under the Export Control Act,* by Sinclair Weeks (Washington, D.C.: Government Printing Office, November 17, 1957), p. 3; Paarlberg to Roswell Garst, July 20, 1957, "Commodities 5," GC 1957, RG 16.

30. J. H. Smith, Jr., to A. J. Goodpaster, December 13, 1957, OF 8-Q, EP; Bulganin to Eisenhower, December 10, 1957, *Department of State Bulletin* 38, #969 (January 20, 1958): 127; Bulganin to Eisenhower, January 8, 1958, OF 225 "1958 (1)," EP; *Public Papers,* Eisenhower, 1958, pp. 75–84, 153–60; Intelligence Report #7681, State, "The Sino-Soviet Economic Offensive in the Less Developed Countries of the Free World," March 12, 1958, "Soviet Economic Penetration," Rand records.

31. *Public Papers,* Eisenhower, 1958, pp. 538–39. This letter did stimulate another interagency review of Soviet trade possibilities. A year earlier when the FAS had projected foreign demand for United States agricultural products in 1965 and 1975 it had not projected United States exports to the USSR and had even worried about possible competitive surpluses of wheat and cotton in the Soviet Union. Nor did FAS foresee Eastern Europe

as an important market, with a "possible exception" in the case of a "genuine accommodation between the West and Russia's East-European satellites," in which case there could "conceivably" be "sizeable" exports. W. T. M. Beale to Paarlberg, July 23, 1958, and Morse to Beale, August 26, 1958, "Foreign Relations 3," GC 1958, RG 16; Raymond Ioanes to Paarlberg, October 14, 1957, "Commodities 5," GC 1957, RG 16.

32. United States Department of Commerce, *43rd Quarterly Report under the Export Control Act,* by Sinclair Weeks (Washington, D.C.: Government Printing Office, May 15, 1958), pp. 18–19; *44th Quarterly Report* (August 15, 1958), p. 17; *45th Quarterly Report* (November 10, 1958), pp. 19–20; John H. Davis to Marvin McLain et al., September 24, 1958, "Commodities 5," GC 1958, RG 16; Frederick H. Mueller to Sinclair Weeks, July 30, 1958, OF 225, EP.

33. Paul Cullen to CFEP, April 7, 1959, enclosing CFEP 579, "Subject File—Communist Trade," Areeda papers; *Department of State Bulletin* 40, #1025 (February 16, 1959): 229, 237–43.

34. Transcript, interview of seven United States governors with Khrushchev, July 7, 1959, OF 225 "1959 (2)," EP; *Department of State Bulletin* 41, #1060 (October 19, 1959): 547–54; #1065 (November 23, 1959): 764; 42, #1077 (February 15, 1960): 239–40; Benson, *Cross Fire,* pp. 472–88.

35. Some members of the USDA were interested in providing food, but State's Douglas Dillon was said to be opposed. Miller Shurtleff to Benson, July 20, 1959, Shurtleff to Clarence Miller, July 20, 1959, Max Myers to Shurtleff, July 24, 1959, all in "Commodities 5," GC 1959, RG 16; Marvin McLain to Vance Hartke, May 19, 1960, "Wheat 5," GC 1960, RG 16; Shurtleff to True Morse and Miller, October 3, 1960, "Title II—PL 480—government-to-government—disaster," Paarlberg papers.

36. William Macomber, Jr., to Jacob Javits, March 17, 1959, *Department of State Bulletin* 40, #1038 (May 18, 1959): 826.

37. Paarlberg to staff secretary, June 8, 1959, OF 1, EP; telegram, American Embassy, Havana, to State, June 5, 1959, and press release, State, June 10, 1959, both in "Sugar," GC 1959, RG 16; press release, State, June 11, 1959, *Department of State Bulletin* 40, #1044 (June 29, 1959): 958.

38. A summary of United States complaints against Cuba is in the aide memoire presented to the Cuban government, June 4, 1960, *Department of State Bulletin* 42, #1095 (June 29, 1960): 994–95; press release, State, May 27, 1960, *Bulletin* 42, #1094 (June 13, 1960): 962; Christian Herter speech, June 22, 1960, *De-*

partment of State Bulletin 43, #1098 (July 11, 1960): 58–59; Keith Thomson to Herter, October 29, 1959, "Sugar," GC 1959, RG 16; Marvin McLain to Paul Rogers, January 5, 1960, John C. Lynn to Harold Cooley, April 12, 1960, telegram, American Embassy, Havana, to State, June 23, 1960, all in "Sugar," GC 1960, RG 16.

39. Don Paarlberg, oral history interview, January 17, 1968; Paarlberg memo, "Sugar," July 5, 1960, "Sugar (1)," Paarlberg papers.

40. Thomas Mann to Benson, July 20, 1960, Benson to Eisenhower, September 9, 1960, both in "Sugar," GC 1960, RG 16; *Public Papers*, Eisenhower, 1960, pp. 646–47.

41. Entire files, "Sugar" and "Sugar 5," GC 1960, RG 16; "Sugar (1)," Paarlberg papers; OF 149-B-2, "Sugar," EP; Christian Herter to Eisenhower, January 15, 1961, OF 110–N–4 "Sugar (4)," EP.

42. Wilhelm Anderson to Don Paarlberg, July 8, 1960, "Sugar (1)," Paarlberg papers; Clarence Miller to Donald N. McDowell, December 9, 1960, "Animals 2-1," GC 1960, RG 16; United States Department of Commerce, *55th Quarterly Report under the Export Control Act*, by Luther Hodges (Washington, D.C.: Government Printing Office, May 15, 1961), pp. 9–10.

43. Benson interview. Benson said he gave the same advice—cash on the barrelhead—to Earl Butz during the Soviet sales of 1972.

CONCLUSION

1. Gabriel Hauge, oral history interview #3, May 31, 1967; Benson, *Cross Fire*, pp. 260, 600.

2. Euphemisms abounded. Dumping was "surplus disposal"; the state trading at the core of PL 480 title I was "facilitating" the sales made by private traders. Some direct state trading was also done, as in a sale to South Africa in October 1958, Resolution of the Board of Directors, Commodity Credit Corporation, October 3, 1958, "Organization 1 (C.C.C.)," GC 1958, RG 16.

3. Earl Butz, oral history interview, January 15, 1968, p. 18.

4. Neil Jacoby reported, "PL 480 shipments of American grains to Taiwan had probably done more harm than good. They had kept down the price of grain, and thereby, inhibited the Taiwanese farmers from developing their own grain production, which they were easily able to do." Neil Jacoby, oral history interview, November–December 1970, pp. 120–21. Studies by various agricultural economists bear him out. See, for example, Jerry A. Fedeler, "An Analysis of Commodity Aid and Policies to

Eliminate Its Negative Effects upon the Commercial Market,"
Ph.D. diss., Iowa State University, 1972; Keith Daniel Rogers,
"Theory and Application of Food Aid in Economic Development,"
Ph.D. diss., Iowa State University, 1971.

5. Marvin McLain to Benson, March 24, 1959, "Pending," reel
11, Benson film; Martin Sorkin to Homer Evans, February 11,
1959, "Wheat 5," GC 1959, RG 16. In an interview on October 7,
1977, Benson said he agreed with McLain. Benson interview.

6. During the Eisenhower administration, the average export
cost per bushel of commercially exported wheat (i.e., the difference between the domestic market price and the export price,
which is then restored to CCC as part of the annual restoration of
capital) ranged from 44 cents to 79.4 cents per bushel. With the
United States commercially exporting up to 300 million bushels
per year, this was a substantial drain on the treasury. True D.
Morse to O. B. Jesness, August 8, 1960, "Wheat 5," GC 1960, RG
16.

7. Interview with Ezra Taft Benson, October 7, 1977; Marvin
McLain to Harold Cooley, July 30, 1959, "Cotton 5," GC 1959, RG
16. The statistics cover the first five years of title I operations.

8. The Indonesian problem is discussed in Douglas Dillon to
Benson, March 20, 1958, and Don Paarlberg to Dillon, April 15,
1958, both in "Rice 5," GC 1958, RG 16.

9. Adams, *Firsthand Report*, p. 391.

10. Earl Butz to Clarence Randall, March 18, 1957, "Butz,
Earl," Francis files.

11. "Policy-level decisions to prohibit . . . either Mutual Security assistance or PL 480 development programs which would result in competition with U.S. agriculture," Joseph Rand to Clarence Randall, February 13, 1958, "Rand, Joseph—General," Rand
records.

12. Clarence Francis to Karl Harr, August 11, 1959, "Operations Coordinating Board," Francis files; Clarence Randall to Wilton Persons, March 4, 1960, "CFEP," Morgan files.

13. Clarence Randall quoted in Herbert Parmet, *Eisenhower
and the American Crusades* (New York: Macmillan, 1972), p. 292.

14. Marvin McLain to Lindley Beckworth, June 4, 1959, "Cotton 5," GC 1959, RG 16; Earl Hughes to Benson, June 11, 1960,
"Books—8 Years—Doubleday," reel 3, Benson film; Paarlberg to
the author, May 18, 1973.

15. Eisenhower's discontent can be seen in a letter he wrote to
Benson in late 1958: "I grow more and more concerned about our
farm program. You and I have rarely, if ever, had any difference

of conviction as to the basic principles we should follow in our attempt to establish the proper relationship between the government and agriculture. I think we have made real progress, but the constant increase in the government funds that we must pay out under present programs suggests the need for critical re-examination of the laws as now written and possibly some changes in them. . . . My feeling is that we should attempt to establish expenditure limits, possibly in several directions. How about establishing a maximum level on loans that could be made to any one individual or any one firm? How about cutting from *any* supports all acreage holdings exceeding a certain size? These might be completely impractical but I think it is nevertheless true that in some instances we have been making millionaires with Federal subsidies." Eisenhower to Benson, November 15, 1958, "President Eisenhower, 1953–55," reel 31, Benson film.

16. Paarlberg, *American Farm Policy,* p. 160.

Bibliography

ARCHIVAL MATERIALS

A. Federal records
   Office of the Secretary of Agriculture, Record Group 16, National Archives
B. Personal papers, Boston University Library
   Jacoby, Neil (microfilm, Dwight D. Eisenhower Library)
C. Personal papers, the Church of Jesus Christ of Latter Day Saints
   Benson, Ezra Taft (microfilm, Dwight D. Eisenhower Library)
D. Personal papers, Dwight D. Eisenhower Library
   Adams, Sherman
   Anderson, Jack Z.
   Areeda, Phillip E.
   Burgess, W. Randolph
   Burns, Arthur F.
   Dodge, Joseph M.
   Eisenhower, Dwight D.
      White House Central Files, 1953–61
      White House Office, Bill Files, 1953–61
      Commission on Foreign Economic Policy, Files, 1953–54
      Commission on National Goals, Files, 1959–61
      Council of Economic Advisors, Files, 1953–61
      Council of Economic Advisors, Office of the Chairman, Files, 1953–60
      Council on Foreign Economic Policy, Files, 1955–61
      Council on Foreign Economic Policy, Office of the Chairman, Files, 1954–61

197

Finder, Leonard V.
Fox, Frederic E.
Francis, Clarence
Hagerty, James C.
Hamlin, John
Harlow, Bryce
Hauge, Gabriel
Hess, Stephen H.
Kendall, David
Kestnbaum, Meyer
Lambie, James M., Jr.
Larson, Arthur
McPhee, Henry Roemer
Martin, I. Jack
Masterson, Charles F.
Merriam, Robert E.
Mitchell, James P.
Morgan, Gerald D.
Morrow, E. Frederic
Mueller, Frederick H.
Paarlberg, Don
Persons, Wilton B.
Pike, Thomas P.
Pyle, Howard
Rand, Joseph
Smith, Walter Bedell
Waugh, Samuel C.
Willis, Charles F.

E. Personal papers, Iowa State University Librarv
Hearst, Charles J.
Russell, J. Stuart
Soth, Lauren

F. Personal papers, United States Department of Agriculture
Roberts, Richard

G. Oral history transcripts, Dwight D. Eisenhower Library
Aiken, George
Benson, Ezra Taft
Boeschenstein, Harold
Bohlen, Charles
Brundage, Percival
Burns, Arthur E.
Butz, Earl
D'Ewart, Wesley A.

Evans, Luther
Francis, Clarence
Hollister, John B.
Jacoby, Neil
Lambie, James M., Jr.
Mann, Thomas C.
Morse, True D.
O'Rourke, Dennis
Paarlberg, Don
Staats, Elmer
Thye, Edward J.
H. Oral history interviews
Benson, Ezra Taft
Garst, Roswell

GOVERNMENT DOCUMENTS

Public Advisory Board for Mutual Security. *A Trade and Tariff Policy in the National Interest.* Washington, D.C.: Government Printing Office, 1953.

Report of the Commission on Foreign Economic Policy, Staff Papers. Washington, D.C.: Government Printing Office, 1954.

Report to the President by the Commission on Foreign Economic Policy. Washington, D.C.: Government Printing Office, 1954.

Report to the President by the President's Citizen Advisors on the Mutual Security Program. Benjamin F. Fairless, Chairman. Washington, D.C.: Government Printing Office, 1957.

United States Congress. *Congressional Record.* Selected portions, 1953–61.

United States Congress. House. *Annual Report on the Operation of the Trade Agreements Program.* 1957–61. Nos. 1–5.

United States Congress. House. Committee on Agriculture. Selected *Hearings,* 1953–61.

United States Congress. House. *Semiannual Report of the National Advisory Council on International Monetary and Financial Problems.* 1956–61.

United States Congress. House. *Report to Congress on the Mutual Security Program.* 1951–60. Nos. 1–16.

United States Congress. House. *Semiannual Report on Public Law 480.* 1955–61. Nos. 1–13.

United States Congress. House. *U.S. Foreign Aid: Its Purposes, Scope, Administration and Related Information.* H. Doc. 116, 86th Cong., 1st sess., 1959.

United States Congress. Senate. Committee on Agriculture and Forestry. Selected *Hearings*. 1953–61.

United States Department of Agriculture. *Agricultural Statistics 1937*. Washington, D.C.: Government Printing Office, 1938.

United States Department of Agriculture. *Foreign Agricultural Trade Outlook Charts*. Washington, D.C.: Government Printing Office, 1959.

United States Department of Agriculture. *The Problem of Maintaining High Level Agricultural Exports*. Washington, D.C.: Government Printing Office, 1957.

United States Department of Agriculture. *Yearbook of Agriculture, 1963*. Washington, D.C.: Government Printing Office, 1963.

United States Department of Commerce. *Quarterly Report under the Export Control Act*. Washington, D.C.: Government Printing Office, 1947–61. Nos. 1–55.

United States Department of State. *Department of State Bulletin*. 1953–61.

United States Mutual Security Agency. *Report to Congress, Mutual Defense Assistance Control Act of 1951*. Washington, D.C.: Government Printing Office, 1952–61. Nos. 1–15.

United States President. *Public Papers of the President of the United States*. Washington, D.C.: Government Printing Office, 1953–61. Dwight D. Eisenhower.

United States *Statutes at Large*, vols. 62–75.

PERIODICALS

American Farm Bureau Federation Newsletter.
Farm Journal.
Journal of Proceedings of the National Grange.
Nation's Agriculture.
National Grange Monthly.
New York Times.
NFO Reporter.
NFU Washington Newsletter.
Official Yearbook of the National Council of Farm Cooperatives.
Wall Street Journal.
Washington Post.

BOOKS

Adams, Sherman. *Firsthand Report: The Story of the Eisenhower Administration*. New York: Harper and Brothers, 1961.

Adler-Karlsson, Gunnar. *Western Economic Warfare, 1947–1967: A Case Study in Foreign Economic Policy.* Stockholm: Almquist and Wiksell, 1968.

Anderson, Patrick B. *The President's Men.* Garden City, N.Y.: Doubleday, 1968.

Andrews, Stanley. *The Farmers' Dilemma.* Washington, D.C.: Public Affairs Press, 1961.

Baldwin, David A. *Economic Development and American Foreign Policy.* Chicago: University of Chicago Press, 1966.

Bauer, Raymond; Pool, Ithiel de Sola; and Dexter, Lewis Anthony. *American Business and Public Policy: The Politics of Foreign Trade.* New York: Atherton Press, 1963.

Benedict, Murray R., and Bauer, Elizabeth K. *Farm Surpluses: U.S. Burden or World Asset?* Berkeley: University of California Press, 1960.

Benson, Ezra Taft. *Cross Fire: The Eight Years with Eisenhower.* Garden City, N.Y.: Doubleday, 1962.

Cochrane, Willard W., and Ryan, Mary E. *American Farm Policy, 1948–1973.* Minneapolis: University of Minnesota Press, 1976.

Craig, Richard B. *The Bracero Program: Interest Groups and Foreign Policy.* Austin: University of Texas Press, 1971.

Cronin, Thomas E., and Greenburg, Sanford D. *The Presidential Advisory System.* New York: Harper and Row, 1969.

Curzon, Gerald. *Multilateral Commercial Diplomacy: The General Agreement on Tariff and Trade and Its Impact on National Commercial Policies and Techniques.* London: Michael Joseph, 1965.

Dmytryshyn, Basil. *USSR: A Concise History.* 2d ed. New York: Charles Scribner's Sons, 1971.

Drachkovitch, Milorad M. *United States Aid to Yugoslavia and Poland.* Washington, D.C.: American Enterprise Institute, 1963.

Eisenhower, Dwight D. *Mandate for Change, 1953–1956: The White House Years.* Garden City, N.Y.: Doubleday, 1963.

———. *Waging Peace, 1956–1961: The White House Years.* Garden City, N.Y.: Doubleday, 1965.

Fenno, Richard F., Jr. *The Power of the Purse: Appropriations Politics in Congress.* Boston: Little, Brown, 1966.

Gardner, Richard N. *Sterling-Dollar Diplomacy.* 2d ed. New York: McGraw-Hill, 1969.

Gray, Robert Keith. *Eighteen Acres under Glass.* Garden City, N.Y.: Doubleday, 1962.

Guhin, Michael A. *John Foster Dulles: A Statesman and His*

Times. New York: Columbia University Press, 1972.

Hadwiger, Don F., and Talbot, Ross B. *Pressures and Protests*. San Francisco: Chandler, 1965.

Hofstadter, Richard. *The Age of Reform from Bryan to F. D. R.* New York: Vintage Books, 1955.

Hoopes, Townsend. *The Devil and John Foster Dulles*. Boston: Little, Brown, 1973.

Howard, Nathaniel R., ed. *The Basic Papers of George M. Humphrey as Secretary of the Treasury, 1953–1957*. Cleveland: Western Reserve Historical Society, 1965.

Hughes, Emmet J. *The Ordeal of Power: A Political Memoir of the Eisenhower Years*. New York: Atheneum, 1963.

Kelly, William B., Jr., ed. *Studies in United States Commercial Policy*. Chapel Hill: University of North Carolina Press, 1963.

Lewis, Cleona. *America's Stake in International Investments*. Washington, D.C.: Brookings Institution, 1938.

Lipsey, Robert E. *Price and Quantity Trends in the Foreign Trade of the United States*. Princeton: Princeton University Press, 1963.

McConnell, Grant. *Private Power and American Democracy*. New York: Knopf, 1966.

McGovern, George. *War against Want: America's Food for Peace Program*. New York: Walker, 1964.

McKitterick, Nathaniel. *East-West Trade: The Background of U.S. Policy*. New York: Twentieth Century Fund, 1966.

Matusow, Allen J. *Farm Policies and Politics in the Truman Years*. Cambridge: Harvard University Press, 1967.

Nourse, Edwin G. *American Agriculture and the European Market*. New York: McGraw-Hill, 1924.

Paarlberg, Don. *American Farm Policy: A Case Study in Decentralized Decision-making*. New York: John Wiley, 1964.

Parmet, Herbert. *Eisenhower and the American Crusades*. New York: Macmillan, 1972.

Paterson, Thomas G. *Cold War Critics: Alternatives to American Foreign Policy in the Truman Years*. Chicago: Quadrangle Books, 1971.

Ploss, Sidney D. *Conflict and Decision-making in Soviet Russia: A Case Study of Agricultural Policy, 1953–1963*. Princeton: Princeton University Press, 1965.

Randall, Clarence B. *A Creed for Free Enterprise*. Boston: Little, Brown, 1952.

————. *A Foreign Economic Policy for the United States*. Chicago: University of Chicago Press, 1954.

————. *Sixty-five Plus*. Boston: Little, Brown, 1963.

Rau, Allan. *Agricultural Policy and Trade Liberalization in the United States, 1934–1956*. Etudes d'histoire economique, politique et sociale, vol. 21. Geneva: Libraire E. Droz, 1957.

Rees, Graham L. *Britain's Commodity Markets*. London: Paul Elek Books, 1972.

Rosenau, James N., ed. *Domestic Sources of Foreign Policy*. New York: Free Press, 1967.

Rowe, J. W. F. *Primary Commodities in International Trade*. London: Cambridge University Press, 1965.

Schapsmeier, Edward L., and Schapsmeier, Frederick H. *Ezra Taft Benson and the Politics of Agriculture: The Eisenhower Years, 1953–1961*. Danville, Ill.: Interstate Printers and Publishers, 1975.

Shapiro, Leonard. *The Communist Party of the Soviet Union*. 2d ed. New York: Vintage Books, 1971.

Talbot, Ross B., and Hadwiger, Don F. *The Policy Process in American Agriculture*. San Francisco: Chandler, 1968.

Toma, Peter. *The Politics of Food for Peace*. Tucson: University of Arizona Press, 1967.

Tontz, Robert L. *Foreign Agricultural Trade: Selected Readings*. Ames: Iowa State University Press, 1966.

Vatter, Harold G. *The U.S. Economy in the 1950's: An Economic History*. New York: Norton, 1963.

Williams, William Appleman. *The Roots of the Modern American Empire*. New York: Vintage, 1970.

Williamson, Jeffrey G. *American Growth and the Balance of Payments, 1820–1913: A Study of the Long Swing*. Chapel Hill: University of North Carolina Press, 1964.

Wilson, Joan Hoff. *Ideology and Economics: U.S. Relations with the Soviet Union, 1918–1933*. Columbia: University of Missouri Press, 1974.

ARTICLES

Allison, Graham T. "Conceptual Models and the Cuban Missile Crisis." *American Political Science Review* 63 (September 1969): 689–718.

Bernstein, Barton J. "Foreign Policy in the Eisenhower Administration." *Foreign Service Journal* (May 1973), pp. 17–20, 23–30, 38.

Farnsworth, Helen C. "International Wheat Agreements and Problems, 1949–56." *Quarterly Journal of Economics* 70 (May 1956): 217–48.

Hammond, Paul Y. "The National Security Council as a Device for Interdepartmental Coordination: An Interpretation and Appraisal." *American Political Science Review* 54 (December 1960): 899–910.

Hardin, Charles M. "The Republican Department of Agriculture–A Political Interpretation." *Journal of Farm Economics* 36 (May 1954): 210–27.

Johnson, Bruce F. "Farm Surpluses and Foreign Policy." *World Politics* 10 (October 1957): 1–23.

McHale, James M. "National Planning and Reciprocal Trade: The New Deal Origins of Government Guarantees for Private Exporters." *Prologue* 6 (fall 1974): 189–99.

Martin, Edward M. "New Trends in United States Economic Foreign Policy." *Annals* 330 (July 1960): 67–76.

Pendleton, Edmund, Jr. "Foreign Currency Loans to Private Business." *Journal of the Bar Association of the District of Columbia,* vol. 25 (March 1958).

Schapsmeier, Edward L., and Schapsmeier, Frederick H. "Eisenhower and Ezra Taft Benson: Farm Policy in the 1950's," *Agricultural History* 44 (October 1970): 369–78.

Smith, Gaddis. "The Shadow of John Foster Dulles." *Foreign Affairs* 52 (January 1974): 403–8.

Sullivan, Robert B. "The Politics of Altruism: An Introduction to the Food-for-Peace Partnership between the U.S. Government and Voluntary Relief Agencies." *Western Political Quarterly* 23 (December 1970): 762–68.

Wells, O. V., et al. "The Fragmentation of the BAE." *Journal of Farm Economics* 36 (February 1954): 1–24.

Williams, William Appleman. "A Historian's Perspective." *Prologue* 6 (fall 1974): 200–203.

UNPUBLISHED MATERIAL

Anderson, William D. "The Intersection of Foreign and Domestic Policy: The Examples in Public Law 480." Ph.D. diss., University of Illinois, 1970.

Fedeler, Jerry A. "An Analysis of Commodity Aid and Policies to Eliminate Its Negative Effects upon the Commercial Market." Ph.D. diss., Iowa State University, 1972.

Rogers, Keith Daniel. "Theory and Application of Food Aid in Economic Development." Ph.D. diss., Iowa State University, 1971.

Acknowledgments

WRITING HISTORY IS A LONELY CRAFT, but it cannot be plied in isolation; the historian is dependent upon others for research materials, advice, criticism, encouragement, and sustenance. I am grateful for a generous fellowship from the American Association of University Women that paid the frightfully high costs of research trips and document reproduction. I am also particularly grateful to Ezra Taft Benson for granting me an interview and permitting me to use the microfilm copy of the Benson papers at the Dwight D. Eisenhower Library, and to True D. Morse, Don Paarlberg, and Thomas Mann for permitting me to use their oral history transcripts. The staffs of the Legislative and Natural Resources Branch of the National Archives, the Dwight D. Eisenhower Library, the Iowa State University Library, and the historical division of the United States Department of Agriculture were consistently helpful. But most of all I am indebted to two men: Professor Ellis Hawley, who directed the original study upon which this work is based, and my husband, Gary, who encouraged me through the long hours of research and writing. Their support has been indispensable.

Index